RAISING
VENTURE
CAPITAL
FOR THE
SERIOUS
ENTREPRENEUR

–RAISING–
VENTURE
CAPITAL
FOR THE
SERIOUS
ENTREPRENEUR

DERMOT BERKERY

New York   Chicago   San Francisco   Lisbon   London   Madrid   Mexico City
Milan   New Delhi   San Juan   Seoul   Singapore   Sydney   Toronto

3 4 5 6 7 8 9 0   DOC/DOC   0 9

ISBN-13: 978-0-07-149602-5
ISBN-10: 0-07-149602-5

This publication is designed to provide accurate and authoritative information in regard to the subject matter covered. It is sold with the understanding that neither the author nor the publisher is engaged in rendering legal, accounting, futures/securities trading, or other professional service. If legal advice or other expert assistance is required, the services of a competent professional person should be sought.

—From a Declaration of Principles jointly adopted by a Committee of the American Bar Association and a Committee of Publishers

McGraw-Hill books are available at special quantity discounts to use as premiums and sales promotions, or for use in corporate training programs. For more information, please write to the Director of Special Sales, Professional Publishing, McGraw-Hill, Two Penn Plaza, New York, NY 10121-2298. Or contact your local bookstore.

This book is printed on acid-free paper.

Library of Congress Cataloging-in-Publication Data

Berkery, Dermot
        Raising venture capital for the serious entrepreneur / Dermot Berkery.
                p.   cm.
        ISBN-13: 978-0-07-149602-5 (hardcover: alk. paper)
        ISBN-10: 0-07-149602-5
        1. Venture capital.   2. Small business—Finance.   3. New business enterprises—
Finance.   I. Title.

        HG4751.B468   2007
        658.15'224—dc22   2007008993

To my mother, Josie. Much missed.

CONTENTS

FOREWORD

The world has changed dramatically over the past 30 years. We have witnessed a number of remarkable technological revolutions ranging from the creation of the biotech and personal computer industries to nascent formation of the nanotech industry. During that period, the venture capital industry has evolved into a major force in financing new ventures. What used to be a tiny cottage industry with only a few players is now a global financial force that helps propel new technologies to successful commercialization.

The roots of the modern venture capital industry trace back to the mid-1940s when General Georges F. Doriot, a renowned professor at Harvard Business School, helped launch American Research & Development (ARD), a publicly traded venture capital firm. ARD started with under $5M in capital. It struggled for several years, partly because it takes time for early-stage investments to get traction.

In 1956, ARD provided $70,000 to a team of scientists at MIT who had a plan to build powerful minicomputers, machines that would compete effectively with the dominant mainframe computers of the day by offering superior performance at a fraction of the cost. In return for that investment, ARD ended up with 70% of the company. The company was Digital Equipment Corporation, which went on to great success. Indeed, ARD eventually made hundreds of times its investment in the company.

But, think about the fact that Ken Olsen and his team had to give up 70% of the company's stock to raise a trivial amount of money. Does that seem reasonable? At the time, Olsen and his colleagues had no choices. There were few investors willing to back such a risky company. Moreover, Olsen and his colleagues had no reasonable ways to benchmark their deal—they didn't have many colleagues starting up companies at the same time.

Today, Olsen could read *Raising Venture Capital for the Serious Entrepreneur* by Dermot Berkery and learn how to level the playing field between venture capitalists and entrepreneurs. He would understand how and why the investors would want to stage their commitment of capital. He would be able to compare the terms he was getting with those being offered similar teams and ideas. He would have a better sense of how growth companies are valued in the public markets.

Berkery's work on financing early-stage, high-potential ventures walks the aspiring entrepreneur through all the steps from conceiving the idea to selling the business. It arms the entrepreneur for negotiations with vastly more experienced venture capitalists and gives the entrepreneurs tools for thinking about their business in productive ways. In short, he increases the likelihood of success for any and all ventures.

If you're an entrepreneur, you should read this book. If you're a venture capitalist, you should read this book. And, certainly, if you're an educator, you should assign this book.

Professor William A. Sahlman
Dimitri V. D'Arbeloff–MBA Class of 1955
Professor of Business Administration
Senior Associate Dean for External Relations
Harvard Business School

PREFACE

Every experienced entrepreneur knows that the process of financing his or her business is a great game full of high drama. Road shows to raise investment are grueling and utterly distracting from the main goal of succeeding in the marketplace. Investors try to grab ownership in the company and are full of promises regarding the value-added they can bring to the fledgling company. Large companies, putting themselves forward as possible strategic investors, are often trying to get control sneakily to stave off their competitors. Different classes of investors in the company pursue different agendas, often dysfunctional from the perspective of the company as a whole. The legal documents governing the investment are mind-numbingly boring and dense—but they can't be ignored. Mistakes in the legal documents can come back to haunt you—a veto granted to a minor investor (sometimes by oversight) can escalate into an intractable standoff a year or two later. Late nights poring over inch-deep legal documents are a far cry from the popular image of entrepreneurs.

If only it were as simple as investing in public companies, where an investment of so-many millions of dollars gives you $X\%$ of the company, and all stock is created equal. It's not. There is little alternative but to play the game on the field set out by the investors. They are the ones with the experience and the money.

The first-time entrepreneur is at a huge disadvantage. While the great game is frustrating and exhilarating, it is also complex and needs to be mastered. You can get advice from your lawyers. But they often understand the words, not the commercial implications. The entrepreneur needs to lessen the learning curve, without taking five to seven years to do it. The venture capitalist has been through it many times before. The old adage applies: "When playing poker, if you don't know who at the table is the fool, it might be you."

In short, entrepreneurs need to get smarter about the rules and the tactics quickly. Mastering the venture capital (VC) method is the key to this.

The VC method has stood the test of time and has proven its worth through extreme peaks and valleys of investment cycles. The shape of a VC deal on the West Coast is much the same as it would be on the East Coast and in Europe. The shape has evolved over the past few decades and will no doubt continue to evolve as investors and entrepreneurs learn and innovate.

As the VC method has been honed and matured through experience, so the business has become institutionalized. There are many VC firms, designed around a standardized limited partner/general partner structure (more on this structure in the chapter on venture capital firms). VC is now a defined investment asset class for pension funds, investment managers, and endowments.

But, while VC has become institutionalized, it is still largely an art rather than a science. Writers on the subject descriptively cover the mechanics of how it works rather than why it works the way it does. Venture capitalists like the fact that the business is opaque; this opacity keeps the market very inefficient. Early-stage investing can sustain the venture capital firms (with a generous fee and profit participation structure as it is) only because the market is extremely inefficient. If the market was truly efficient and the VC process a science, extremely bright 25-year-olds would be throwing the darts instead.

Thankfully for venture capitalists, VC doesn't work this way. Wisdom and judgment are more important than are smarts. The potential to build a company around good technology or a good team is extremely difficult to spot and immensely harder to make happen. Long-in-the-tooth venture capitalists joke that it takes five years and $5M in failed investments to train a new venture capitalist. Many ventures that should get funded do not get funded and vice versa. First-class venture capital managers exploit this inefficiency in the market to earn supernormal returns for their investors and to build their personal wealth. Demystifying the process is not in their interest. Nor is it fully possible.

Dermot Berkery

ACKNOWLEDGMENTS

Many thanks to everyone who helped along the way in pulling together this book.

Becoming a venture capitalist is a long apprenticeship in which money is lost and tears are shed. There are lots of discussions along the way that begin with the phrase: "Well, I won't make that mistake again." My colleagues at Delta Partners helped me to avoid some of the most egregious mistakes along the way with gentle suggestions, such as, "You might want to think about . . ." We have been in the business too long and are humbled too often not to value the opinions of others we respect. Frank Kenny, our managing partner, is a long-term investor who has been in the business for decades. Maurice Roche, Shay Garvey, Joey Mason, Rob Johnson, and John O'Sullivan have all helped in their own special ways to make me to be a better investor. Karen Clarke, my secretary, has kept me in line for many years.

In the spirit of learning in the school of hard knocks, I owe a lot to the CEOs and senior executives of companies in which I invested, all of whom endured (and some continue to endure) me as I go through the lifelong apprenticeship of becoming a better investor. Sometimes things worked out great, and sometimes things got ugly—at no time was it ever dull. Every new company was a baptism of fire for all of us. Thanks to Garry Moroney, Tony McEnroe, Joe Gantly, Joe O'Keeffe, Carl Jackson, Charles Nicholls, Andy Walker, Adrian Cuthbert, Jon Billing, Vincent Browne, Peter Branagan, Mark Suster, and many others. Some of them still send me a Christmas card.

Thanks also to Professors Mike Roberts and Bill Sahlman of Harvard Business School for their input and support.

I owe Dianne Wheeler, my executive editor at McGraw-Hill, a debt of gratitude. Her thoughts on the book structure in particular were excellent, and I listened assiduously to all her advice.

My dad, John Berkery, and father-in-law, Doug Mason, sorted out the worst of my grammar. Jane Palmieri at McGraw-Hill sorted out the rest.

Sally, my other half in all the best senses of the phrase, tolerated me through prolonged periods of radio silence while I was writing this book. Where would I be without her? My three wonderful, zany children, Cormac, Rory, and Kathleen, did everything possible to disrupt the writing of this book. By so doing, they forced me to write quickly and to get it right the first time as much as possible. For this, I suppose they deserve some gratitude.

– RAISING –
VENTURE
CAPITAL
FOR THE
SERIOUS
ENTREPRENEUR

INTRODUCTION

New companies are guilty until proven innocent.

Most of them fail. Investors know this. Entrepreneurs don't—or at least choose not to believe this. Their company will be different from all the others.

Is this clash of views a problem? Businesses need capital so that they can invest in people, physical assets, inventory, and so on. But investors are gripped by the fear of failure and the possible loss of their precious capital. Of course, they are intrigued by (yes, greedy for) the prize if the venture succeeds. Entrepreneurs are captivated by the opportunity and are blind to the possibility of failure. They have to be. Otherwise, they wouldn't set out on the crazy journey of building a new company.

How can the two sides come together? Is it a zero-sum game in which either the investor buys the entrepreneur's story hook, line, and sinker or the entrepreneur submits to the investor's view and abandons the project? Regardless of which, the two minds will seldom meet, and great opportunities to launch new businesses will be missed. We all lose.

The venture capital (VC) method of investing solves this conundrum. It acts as a bridge between the fears of the investor and the hopes of the entrepreneur. Neither party needs to accept the other's view entirely. Rather, the VC method recognizes that both points of view are valid, and it provides a dynamic financing structure for navigating between the two.

This book covers the primary elements of this dynamic financing structure. It starts with a case study of a fictional company called Creditica Inc. Creditica is a software company with a very generic business plan. It intends to start with a beta product, gather early reference customers, and build the business from there. Throughout the book the VC method is applied to Creditica; therefore, it is important to get a feel for Creditica prior to jumping into most of the chapters.

Chapter 1 outlines how the long journey (5 to 7 years or more) of building a valuable business should be broken into a series of stepping-stones—with typically a 12- to 18-month gap between the stepping-stones. Each stepping-stone comprises an integrated group of milestones (related to the product, market, customers, management, etc.). These stepping-stones are analogous to resting points on a long journey. They represent demonstrable progress on the way to the goal. They also are a good place to stop and think about the remaining journey. Is the planned route still the correct one? Have other less risky or shorter routes opened up? In fact, is the destination we were originally heading toward still the best one?

The stepping-stones provide a structure that can be financed. Investors do not have to sign up to finance the whole journey facing the business; they will rarely have enough confidence in the plan up front to do this. They need to provide only enough capital to finance the company to the next stepping-stone. Entrepreneurs get enough capital to start moving on their journey and to achieve milestones that should entice more investment later which in turn finances the journey farther. As new stepping-stones are reached, the chances of reaching the prize are improved and the cost of the investment capital should decline.

Chapter 2 focuses on the first of the stepping-stones. What sort of milestones should be included in it? What are the different first stepping-stones that might be open to the company? What role should the CFO play in the development of the strategy of the company?

The next 12 to 18 months on the way to reaching the first stepping-stone will be very telling. Will the entrepreneur execute well and get the business to the first stepping-stone thereby reaching important milestones with the initial capital? If so, will new investors buy into the dream at that point and invest more capital to take the business further? If not, should the early investors abandon the journey and let the company fail? Or should the company be restructured (making the entrepreneur a casualty in the process)?

Breaking the journey into a series of stepping-stones offers innumerable options for midcourse shifts in strategy, financing approaches, and personnel.

Because of the stepping-stone structure, an early-stage company has only, at most, 12 to 18 months of financing available to it. This creates a series of unusual cash flow and risk dynamics. There is always a ticking clock at work in the background. Each company has a time runway; if the airplane doesn't take off and build value before the end of the runway, the consequences will be severe—perhaps catastrophic. Chapter 3 enumerates 10 unique cash flow and risk dynamics—all of which are derived from the stepping-stone financing structure.

Chapter 4 establishes how much capital a company should seek to raise in a round of funding and, more importantly, what it should spend the capital on. Simply categorized, entrepreneurs can spend their VC investment on five items—capital assets, product development overhead, leadership and administration expenses, working capital, and sales ramp-up costs. The return on investment of some of these items is inherently very low. Only some have the potential to create enormous value. Entrepreneurs need to know which items have the potential to yield a venture return; they must avoid or minimize the others or, even better, get someone else to pay for them.

Venture capital funds are normally fixed-term partnerships. The compensation for the venture capitalists comes in two forms—a management fee and a share in the gains ("carry"). Chapter 5 describes how the structure of a fund and the compensation approach drives a venture capitalist's behavior and thought process.

There have been far too many books and articles written about business plans, listing the topics to include. Most miss the point. A business plan is simply a vehicle for outlining how a business will create and exploit market power in its target market. The business plan needs to identify the source of market power, marshal the evidence to support the case as to why the company can capture and sustain it, and present the evidence in a simple, absorbable form. Chapter 6 covers the blocks of evidence a typical investor will want.

Valuation of new companies is a black art to most people who are not involved in the business on an ongoing basis. The traditional methods of discounted cash flow and earnings/revenue multiples don't work. Yet, investors and entrepreneurs need to agree on a valuation. How does it happen in practice? What are the rules of thumb, and why do they make sense? Chapter 7 addresses the area fudged by other books on VC—how to set a fair valuation for a new or early-stage company.

Chapter 8 introduces the concept of term sheets. In a public company, all units of stock are created equal. In a venture-backed company, the investors typically buy preferred stock. This preferred stock gives them three primary advantages. First, it allows the returns to be skewed in favor of the preferred stockholder—at the expense of the common stockholder. The mechanisms for achieving this are covered in Chapter 9. Second, it enables investors to exercise control that is disproportionate to their level of shareholding. Retaining certain decision rights or appointing board members can achieve this. All these issues are covered in Chapter 10. Third, it helps to closely align the economic interests of the investor and the entrepreneur through techniques such as vesting and warranties; this is addressed in Chapter 11. Chapters 8 through 11 also provide the entrepreneur with tips regarding pitfalls to look out for and suggestions for negotiating tactics on each point.

The last chapter of the book—Chapter 12, Term Sheet Exercises—pulls together the lessons from across all the chapters into a series of financing situations facing companies. If you can figure out the investor's thought processes in each of these mini cases (without reading the answers!), you are well on the way to being versed in the VC method. It doesn't make sense to go through these exercises until you have at least covered the chapters on term sheets and venture capital companies.

There are two appendixes. The first is a case study called Security Portal Inc.; it illustrates another stepping-stone map. The second is a real-life term sheet used in practice by venture capitalists. This term sheet supports the term-by-term review in Chapters 8, 9, and 10.

Let's be clear. The VC method is not a smooth, seamless step-by-step production line for funding new ventures successfully. It is messy, complicated, legalistic, dynamic, and often acrimonious. It is not surprising that it is this way. It is not a cooperative arrangement in which investors benignly help entrepreneurs to realize their dreams. It is a hard-nosed bargain in which investors and entrepreneurs carve out enough to satisfy their incompatible hopes along the journey.

If you can develop an appreciation for the stepping-stone approach, valuing start-ups based on future multiples, venture capitalist psychology, and the nuances of term sheets, you should acquit yourself well in the cut and thrust of the great financing game.

CREDITICA SOFTWARE INC. CASE STUDY

Although the software industry is starting to mature, many investors continue to view it as an attractive target investment sector. Software companies offer the potential for high growth with only a modest amount of capital required. They fulfill the criterion of "write-once, use-often" necessary for the business to be scalable. They have very high gross margins. They are knowledge-based businesses in which domain knowledge is more important than physical assets. For these reasons, they continue to consume a large share of the capital of venture capital companies and will do so until the sector fully matures.

Introduction

Creditica Software Inc. is a hypothetical software company with all the challenges of a typical early-stage venture. It intends to develop algorithms to identify good credit risks for credit card issuers and to package the algorithms as a software product. It starts with some great assets—people who deeply understand their domain, a track record of previously developing a good product (albeit for a large company), and a highly important problem on which to focus.

The financing side of the business is a blank sheet of paper. The founders have never encountered the venture capital industry before. They have yet to realize that the dominant axis of their lives for the next five to seven years will be the navigation of the company through several rounds of investment. The company will at all times look forward and see a cliff where the funding might run out and where the team needs to meet milestones in order to excite investors enough to support the company to the next stage.

This is the essence of the venture capital method—a treadmill for the company on which it needs to meet milestones relentlessly and periodically in order to justify the value of the prize to new or existing investors.

This case study is referred to throughout the book. So it is advisable to familiarize yourself with all the details.

The Creditica case is wholly fictional. Any similarities to any existing company are purely coincidental.

Creditica Software Inc.

Background

It is June 2008.

Creditica was incorporated in March 2008 when four senior technology professionals resigned from the credit card division of a large midwestern bank. At the bank, the four had created a scorecard for determining to whom the bank should offer a credit card, how much of a balance to allocate to them, and how to monitor the ongoing risk of nonrepayment. This scorecard had been extremely successful in helping the bank reduce bad debts and ferret out new low-risk customers ignored by other credit card companies.

With the blessing of the bank, the four had decided to leave to form a new venture. Their ambition was to design a next generation scorecard, building on the lessons learned from their work at the bank.

Product Proposition

Creditica aims to be the first dedicated third-party scorecard company utilizing prior financial history, sociodemographic data, behavioral patterns, and prior mailing addresses.

Scorecards are not new. Credit card issuers have used them for years as a means of speeding up the process of approving new card applications and eliminating the vagaries of human judgment. However, the scorecards tended to focus purely on financial data and payment/credit history. These scorecards had been developed in-house at each bank, which meant that it was impossible to transfer lessons learned from one credit card issuer to another. In fact, many issuers viewed their in-house scorecards as their competitive weapon (our scorecard is better than everyone else's).

Creditica's mission is to prove that its algorithms and software will perform far better than the in-house algorithms of any individual credit card issuer. Its founders want the scorecard to yield the lowest level of bad debts and to be smarter at identifying good-quality, overlooked customers. The scorecard will draw on prior financial history, sociodemographic data, behavioral patterns, and other new information sources to develop a best-in-class scorecard to sell to all the credit card issuing companies.

Creditica's secret weapon is a history of prior mailing addresses. The company aims to predict poor credit risks better than any other financial institution by tracking different addresses (and the length of time spent at each address) and cross-referencing the payment patterns of individuals in each locality. To achieve this, Creditica has built an enormous database of prior addresses. Built up over the previous 10 years, this database has been enriched each week with address changes and new sources of information on old addresses. This database would be very difficult to replicate—it would take a competitor five or more years to attain anything comparable. In addition, Creditica plans to maintain its advantage by capturing the lessons learned by each issuer that bought its scorecard—these lessons would be used to tweak the scoring algorithms, thereby making the scorecard ever more effective over the course of time. Creditica will tailor the algorithms by country to ensure that they are fully optimized to the local environment.

Creditica is also planning to issue new scorecard algorithms each year (on the same software platform) to customers for an annual fee (see below). These algorithms will take into account the lessons learned from the use of the scorecard by all its customers.

All in all, the company plans to attain an unassailable position by developing better algorithms, capturing richer data on customers, and continuing to tweak the algorithms based on the lessons learned across an ever-increasing customer base of credit card issuers.

Target Market Size

Creditica will sell its products to banks and to nonbank institutions (e.g., supermarkets, specialist card issuers, affinity schemes) that issue credit cards or that are interested in entering the credit card business.

The total number of potential customers and the expected pricing per customer are presented in Exhibit C.1.

The market forms a classic pyramid. A large number of less valuable customers at the base of the pyramid dwarf a relatively small group of highly valuable ones at the top.

Exhibit C.1 Market Segments for Creditica

	Number of Banks in the World	Number of Nonbank Issuers in the World (Today)	Potential New Issuers of Credit Cards	Projected Pricing to Creditica
Large	500	200	?	$1M year-one license fee $400,000 annual fee for updated algorithms 20% maintenance revenues each year on initial license
Medium	1,000	500	?	$500,000 year-one license fee $200,000 annual fee for updated algorithms 20% maintenance
Small	10,000	8,000	?	$300,000 year-one license fee $100,000 annual fee for updated algorithms 20% maintenance

One noticeable feature about the business is that the largest bank issuers of credit cards are not necessarily the largest banks in the country. Clearly it would be easy to become the largest credit card issuer in the country by issuing credit cards to all applicants regardless of their ability or willingness to pay their balances. This is a recipe for losing a lot of money very quickly. A profitable credit card business should be built on brains rather than brawn.

Surprisingly, a small number of modestly sized banks have become large, highly profitable issuers of credit cards based on their ability to identify, target, and capture the best customers. The best customers are those who revolve large outstanding credit balances on their cards from month to month and accrue high interest payments but who have a good payment history. The best revolvers—as they are known—always make the minimum required payment each month and maybe once every year pay the entire balance on the card.

Creditica's management team believes that its algorithms will be suited best to medium- and small-sized issuers. The biggest existing issuers of cards already have the best statisticians in-house and would guard their algorithms jealously. Smaller, hungrier credit card issuers or banks with a small credit card operation would be keen to move out of the also-ran group. On the other hand, they wouldn't be willing to invest in large teams of mathematicians and statisticians to develop proprietary algorithms. Creditica wants to be the vehicle through which these types of institutions can become big profitable card issuers based on better identification and targeting of prospects.

This is the value proposition.

Timing and Key Milestones

The business plan put together by the four founders is based on the usual model pursued by a software company. They will build an early beta version of the product, engage with a few customers that could be good references, use these references to seed the market, and grow the company from there.

Exhibit C.2 Elements of the Business Plan

Q3 2008	• Make initial hires to technical team. Start product design.
Q4 2008	• Ramp up product development team to 10 people (including founders).
Q1 2009	• Hire new CEO who will act as interim head of sales.
Q2 2009	• Finalize beta version of product. Sign up two banks as development partners (i.e., they won't pay up front, but they will commit to providing feedback and testing product against their data).
Q3 2009	• Make first customer release available for sale.
Q4 2009	• Make two initial, small sales (perhaps to development partners) of $200,000 each. Quantify savings to each development partner clearly.
In 2010	• Make 1 sale to a large customer (see price list above in Exhibit C.1). Make 1 sale to a medium-sized customer. Make 2 sales to small customers.
In 2011	• Make 6 sales to a large customer. Make 5 sales to medium-sized customers. Make 7 sales to small customers.
In 2012	• Make 30 sales to large customers. Make 15 sales to medium-sized customers. Make 50 sales to small customers.

The specific steps set out in the business plan are presented in Exhibit C.2.

Resources Required

Like an army marching on its stomach, an early-stage company needs to pay for product development and other monthly overhead. This creates a need for investment capital because sales are generally one to three years away from the start-up date.

The planned hires are presented in Exhibit C.3.

The cost structure of the company is made up of the following elements:

- Up-front capital expenditure and company setup $100,000
- Fully loaded cost per developer/founder (including. premises, travel, etc.) $100,000 each
- Fully loaded cost of CEO/senior executives $200,000 each
- Fully loaded cost per salesperson $150,000 each

Exhibit C.3 Planned Hires

	Q3 2008	Q4 2008	QI 2009	Q2 2009	Q3 2009	Q4 2009	QI 2010	Q2 2010	Q3 2010	Q4 2010
CEO/senior executives			I	I	I	I	2	2	2	2
Technical team	4	4	10	10	10	10	15	15	20	20
Salespeople				2	2	2	10	10	10	10

Ownership

The company founders have raised only $100,000 from friends and family to cover the basic expenses associated with the establishment of the company. Friends and family now own 8% of the company's common stock. Each of the four founders owns 23% of the company, issued to them as common stock. In any future round of finance, they will suffer dilution in their ownership position.

Valuation of Companies in the Sector

It is always very difficult to find comparable companies. Each new early-stage technology company is interesting to investors precisely because it is unique—doing things that no other company is currently doing. But there are a few companies that have some similarities to Creditica. See Exhibit C.4.

The first two companies named in Exhibit C.4 are large software companies from the enterprise resource planning (ERP) and customer relationship management (CRM) sectors. The other three companies are specifically from the financial services software sector:

- *Company 1.* This company sells credit card processing software to credit card companies. Transactions by customers are processed and checked by this system. It has been the leader in its field for the past five years. The average sale value per customer is about $1M.

Exhibit C.4 Comparable Companies

Company	Market Capitalization ($M)	Units of Stock (M)	Revenues ($M)			Net Profits ($M)			Enterprise Value/ Revenues			Price/Earnings Ratio		
			05	06	07	05	06	07	05	06	07	05	06	07
Large Software Companies														
ERP Company	20,000	1,000	5,400	5,800	6,100	600	700	800	3.7	3.4	3.3	33	29	25
CRM Company	2,404	200	300	400	500	300	200	400	8.0	6.0	4.8	8	12	6
Financial Services Software Companies														
Company 1	120	30	60	60	62	5	6	10	2.0	2.0	1.9	24	20	12
Company 2	117	10	100	105	109	3	4	8	1.2	1.1	1.1	39	29	15
Company 3	1,200	15	1,000	900	920	60	60	80	1.2	1.3	1.3	20	20	15
								Average	3.2	2.8	2.5	25	22	15

Market capitalization is assumed to be the same as enterprise value (EV).

- *Company 2.* This company sells leasing management systems to financial institutions. It manages the establishment of lease finance through car dealers when the car is sold initially, then processes the payments as they are received, and handles the termination of the lease. It links car retailers to the financial institution over the Internet. Average sale value per customer is $500,000, but it also sells software to car dealers at a much lower price.
- *Company 3.* It develops and sells bank administration systems. This front office software handles new sales and also does the initial checking and processing of customer transactions. Average sales price per branch is $100,000.

Thoughts on Possible Exits

While there is the hope of an initial public offering, Creditica's founders believe that it is more realistic that the company might be sold to a large credit card software company, such as one of the large companies that processes transactions. Alternatively, a sale to a general financial services software company might be a possibility.

PART I

UNDERSTANDING THE BASICS OF THE VENTURE CAPITAL METHOD

CHAPTER 1

DEVELOPING A FINANCING MAP

There is a clear destination, and the prize for reaching it is intoxicating—the fabled initial public offering (IPO) or the successful trade sale of the company that turns the founders and investors into latter-day robber barons. There is a generic five- to seven-year map that has been established by prior generations of entrepreneurs regarding how to build a business.

But this is new terrain. Every new business that has world-beating aspirations is unique. There are lots of issues. What competitors are out there lurking in the tall grass? If a competitor or some other roadblock thwarts the company, is there a way around? Are there small steps that the company might take up front to block competitors? Is the destination as clear as it seems at first glance? Or are there multiple possible destinations—might some of them be even more interesting than the most obvious destination?

Take the example of Creditica. Clearly, it is a modest creation today. At its simplest, it is a 20-page slide presentation containing insightful perspectives on the opportunity, put together by some smart mathematicians. It is plausible to look forward five to seven or more years and to see it as a good-sized company capable of undertaking an IPO. The situation is pregnant with possibilities. But it is dizzying to think of everything that needs to be done on the journey from here to there. What should be done first? Who should be hired and when? Which customers should be approached first? What happens if competitors get to the market first? How is Creditica going to be financed?

Communicating the complexity of all these execution issues to investors, while still conveying the sense of opportunity, is very difficult.

An early-stage venture should simplify its business plan by breaking the planned development of the company into three to four major stepping-stones on the way to the prize. These stepping-stones should become the financing blueprint for the business. This concept of building a valuable business through multiple staging posts, each of which is financed separately, is the core tenet underpinning entrepreneurial finance. All the complexities and incongruities on the way are derived from this one concept.

The best place to start is to show how the five- to ten-year plan for a business can and should be split into a series of major stepping-stones, normally three to four.

Creating a Set of Stepping-Stones for a New Business

The founders of Creditica have set out a four- to five-year high-level plan for their business. They expect the business to achieve its potential within this period. What they have also done implicitly in the plan (even though they might not have intentionally done so) is to split the journey into three to four major stepping-stones. Exhibit 1.1 shows the implied steps from the establishment of the business in early 2008 to the possible exit of the business in 2012 or later.

Creditica's is a straightforward path of stepping-stones. It is a classic software company path seen by venture capitalists in hundreds, if not thousands, of business plans every year. It has proven itself over the years. Many companies have followed such a path and built valuable businesses. Of course, many have also failed.

Stepping-stones represent groups of major milestones for the company. The milestones might relate to product development, acquisition of customers, recruitment of top-class management, and so forth. The groups of milestones then become stepping-stones. Each stepping-stone

Exhibit 1.1 Creditica Stepping Stones

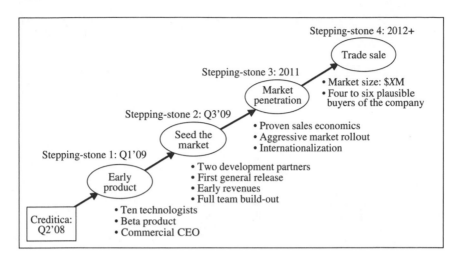

provides an integrated perspective on the progress (and potential valuation) of the company.

The best stepping-stones are ones that the company can point to with hard evidence and that demonstrate real momentum in the progress of the business. It is the team's task to articulate the major stepping-stones because it is impossible for an investor to absorb all of the micro steps a company will take in the course of its development.

Matching the Financing Strategy to the Stepping-Stones

The stepping-stones should then seamlessly match the financing strategy for the business.

Consider the example of Creditica in Exhibit 1.2. If the team has established a workable set of stepping-stones and if the company executes the plan well, it will raise four rounds of investment in the course of its development. In the VC business these are called Series A, B, C, and D and so forth.

Exhibit 1.2 Link to Funding Strategy

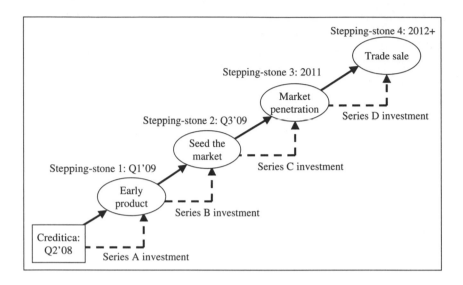

Many software companies before Creditica have proven that moving from stepping-stone to stepping-stone, while continuing to convince investors of the size of the ultimate prize, is a good financing strategy for a company.

The Series A round should be big enough to get the company to stepping-stone 1 (with some margin of error since plans generally take longer to execute than expected). In theory, from start-up, the company could consider raising enough money to take itself to stepping-stone 2 or beyond—if it can find a willing investor. But this misses the point. At start-up the company will probably be at the lowest valuation of its existence. Therefore, if it raised the capital to get it all the way to stepping-stone 2 or beyond, the initial shareholders would suffer far more dilution in their ownership percentages than is necessary. Better to raise just enough capital now and raise more later at a higher valuation.

This is the essence of the early-stage venture game—raising just enough to get to the next stage of development of the company (with a reasonable margin of error) in the hope and expectation of raising more capital on much more attractive terms later. This trade-off is covered more extensively in subsequent chapters.

To get started, the entrepreneur needs to convince the investors of three propositions:

1. The ultimate prize is worth going for. (The opportunity is big enough for early investors to get a 10 to 20 times multiple return on their investment.)
2. There are logical, achievable stepping-stones between start-up and the prize. (There are future points in the development of the company where new investors can be enticed to come on board and where the risks of the business have been progressively stripped away.)
3. The first stepping-stone on the way to the prize, by itself, is a stepping-stone worthy of investment by the investor. (A second-round investor will pay a price per share two to four times the price the early investor paid.)

Developing a Map of Possible Stepping-Stones

Given the way in which business plans are prepared and written, they almost inevitably set out the future development of the business in a linear fashion. The earlier approach of thinking in terms of stepping-stones seems to reinforce this. This linearity does not do the entrepreneur justice.

No business is linear. It is a living entity full of possibilities and dangers. There are many possible destinations and many possible sequences of stepping-stones for getting to each destination. The prize being sought by Creditica in Q2 2008 might not end up being the prize attained in 2012 and beyond.

If there were only one way for Creditica to pursue its business plan, investors would be concerned. Every entrepreneurial business goes through a series of existential crises. The best-laid plans often don't survive the first contact with customers or competitors. Executing strategies in the real world takes longer than it does on paper. It is extremely difficult to predict the future for a business five to seven years down the road. If the path being pursued terminates (e.g., because of the emergence of a dominant competitor), the business could die.

What is needed is a map of possible stepping-stones rather than a deterministic single path. A good map will excite an investor much more than a path. A map should communicate options and possibilities. As any financial theorist will tell you, options have value.

All investors usually ask themselves the following questions:

1. What are the big things that could go wrong (and how will the business handle them)?
2. What are the big options that might open up further down the road (and how might the business take advantage of them)?

Big Things That Could Go Wrong

If there are a few big potential roadblocks ahead—even if there is only a small chance of them happening—investors will want to see a plan B. In fact, they will want to know that there are many plan Bs.

An investor might look at Creditica and see the following potential roadblocks (no doubt you will see others):

-   Credit card issuers might view their proprietary algorithms as so fundamental to their competitive advantage that they will not utilize third-party algorithms from a company such as Creditica.
-   Creditica's algorithms are a "black box" giving out results (target customer names). The results, although accurate, are hard to rationalize simply. Therefore, the results might not be trusted.
-   New personal privacy legislation might prohibit sharing of data from one company to another.
-   The bank from which the team originated might change its mind and attempt to block the business.

All businesses have inherent risks. The business plan should establish how to mitigate the likelihood of them occurring, but it should also establish the possibilities that might still be open to the company in the event that they materialize.

Big Options That Might Open Up Later

On the positive side, the entrepreneur and the investors might foresee ways in which the sequence of stepping-stones the company is pursuing might lead to new possibilities that will open up later. These options must have some value for the investor considering an investment today. These options might not be open to the company today, but the company, having reached the first few stepping-stones along a chosen path, might find them open at a later stage. For Creditica these might include:

- *Becoming a credit card issuer itself.* If Creditica genuinely develops the best algorithms in the world, then maybe the best way of monetizing this advantage is to set up its own credit card issuing company. It could exploit the algorithms itself rather than selling them to others. More plausibly, Creditica might set up a joint venture with one of the smaller credit card issuers to attack the market.
- *Developing managed service for issuers.* If Creditica's software becomes complex to administer, perhaps Creditica could run a managed service. The customer could set broad parameters (e.g., only customers in the northwest with a lower risk exposure than other issuers are willing to accept), and Creditica could generate a list of target names. Maybe the customer would pay per name instead of paying an up-front license fee.
- *Expanding to become a database marketing company.* If Creditica could start to collect the transactional purchase data (what people purchased) on the credit cards issued resulting from Creditica's targeting software, perhaps it could become a world-class database company—selling slices of data to companies in many different industries.
- *Becoming an expert source on targets for financial products other than credit cards.* The excellent data gathered and enriched by Creditica might be usable to identify target customers for other financial products—credit products such as mortgages or personal loans or even asset products such as mutual funds and savings products.

Each of these four possible endgames for Creditica could yield a prize significantly larger than the basic prize of trying to become the leading independent credit card scorecard company.

The point here is not to show that there are infinite paths open to Creditica. Rather, it is to convey to the investor that there are future options that might open up as a result of developing the business in a certain way. Also, the potential roadblocks that might arise can be bypassed in some way.

Generating a Map

It is impossible to articulate all the twists and turns that might occur throughout the future life of the business. But it should be possible to develop a high-level map of the major alternative sequences of stepping-stones. At a minimum, all entrepreneurs should develop their thought processes along these lines, even if they haven't put them down on paper.

One advantage of putting ideas down on paper is that it encourages the team to think laterally. The sequence of stepping-stones for Creditica presented in Exhibit 1.1 is typical of most software companies. But maybe there is a completely different way to chart the future development of the business.

Exhibit 1.3 shows that there is a very early choice for Creditica that was not discussed in the case study. Instead of raising capital from financial investors and advancing to the "early-product" stepping-stone, the company could decide instead to go with a primary development partner. Under this strategy, the company would raise capital from a customer (a credit card issuer) and develop the product in conjunction with that customer. This would have the advantage of getting valuable customer input at the start of the project. It might be possible to perfect the algorithms by running ongoing pilots with the development partner on live data. Of course, this strategy also has the disadvantage of the company being seen as compromised by its close relationship with one large issuer. Such compromises are often dealt with by early-stage companies.

If Creditica decides to go ahead with the early-product stepping-stone without working with a development partner, then once again it

Exhibit 1.3 Creditica Map of Possible Stepping-Stones

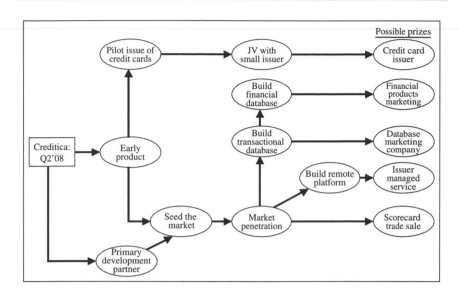

has a fundamental choice. Should it seed the market and make some license sales of the software? Or should it keep the algorithms in-house and run a pilot program to issue some credit cards itself (in conjunction with a partner)? If the software provides huge advantages in issuing cards, then it might be more valuable to Creditica to be an issuer rather than a technology provider. One advantage of the stepping-stone approach is that the company doesn't have to make this decision right away; it can decide in a year or so.

The map shown in Exhibit 1.3 is clearly very simplified. It should be overlaid with the specific steps that should be taken and a preliminary view of the capital required to progress from stepping-stone to stepping-stone.

One advantage of the stepping-stone approach is that only the jump to stepping-stone 1 needs to be costed out to a very low level of detail. This is the part that the initial investor will be asked to finance. The Series A investor will need to be convinced that it will get an economic return for financing the jump to the first stepping-stone. In practice the Series A investor will need to be convinced that the company will be attractive to new investors if it gets to the first stepping-stone and that the Series B investor will pay a price per share that is two to four times greater than the price the Series A investor pays. If the Series A investor cannot convince itself of this, it should not invest and perhaps wait for the opportunity to invest in the Series B round instead.

Convincing the investor of this proposition is covered in more detail in Chapter 7, "Valuing Early-Stage Companies."

Action Steps for the Entrepreneur

In summary, the entrepreneur should think about taking the following actions:

1. Identify the primary prize that the company is going after.
2. Unearth other, potentially larger, prizes that might be possible to pursue if the company is thwarted in pursuing the primary prize because of competitors' actions, regulatory changes, and so forth.
3. Conceptualize, up front, the stepping-stones on the way to the primary prize and the stepping-stones that might branch the company off in the direction of the other prizes.
4. Figure out, at a high level, the amount of resources required to jump from stepping-stone to stepping-stone on the way to the prize. In particular, develop an in-depth view of the resources needed to jump to the initial stepping-stone.
5. Find an investor to finance the jump to the first stepping-stone. Convince the investor that the value of the company will increase by two to four times if the company can jump to the first stepping-stone.
6. Negotiate a win-win deal with the investor that:
   - Gives the investor a share in the ultimate prize compatible with the risk that must be taken in funding the company.
   - Gives the entrepreneur a continued strong interest in pursuing the prize. Don't forget that all the investors who will finance the jumps to future stepping-stones will need to be allocated a piece of the prize as well.

Experienced entrepreneurs looking back on their company will define their lives to a large degree in terms of investment rounds and the stepping-stones along the way.

At each stepping-stone, the company is materially different from what it was at the prior stepping-stone. And to jump from one stepping-stone to another probably requires a new round of capital. Raising each round of capital represents a true test of character for the company. It is enormously time-consuming and challenges a company to examine closely what it is trying to achieve. Entrepreneurs tend to resent the huge time commitment and the distraction from running the business that raising new capital requires.

Each stepping-stone is the true macro milestone for the company that encapsulates commercial milestones such as reference sales, key hires, product completions, new market entries, and an associated investment round to finance all the activities on the way to meeting the commercial milestones. If good commercial milestones are met that are attractive to investors, the company can raise additional investment capital at a good price. If good milestones are met which investors do not value, the company is in trouble. It won't raise new funds, or it will raise new funds only at a punitive price.

Thus (in general, but not always) the best path for the entrepreneur is the one with clearly defined stepping-stones containing milestones that are attractive to investors and that will boost the price per unit of stock at each stage. If a few valuable milestones can be met quickly, it might make sense to raise a small amount of capital up front and raise more at a high price later. Alternatively, if a lot of capital is available now at a good price, it might make sense to take it.

Each stepping-stone on the journey is made up of a series of challenges that provides an enhanced level of proof to the investor (and to the entrepreneur) that the prize is attainable. Designing the right bundle of challenges to overcome is the true creative task in the entrepreneurial process. At the start of the journey, the risks are enormous. Any investor that puts up $100 at stage one of the journey for the right to 10% of the prize wants to know that an investor who later puts up $100 for stage two of the journey will get less than 10% of the prize. Otherwise the first investor will realize that waiting to fund the venture in stage two would offer more of the prize for less risk. The challenges undertaken need to improve the chances of winning the prize.

The entrepreneur has to figure out which challenges to overcome and milestones to reach in stage one with investor one's money that will lessen the risks and catalyze investor two to provide money at a low cost. The range of possible challenges to undertake is limitless. The true art of entrepreneurial finance is to pinpoint the smallest number of achievable, yet valuable, challenges to overcome in the upcoming stage.

The challenges typically fall into the following groups:

- *Product.*   New ventures can happily lose themselves in developing their product. But entrepreneurs need to remember that building the product is a necessary but not sufficient milestone. If the Series A investment just allows the company to develop its product, it will often fail to garner Series B investment because the challenges that were overcome may not have provided evidence sufficient to excite the Series B investor to support the project.
- *Market.*   The size of the prize, from a revenue perspective, is the number of possible customers multiplied by the value that can be extracted from each customer. At every point along the journey, the entrepreneur should be gathering evidence regarding these two factors. One of the tasks to undertake with the Series A capital might be to figure out how much an average customer would be willing to pay. How much value would the entrepreneur's product or service provide to the customer? If investors perceive the market as not particularly big, should part of the Series A capital be carved out to recraft the product to address a completely different market segment?
- *Team.*   Who are the critical people to hire? Which members of the team are critical to the early stages, but will be less necessary later? Since the most important members of the team will want a piece of the prize (a shareholding) and cost a lot of resources along the way, which ones should the entrepreneur take on now? Of course, if the company waits and takes them

on later, the risks will be diminished, and the prize will be more apparent—and they will need to be given a lesser percentage of the prize. The ability of entrepreneurs to hire people of a quality far superior to the norm (without paying them an excessive level of compensation) is a key attribute sought by investors. Investors see hiring great people as a significant milestone.

- *Competitors.*   In which customer accounts should the company aim to prove that it has a superior value proposition? Are there actions the company can take (partnerships signed, key accounts captured, senior staff poached, support from industry analysts, etc.) that can negate competitors' activities in the market?

Creatively combining different challenges can reveal new paths that might make it easier to capture the attention of investors.

Most founders of a new business are not creative enough in designing alternative paths to the prize. They tend to follow approaches pursued by prior entrepreneurs.

Capturing as Much of the Prize as You Can

The popular image of early-stage venturing is of benign venture capitalists working with great entrepreneurs as they build world-class businesses. Every entrepreneur knows that this is stretching the truth. Great entrepreneurs build great businesses; occasionally an experienced venture capitalist can help.

The goal of every entrepreneur with regard to finance is to capture as many dollars out of the ultimate prize as is possible. This has a few implications:

- It might be worth giving investors a larger share of the prize by using more resources in the interest of getting to the prize before competitors. On the other hand, if the competition proves relatively benign, the entrepreneur might target consuming fewer investor resources along the way and holding onto a higher percentage. Sometimes, it might be worth going for a smaller aggregate prize if the cost of the resources associated with chasing the bigger prize is overwhelming.

- The entrepreneur must structure the challenges and milestones for each stepping-stone in order to provide the proof required by the likely investor in the subsequent stage. In particular, the milestones met should be such that investors will be encouraged to provide the funds at a low cost of capital—to minimize the investors' claim on the ultimate prize.

CHAPTER 2

GETTING TO THE FIRST STEPPING-STONE

Getting to the base camp is the first step for any team that wants to conquer Mount Everest. If Chapter 1 set out a team's broad multi-stepping-stone plan for scaling the mountain, then Chapter 2 covers the journey to the base camp—the first stepping-stone.

Once at the base camp, the possibilities open up. It is the jumping-off point for a variety of routes. Resources can be replenished, and intelligence on weather and conditions gleaned. If the weather is particularly favorable, the trip might be expedited. The merits of alternative routes can be explored. But there is a downside; the group funding the trip can decide to abandon the trek to the summit if the possibility of reaching the summit is remote. Groups take the trip to the base camp with the hope of getting to the top. But they know that the chances of getting there are modest.

The same is true for the way in which early-stage companies are financed. Venture capitalists aim to reach the top, but they hedge their bets and stay flexible along the way. In short, early-stage ventures are not assumed to be a going concern and to have an infinite life. Business plans are rarely, if ever, fully funded to a cash flow breakeven point. In essence, the investor sets a test for a company: "Here is a defined amount of money to achieve some milestones (to jump to the next stepping-stone)." If the milestones are met, the value of the company will have gone up and the company can probably raise more money from the initial investor or others. Each round of funding is therefore targeted at meeting certain milestones. If milestones are not met, the company can be liquidated, merged, financed again (if the prospects for the company continue to be perceived as attractive), or restructured.

The company has no assumed life beyond the next important stepping-stone. It lives its life from round to round of investment. CEOs regularly claim that they are perpetually in fund-raising mode which distracts them from the business at hand of building the value of the company.

All this emphasizes that the goal is to get to the first stepping-stone.

Why New Ventures Are Not Fully Funded from the Start

Entrepreneurs would like to have their business fully funded to the point where they are cash-flow-positive based on revenues. Once cash-flow-positive, they should be able to sustain themselves, in the absence of the need to finance a new growth curve. But there are a number of good reasons why new ventures do not get (or deserve to get) up front the entire amount of capital required to sustain them up to the point where they become cash-flow-positive.

1. *The risks at the outset of a business are daunting.* No investor is likely to cover the risks in one fully committed investment. The end point is so far in the future and the level of risk on the way there is so high that investors would shy away. The investor needs the entrepreneur to break the project down into logical, plausible steps that demonstrate progress toward the end goal. These logical steps might then be financed.

   Designing these steps is like designing a bundle of trials for the company to undertake. If designed correctly, the bundles of trials inherent in each step progressively reduce the risk of the project—the quicker the better. The investors in each round get comfort in knowing that the value of the company is being enhanced with their investment. As the risks fall away, the entrepreneur can sell units of stock at a progressively higher price and suffer less onerous dilution in his or her ownership.

2. *The situation is too dynamic to make the full commitment up front.* The best investment opportunities are those that offer lots of flexibility and multiple potential prizes. If one avenue closes off, there are others to pursue. Investing all the capital up front might put a company on a lockstep path toward one particular prize.

    As well as giving flexibility regarding the prizes to pursue, staging the investment also gives the investor the chance to fix the company midstream if the company is not making sufficient progress. Removing an underperforming CEO is very difficult without the threat of refusing to provide the investment required to keep the company going.

3. *If someone was willing to cover all these risks in one single investment, he or she would require a huge percentage of the ownership of the company, leaving little for the entrepreneur.* If an investor was willing to fund the entire development of the company in one go, then the essence of entrepreneurship is lacking and the entrepreneur truly deserves only a small ownership position. The early stage of a business represents its lowest likely economic value. Raising all the capital at this point, at a low valuation, would lead to punitive levels of dilution.

Fleshing Out the First Stepping-Stone

The first stepping-stone is the most important. The entrepreneur needs to think carefully about the trials he or she is going to have to deal with on the way to this stepping-stone. It is a period for gathering evidence regarding the attractiveness of the ultimate prize and the ability of the company to attain the prize. Consider the following mini case.

An entrepreneur wishes to set up a chain of 300 high-end audio-video equipment stores across the United States. These stores will provide a high-service experience for customers by employing expert staff. Approximately $100M will be required to cover the capital and start-up costs of rolling out 300 new stores.

Investors have refused to finance the full plan with one investment—it is simply too risky. But they are intrigued by the opportunity and have asked the team to recraft the plan so that the business will utilize less capital, but keep the potential upside of rolling out 300 stores over time.

The first place for the audio-video entrepreneur to start is to establish an overall set of stepping-stones for the business. One path of stepping-stones, assuming a successful one-store experiment, might be along the following lines:

1. ***Stepping-stone 1: Prove the economics of one store.*** This involves setting up a supply chain, creating a differentiable customer experience, building a customer base, figuring out the staffing model, and so on. At the end of this stage, the entrepreneur and investors should be able to run focus groups of customers to assess whether the customers appreciated the higher level of service and determine the size of the premium they are willing to pay for the service.

2. ***Stepping-stone 2: Prove the manageability of a small group (10–20) of stores.*** This means that the repeatability of the format needs to be determined. It involves creating the position of a professional store manager separate from the entrepreneur, mastering multilocation logistics, controlling a more complex operation, and so forth.

3. ***Stepping-stone 3: Prove the ability to scale up to 300 stores and the incremental economic advantages of size.*** This is the final roll-out stage when the business model is clear and repeatable. A large amount of capital can be committed at this point because the project now has much lower risk than it did during the first stage.

Once the overall stepping-stones have been identified, the entrepreneur needs to hone in very precisely on the first stepping-stone and figure out the specific bundle of trials that must be undertaken on the way to it.

Crafting a Good First Stepping-Stone

Clearly, there is significant risk associated with the scale up from a small number of stores to a large number of stores. These risks are execution risks.

However, there are some basic first-stage risks that need to be tested up front. The smart investor and entrepreneur will flush out these risks and package them into a work program while establishing milestones to be achieved on the way to the first stepping-stone. Proving the economics of one store might involve testing the following issues:

- Can the entrepreneur get a quality supply chain in place and procure product at a price that will allow him or her to achieve a 40%+ gross margin?
- Can working capital terms (determined by days of accounts receivable, days of accounts payable, and rate of turning inventory) be set so that the business does not consume significant amounts of working capital as sales increase?[1]
- Can a run rate on sales (and gross margin) be achieved that will cover the overhead of running a shop and yield an annual per-shop profit of, say, $250,000?
- Can the entrepreneur find good sites for the stores that will provide enough passing customers in the target segment?
- Can the entrepreneur find and train high-quality staff at the salaries established in the business plan?
- Do customers appreciate and value the high level of service? Most importantly, are they willing to pay a premium price for this service? Will this premium cover the incremental cost?

The investor and the entrepreneur might decide that, by setting up just one store, these issues can be tested. The investment would then be structured to cover just the cost of testing these issues. This should require a very modest amount of

---

1 More on the capital implications of working capital terms in Chapter 4.

capital, and the entrepreneur might have to give up a small amount of ownership in return. If the experiment with one store is not successful, then the plan can be abandoned without the waste of large amounts of capital.

Options at the End of Each Stage of Investment

By staging the investment to coincide with the stepping-stones, the investor is presented with a wide variety of options. Implicit in funding against stepping-stones is the expectation that the company will run out of money at some point. When this point is reached, the investor can decide to fund it to the next stepping-stone, accelerate or decelerate, abandon the investment, restructure it, and the like.

This sort of dynamic decision making is central to the VC method. If progress is swift toward milestones, the financing strategy might be pursued as set out in the initial plan. But things don't always go according to plan. Experienced investors factor slow performance with respect to the plan into their thinking.

The investors in a private company have fairly limited power once the check is written and the investment is made. In theory they have a broad set of rights as set out in the shareholders' agreement. In practice it is hard for them to direct changes in the company—the entrepreneurs have the money, and, in the absence of fraud or gross incompetence, they can pretty much do with it as they see fit. But this all changes when the company has an impending need for fresh capital. This is the point at which investors have the leverage to effect changes that might be problematic for the entrepreneur. The investors have the implied threat of not continuing to fund the company. If the CEO needs to be changed, the cost base needs to be dramatically reduced or the strategy adjusted—against the wishes of the founders. The investors might be able to make this happen only when the issue of making a new investment arises.

The broad set of options open to the investors at the time of the new funding round is presented in Exhibit 2.1.

Exhibit 2.1 Finite Life of Business—the Implications

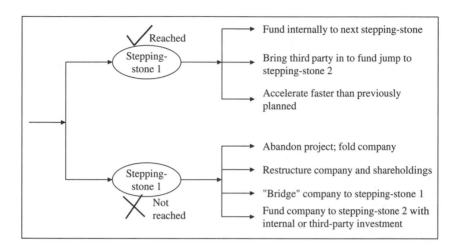

The wide variety of options provides a period of analysis at the end of each stage when the investors can take stock of the situation. The goal of the entrepreneur is to have collected sufficient "proof" of the viability of the business to convince the existing investors or new investors to fund the company to the next stepping-stone, with a modest amount of dilution.

The Chief Financial Officer as Strategist

Chief financial officers (CFOs) in most established companies are numbers-focused and analytical. They translate the strategy of the company into its financial implications. Then they assess whether the business will generate sufficient capital from its ongoing operations to fund the strategy. If there is a gap, they arrange for the finance to be available— through debt or equity. In effect, the CFO generally plays a subsidiary role in the development of the strategy.

The CFO in an early-stage company plays a different role. The strategy is not a given because the strategy is irrelevant unless the finance is available. The CFO becomes integral to strategy formulation.

Strategy and the finance to implement it are two sides of the same coin in an early-stage venture.

At its most simple, the best stepping-stone for an early-stage company is the one that allows it to capture the necessary funding in the next investment round at the highest price.

While this is not necessarily true in all instances, it is a good guideline for the CFO of an early-stage company to follow. The highest price will take into account factors such as progress with customers, moves to thwart competitors, and achieving product development milestones.

If CFOs are purely reactive to a strategy developed by a board or a CEO, they are not doing their job. While the CEO might have an intuitive feel for the best strategy for the company, the CFO needs to ask the hard questions:

- Taking into account the cash resources on hand, which milestones are likely to be attainable? What is the margin for error for each of these milestones?
- By how much will the valuation of the company increase in the eyes of the investment world if different types of milestones are met?
- If $5M, for example, is invested in the company, will the milestones reached by spending the $5M boost the valuation of the company by $20M or $30M at least? If not, the entrepreneur is not utilizing the capital efficiently, and the investors are not likely to get a reasonable return on their investment.
- Which milestones are most at risk of not being met? If the major identifiable milestones are not achieved, will the company have established enough proof of its viability by reaching the other milestones to convince the investors to invest more?
- Some milestones tend to have all-or-nothing outcomes; others can be achieved in part and still yield value to the company. Do the CEO and CFO accept that all-or-nothing milestones might mean that the company could fold if the milestones are not met?
- What alternative sets of milestones could the company possibly pursue? What impact might reaching the different sets of milestones have on the next round valuation of the company?

- Should the company take on a lot of capital now or a smaller amount of capital now in the hope of boosting the valuation of the company prior to taking on more capital? How risky would this be?

Many CFOs of early-stage companies are not creative enough in developing alternative sets of milestones to submit to a board and CEO. Milestones tend to be created by the technical development group or the sales and marketing division without explicitly assessing how the resources spent on these activities will earn a high enough return on capital.

Most investors want the chance of earning a 10-times multiple on their investment. Consequently, on average every $1 of resources spent by the company today must boost the value of the company by at least $10 tomorrow. Most CFOs don't think about resource consumption with this degree of discipline.

Unfortunately, the cost budget in many early-stage companies is often defined as follows.

- Sales and marketing establish high-level sales targets for the next year or two.
- Sales and marketing determine that to reach these targets the product needs to incorporate certain features to satisfy customers (or the next generation of the product will be required). In addition, sales and marketing decide how many people will be required to meet the targets, given the typical sales level of a quota-carrying salesperson.
- Product development translates these needs into a product road map and estimates how many people (and the requisite skills) are needed to achieve what's been established in the product road map.
- Finance costs out the increased resources.
- If the capital is not available, there is an iterative process among finance, product development, and sales and marketing to reduce the projected costs or boost projected sales to fit the capital available.

The CFO must be deeply involved in developing the strategy alongside the CEO. Consider the following mini case concerning an early-stage software company that is developing its strategy and trying to identify the best first stepping-stone.

MINI CASE: A SOFTWARE COMPANY DEVELOPING ALTERNATIVE FIRST STEPPING-STONES

The software company has just closed a $3M round of funding. The team is primarily a technical team with plans to add a top-class CEO and a head of sales over time. If the CFO is good, he or she will push the executive team to figure out alternative sets of milestones beyond the usual sequence of stepping-stones.

The alternatives might include the three below:

Alternative	Milestones and Actions	Considerations
1. World-class product first	Over 18 to 24 months, build a complete world-class product that will be clearly superior to that of the competition. Aim to close some very early direct sales with trial customers (value of $200,000). Plan on hiring a CEO in 18 months when the product is finished. Save the cost in the meantime.	Will the product be built on time? Can the team build a world-class product without close engagement with the market? Is it important to avoid having competitors see the product prior to it being ready for market? If the product is late and no sales are made, how will investors in the next round validate the superiority of the product and its market potential? Without a CEO, will the company go astray?
2. Proof of concept	Hire the CEO immediately. Build a simple proof-of-concept product in 6 to 8 months. Using the proof of concept, aim to sign up two companies as development partners who will work with the company to specify the product (they will get a good price on the product for their early commitment).	Can a great CEO be attracted when there is, as yet, limited external validation of the opportunity? Would the company be better served by getting a first-class CEO later? Are there some good prospects in the picture today that might be willing to act as development partners? Will the development partners help to build a product that is

		valid for the broad market or will the company get pulled into serving their unique needs?
3. Original equipment manufacturer (OEM) route	Target one large software company that is likely to want your product included as part of its product line. Try to strike an up-front OEM deal (where the early-stage company will receive a royalty on each sale of the larger company's product). Build the product to meet the large company's specifications. Add the CEO later.	Is there an OEM partner in the picture today? If the company works with one OEM, will that inhibit it from selling its product directly to customers? Will a close relationship with one large company be a barrier to the company working with its competitors later?

There are a large number of other alternatives available as well. By teasing out alternatives and developing a broad view of the likely next round valuation and the strategic implications with respect to each alternative, the company can ensure that it uses its capital most effectively. The CFO will need to have a good feel for the venture capital financing market to make a useful contribution on this front.

One way to formulate alternatives is to consider the big risks and big possibilities facing the business and to flesh out steps the company could take cheaply and quickly to "clear the fog" in relation to them.

The right alternative won't depend only on the valuation possible. It must take into account the risks of getting there. Not reaching a stepping-stone could have a catastrophic impact on the future existence of the company.

Why Corporations Fail in Creating New Businesses

Large corporations are famously bad at creating new businesses. The main reason for this is that they are organizationally unwilling or unable to stage the investment with stepping-stones and to be ruthless about abandoning (or accelerating) the project midstream.

Executives in corporations who are on the fast track don't want to be associated with failure; therefore, they always want a new venture to be funded "properly." Properly to them means that it be fully funded, regardless of the positives or negatives that might arise in the course of the company's development. Career progression in a large company often requires that executives avoid any link to failures. But failure is a consistent variable in venture capital. Consequently, it is very hard to inject a venture capital mindset into decision making in a large company.

Some companies have tried to segregate new ventures into a protected part of the organization, in which compensation structures mirror those of executives in entrepreneurial ventures (highly leveraged pay and stock participation). But if taken too far, other established business units in the large corporation can become hostile to the new ventures unit, resenting the compensation structures and the looser attitude to losing money. As a result, the theoretical benefits of starting a small company as part of the large corporation (access to the distribution power of other business units, skills and expertise, etc.) often fail to materialize.

For many investors, an investment in an early-stage company is an option. An option can be exercised or abandoned at any point. Large companies find it hard to pursue investments in new ventures in this manner.

Exhibit 2.2 Large Corporations Innovate by Buying Small Companies

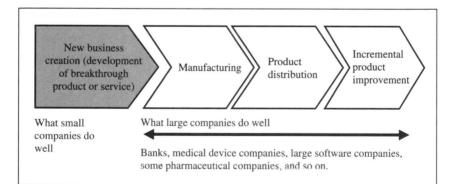

Given this, many large corporations have, in effect, outsourced new product and service development to early-stage ventures. They simply buy smaller companies if they like the products or the market progress they have made. This is often the most effective way for large companies to develop new lines of business. The strength of many large corporations is in their distribution power (large sales forces, relationships with customers and channels, strong brand names, etc.), their manufacturing scale, and their large capital base. If they can buy a small, innovative company with good products, they can manufacture the product more cheaply than the small company can, and they have a much more powerful distribution footprint. In industries such as medical devices, pharmaceuticals and biotechnology, software, and communications this has created a symbiotic relationship between small ventures and large corporations. This relationship can be seen in Exhibit 2.2.

CHAPTER 3

THE UNIQUE CASH FLOW AND RISK DYNAMICS OF EARLY-STAGE VENTURES

Early-stage businesses are peculiar in the way they are financed. Valuing them appears to be an art rather than a science, particularly when compared to the rigorous analytical techniques used to value established companies. Authors of the standard finance textbooks steer clear of them—they just don't understand them. The types of investors are different—angels and venture capitalists, rather than banks and public stock fund managers. The instruments of investment (preferred stock) used in early-stage companies are crafted intricately. The investment contracts are full of their own arcane language (e.g., pay-to-play antidilution, participating preferred, protective provisions, liquidation preferences, tagalong, dragalong). These peculiarities are there for a reason. They have been tried and tested under stress by investors and entrepreneurs over time, and they exist on the West and East Coasts and overseas. They simply work.

But all of the above differences are just symptoms of one crucial underlying difference—the life of a new venture is assumed to be finite. This finite life creates a unique set of cash flow and risk dynamics for investors and entrepreneurs.

If you develop an appreciation for these unique cash flow and risk dynamics, then the peculiarities in valuation techniques, investment instruments, types of investors, and so forth that are covered in subsequent chapters will start to make sense.

If investors and executives in early-stage companies compared notes with their peers in established companies, they would see the following 10 unique dynamics:

1. Costs known—revenues unknown.
2. J curves and peak cash needs.
3. Milestone funding: option or investment?
4. A 12- to 24-month ticking clock.
5. Timing is everything—buy low, sell high.
6. A five- to seven-year marathon in three to four stages.
7. Gross margins of 80 to 100%.
8. No correlation between the amount of money raised and the company's success.
9. A tension between the "lemons ripening early" and the "valley of death."
10. A binary payoff profile.

Costs Known—Revenues Unknown

Established companies have tried, trusted, and administratively smooth approaches for evaluating whether to purchase a new piece of equipment and how to finance it. They can generally make a fairly good estimate of the up-front capital cost and the likely annual cost savings, which can be planned as shown in Exhibit 3.1.

In this case the up-front capital cost is $300,000, and the yearly savings are $100,000. The payback period (three years) is reasonably predictable. Consequently, if the company makes a good enough case to a bank or a leasing company, it should be able to avoid expending valuable equity in financing the equipment. Cheaper debt should be available. While the go/no-go purchase decision will, of course, require good managerial judgment, the decision can be underpinned by rigorous analysis. Most large companies have good processes for distinguishing worthwhile capital investment projects from wasteful ones.

Go/no-go decisions regarding an investment in a new venture are a lot trickier. Entrepreneurs approaching investors with a business plan

Exhibit 3.1 Financing a Piece of Equipment

New Piece of Equipment ($000)

					Years			
	0	1	2	3	4	5	6..........X	
Outflows	(300)							
Savings	0	100	100	100	100	100	100.......100	
Cumulative	(300)	(200)	(100)	0	100	200	300....... X	

- Three-year payback
- Predictable
- Financed by debt or lease finance
- Good analysis rather than good judgment required

for a new venture generally present detailed three- (or more) year projections setting out the revenue, cost, and cash flow expectations for the company. Hockey stick projections showing revenues growing to $75M over five years and the company breaking even in three to four years seem to be the norm!

The shape of the projections presented by the entrepreneur to the investor might look like the simplified projections in Exhibit 3.2. The entrepreneur with projections like this will seek $4M of investment over the life of the company—the peak cash need is $3.6M (in Q4 2007), and a small amount of capital would be useful as a margin for error. The entrepreneur might split the investment required in two tranches—the first one of, say, $2.5M and the second of $1.5M.

Both the entrepreneur and the investor know that these projections are make-believe because it is impossible to get an accurate view of the future financial prospects for the business. There are just too many moving variables, risks, and pitfalls.

More importantly, the thought process inherent in the construction of the entrepreneur's projections is completely at odds with that of the

Exhibit 3.2 Entrepreneur's View of the World

$000

	2006				2007				2008			
	Q1	Q2	Q3	Q4	Q1	Q2	Q3	Q4	Q1	Q2	Q3	Q4
Revenues	0	0	300	500	600	800	1,000	1,200	1,500	2,000	3,000	3,500
Costs	500	800	900	1,000	1,000	1,100	1,200	1,500	1,500	1,500	1,600	1,800
Net profit (loss)	–500	–800	–600	–500	–400	–300	–200	–300	0	500	1,400	1,700
Cumulative cash need	–500	–1,300	–1,900	–2,400	–2,800	–3,100	–3,300	–3,600	–3,600	–3,100	–1,700	0

typical early-stage investor. Investors don't tend to think in terms of spreadsheets and sensitivity. Rather:

- *Investors want to know how many months the company has, in a downside scenario, to achieve some basic milestones.* Shortly after meeting a new opportunity, an investor tends to quickly zero in on an amount that he or she is willing to invest. Rather than thinking about how much the business needs, the investor tends to come up with a preferred investment amount. This amount is framed by the likely J curve facing the business (more on J curves later in this chapter). But he or she will also be thinking about the size of his or her fund. The size of the fund generally has a big bearing on the amount to be invested; the investor will want no more than 5 to 8% of his or her fund invested in a deal over its life.

    The investor will then start thinking about how far the business can get with the amount of capital that he or she is willing to invest (alongside potential coinvestors). Will the business reach a major stepping-stone with that amount? If not, could cash expenditure be cut back or the company's plan be reshaped such that a good stepping-stone could be reached?

    Entrepreneurs are often not clued in to the fact that investors are not necessarily thinking about what the business needs; rather they are focused on what it deserves and the amount of capital the investor is willing to commit.

- *Investors inject realism and prior experience into the projections.*
  The early-stage investor will take the entrepreneur's projections
  and red-line the revenues—for at least the first 18 to 24 months.
  When it comes to revenue projections from entrepreneurs,
  investors regularly utter the maxim, "Half as much and twice as
  long." It is not that entrepreneurs maliciously overestimate
  revenues. Because of optimism, naïveté, or the desire to capture
  the investor's attention, they systematically underestimate the
  challenge a small company has in closing its first sales. On the
  other hand, costs should be fairly predictable in the first 18 to
  24 months. The primary cash-consuming activity will be to feed
  the "marching army" of the product development team and the
  monthly overhead. These are straightforward to project.

Therefore, after reworking the entrepreneur's numbers,
investors might end up with projections for the same project like
those shown in Exhibit 3.3.

An 18- to 24-month horizon indicates a capital requirement of
$8M, rather than the $4M suggested by the entrepreneur's
forecasts. Note that a cautious view of revenue flows can lead to
a dramatic increase in capital requirements.

In practice, the investor will allow for certain modest revenues,
perhaps where there are early indications from customers of
potential sales. This is why investors examine the near-term sales

Exhibit 3.3 Investor's View of the World

$000

	2006				2007				2008			
	Q1	Q2	Q3	Q4	Q1	Q2	Q3	Q4	Q1	Q2	Q3	Q4
Revenues	0	0	0	0	0	0	0	0	?	?	?	?
Costs	500	800	900	1,000	1,000	1,100	1,200	1,500	1,000	1,500	1,600	1,800
Net profit (loss)	–500	–800	–900	–1,000	–1,000	–1,100	–1,200	–1,500	?	?	?	?
Cumulative cash need	–500	–1,300	–2,200	–3,200	–4,200	–5,300	–6,500	–8,000	?	?	?	?

pipeline very closely and form a customer-by-customer view concerning the revenues that should be included. Investors don't like revenue projections based on top-down analysis such as, "The company will capture 2% of a $500M market in two years."

In effect, the investors test the entrepreneur's numbers against their own gut feelings. They will usually have the benefit of a much larger data set of start-ups and the typical pitfalls and time frames involved.

- *Investors tend to be obsessively focused on the short term (one to two years) and the long term (five to seven years or more when the venture might be exited).* They don't pay a lot of attention to the medium-term (two- to four-year) projections.

As the chapter on valuation discusses, in the short term investors will be concerned about ensuring that the resources required have been specified correctly and that the company is heading toward valuable milestones. Most importantly, they will want to ensure that the capital they are investing will be sufficient to get the company to a new stepping-stone—milestones that can be used as a basis on which the company can raise more capital at a higher price per unit of stock.

For the longer term, they will be focused on the ultimate potential size of the market for the company and the odds that the company will become a leader in the market. This is because the payoff structure for an early-stage venture is generally, but not always, binary—the investor either gets a very good return or loses his or her capital. There is more on this under the section "A Binary Payoff Profile" below.

Investors are much less concerned with the three- to four-year horizon for a business, which is where many entrepreneurs focus, albeit erroneously. The investor wants to know that management will meet a number of milestones in the next 18 months or so that will justify the company raising more capital (at a higher valuation). The investor really won't be too concerned about whether the entrepreneur is projecting sales per quarter in year 3 or 4 of $6M or $10M.

J Curves and Peak Cash Needs

Every new venture faces a J curve—the cash goes down before it comes back up, if it comes back up at all. Smart investors, implicitly or explicitly, always have a feel for the J curve that they will likely face over the life of an investment. They also have an idea of the point on the J curve where their cash should fit in during the course of the development of the company.

The *J curve* is the expected cash flow profile of the venture over its life. It incorporates key factors such as the likely size and timing of required capital injections, the elapsed time to first revenues, the elapsed time to operating cash flow breakeven, the elapsed time to cash flow breakeven on the project as a whole (including payback of the capital), and the ultimate potential cash flow upside. An example of a J curve is shown in Exhibit 3.4.

As you can see, according to the investor, the peak cash need, in this example, is around $12M, the time to operating cash flow breakeven (where quarterly cash-in exceeds cash-out) is four years and full cash

Exhibit 3.4 J Curve and Peak Cash Need

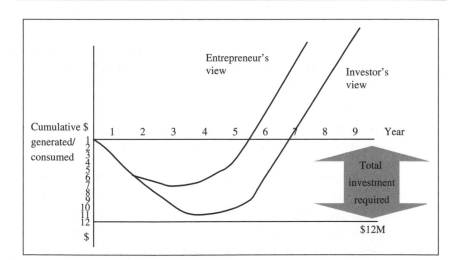

flow breakeven (including repayment of the capital invested) is seven years. This is where the optimism of the entrepreneur contrasts sharply with the cautiousness of the investor. The entrepreneur is forecasting a peak cash need of $6M. With relatively modest changes to the expected size and timing of revenues, the J curve can deepen significantly.

Link between Peak Cash Need and Exit Value Expectations

An informed view of the peak cash need is critical. Consider the example presented in Exhibit 3.4. If the investor is correct, then the capital need is $12M. If the entrepreneur is correct, then it is $6M. Assuming that the investor ends up owning half of the business in each scenario, the investor's final average company valuation (after all the rounds of investment) will be either $24M or $12M.

Most investors involved in early-stage investments want to have a chance of making at least 10 times their money. If the entrepreneur's view of the capital required is correct, the company needs to have a chance of being valued at $120M on exit. If the investor's view is correct, the company must have a chance of being valued at $240M on exit.

Experienced investors turn that sort of analysis on its head. When they see a company, they instinctively form an opinion as to whether it is a $500M opportunity, a $250M opportunity, or an opportunity worth less than $100M. Businesses that are a $250M or less opportunity had better not have a peak cash need of more than $15M to 20M.

Link between Size of the Venture Capital Fund and the Projected Peak Cash Need of the Business

Venture capital firms with large amounts of capital under their management will want to know that there is the possibility of investing a material percentage of their fund in the deal over its lifetime. For example, if the venture capital fund has $500M in capital, it will not want to be investing in deals that have a likely peak capital need of $5M to $10M. It would simply have too many investments to manage if it were involved in a number of deals of that size. A view of the J curve for each investment can screen out investments that do not fit with the venture firm's strategy.

A view of the J curve on an investment is more important in the reverse case, where the investor does not have the ability to sustain an investment through its life. This is a far more likely case than the investor with too much capital. In such an instance, each investor needs to know what the journey is going to be like and where he or she fits in the overall funding structure. If the capital needs are going to be substantial over multiple rounds, then the seed investor must be very careful. As the round size gets bigger and bigger, an inability to "play" for his or her pro rata allocation in the round could lead to his or her position being wiped out in a down round. A down round of investment is one in which the price per unit of stock in an investment round is less than the price per share in the previous round—in essence, the value of the company has declined.

The J curve will help the early investor spot points in the future when fresh injections of capital will be critical for the company. It will help the early investor figure out his or her exact role in the upcoming multitiered capital structure of the company. See the mini case about a VC firm with a $100M fund.

MINI CASE: HOW MUCH SHOULD AN INVESTOR INVEST IN A PARTICULAR ROUND OF INVESTMENT?

If an investor with a $100M fund has set aside $5M to invest in a particular company over its life, what proportion of the $5M should it invest in the first round, and how much should it reserve for future rounds?

Should it invest all $5M in the company in the first (or upcoming) round (when the price per unit of stock is likely at its lowest point)? Should it invest $3M to $4M now and reserve $1M to $2M for later rounds? Or maybe invest $2M now and hold a lot of capital back in reserve?

Unfortunately, the answer to this issue is, it depends. If the initial round of investment in the company is $3M (for 40%) but it is likely that two to three more rounds, each progressively larger, will be required, the investor might decide to only invest $1.5M for 20% in the first round alongside another similarly sized investor and reserve $3.5M for future rounds. This gives the investor full protection for future rounds of investment in aggregate of $17.5M or less ($3.5M would allow the investor to play for 20%). An inability to play for 20% of all likely future rounds of investment could mean heavy dilution of the investor's ownership position if the price per share is set very low.

The investor who has decided to allocate $5M to the company over its life could decide to cover the full initial investment round of $3M for a share of 40% and reserve $2M for future rounds. This would make sense only in the following two cases:

1. The future investment needs are likely to be limited. Thus the need for protection is limited.
2. The company seems likely to meet some very important value milestones with the initial $3M, and there is a good chance of a serious uplift in valuation (price per unit of stock) in subsequent rounds. In this instance, the investor is taking a substantial funding risk—will future investors come onboard at a high price without requiring the early investors to play for a high percentage of the subsequent round? While this risk might be high, the early investor is betting that the rewards of owning 40% of the company outweigh the risks.

Early investors need to be aware that investors in later rounds often want the early investors to invest in later rounds "to show good faith." They want to see that the early investors still believe the company has good prospects; the only way for the early investor to do this is to invest more money at the same price per share as the new investor.

Consider the following three investment opportunities. What shape would you expect the J curve to be for each?

1. *Purchase of an existing retail business.* The entrepreneur wishes to buy a well-run toy store in an established area from an owner planning retirement.

2. ***Establishment of a new software business.*** The entrepreneur wishes to develop a new software product for sale to large corporations.
3. ***Development of a new biotech drug.*** The basic research of the drug compound is completed, and the entrepreneur is looking for investment to sustain the business through four rounds of clinical trials and regulatory approvals.

The expected shape of the J curves for these businesses is shown in Exhibit 3.5.

The shape of the J curves in Exhibit 3.5 for the three businesses is determined by the following dynamics:

1. ***Retail toy business.*** The capital required to buy this business will go out on day 1, in the absence of any earn-out payments over time to the former owner. From day 1 forward, the revenues and costs (and, consequently, operating cash flow by month) should be fairly predictable. There might be an upward turn in the angle of the curve as the new owner will no doubt have plans for

Exhibit 3.5 Expected J Curve by Type of Business

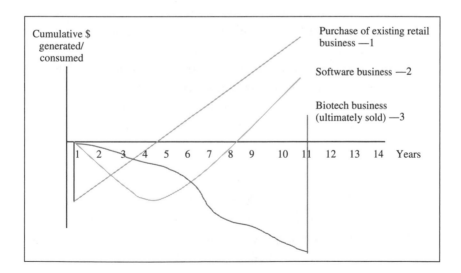

improving operations and enhancing profitability. Again, these plans might require some investment. Note also that an increase in the rate of sales will probably have a negative impact on cash flow in the near term because of the demands of working capital—see Chapter 4 for a full review of the impact of working capital on the investment requirement.

2. **Software business.** Up-front product development, prior to initial sales, might take 18 to 24 months. Thereafter, the business might accrue some modest revenues for a few years, but these are unlikely to cover the ongoing monthly costs. In years 3 to 5 the company might see operating cash flow breakeven—the incoming cash from sales covering the outgoing costs. Software businesses sometimes take four to six years or more to get to breakeven on a cumulative basis—the point at which the cumulative cash flow deficits in prior years (including the up-front capital cost) are made up by sales receipts.

3. **Biotech business.** This business will require large—potentially enormous—amounts of capital. One positive feature is that there will be a number of clear go/no-go decision points after each set of clinical trials. These can be based on objective evidence. At each stage, the valuation will hopefully be enhanced, as the capital investment required will mushroom. With the valuation increasing, the hope of the entrepreneur is that the increasing capital requirements will entail proportionately declining amounts of dilution. In practice, rather than a biotech business achieving positive operating cash flow by building sales, it is likely to be sold. Building distribution for a new therapeutic treatment through clinical networks is incredibly expensive. Large pharmaceutical companies have strong distribution networks that can accelerate access to market for product-rich biotech businesses.

While the J curve is rarely drawn and discussed between investors and entrepreneurs, good investors will have a mental picture of what will match their investing strategy. For example, investors in semiconductor start-ups will often say that it takes $30M to $60M in peak capital need to bring one of these companies to a logical exit point. Similarly, some investors in life sciences with modestly sized funds will avoid biotech investments (given their voracious capital appetites) and stick to medical devices or similar investments that have a J curve more like a software company than a drug development company.

Milestone Funding: Option or Investment?

As prior chapters make clear, milestone investing is the standard financing approach for early-stage ventures. No early-stage business is funded to break even. This means the commitment of capital to a business in tranches at, hopefully, an increasing valuation each time. The larger amounts of capital are taken on when the valuation is highest, thus mitigating the dilution impact. In general, the amount of capital required by a company increases as it moves from product development into market rollout. Building a distribution network is often, but not always, the most capital consumptive part of the development of a business.

Applying milestone investing to the J curve example in the last section might lead to the $12M investment that must be tranched into four investment rounds as shown in Exhibit 3.6.

The investment round sizes should match the shape of the J curve. Most companies will aim to raise new capital no sooner than every 12 to 18 months.

One classic example of a business requiring milestone-based investments is the rollout of a new telecommunications service. Exhibit 3.7 outlines the typical investment phases of a new mobile phone company. In phase 1, a small amount of money is required to fund the process of applying for a license. In return, the investor can expect a good share of the equity because the risks are very high—the most immediate being whether the company will win the license competition in the first place. If the license is won, the value of the company might go up significantly since mobile phone businesses were traditionally viewed by investors as offering the potential to participate in a sheltered market with good premium pricing (if not, predatory!) power for those with licenses. A lot of money will be required to build the network and launch the

Exhibit 3.6 Milestone Funding

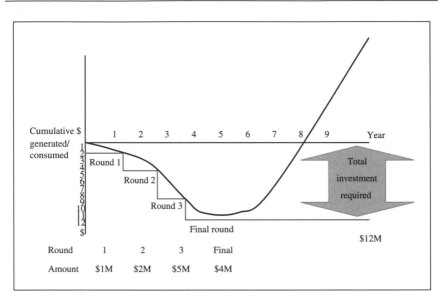

Round	1	2	3	Final
Amount	$1M	$2M	$5M	$4M

Exhibit 3.7 Example: Mobile Phone Business

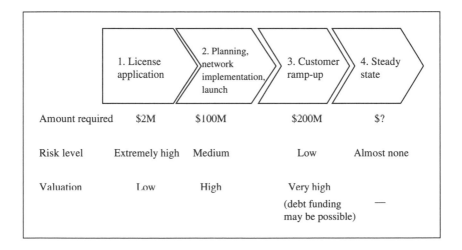

	1. License application	2. Planning, network implementation, launch	3. Customer ramp-up	4. Steady state
Amount required	$2M	$100M	$200M	$?
Risk level	Extremely high	Medium	Low	Almost none
Valuation	Low	High	Very high (debt funding may be possible)	—

company in the market. Typically, the amount of money raised will allow for early customer acquisition. This will provide some sense of the cost of customer acquisition and the likely revenue per customer. With clarity on these factors, a new round of investment might be initiated to fund customer ramp-up. Since the business has been substantially derisked at this point, debt providers might be willing to fund the next stage of the business.

Spreading the investment out over these three to four steppingstones helps the investor in three ways:

1. *It matches the risk-reward profile of the stage of the investment.* In simple terms, early-stage investors invest at the riskiest point of the cycle; as a result, they expect the highest return on their investment.

   Exhibit 3.8 shows a simplified view of the proportionate relationship between the level of risk and the return likely to be demanded by the investor. (Chapter 7 covers the detail of the expected multiple and percentage returns that investors at each stage should aim to get.)

Exhibit 3.8 Milestone Funding Matches Risk to Reward for Investors

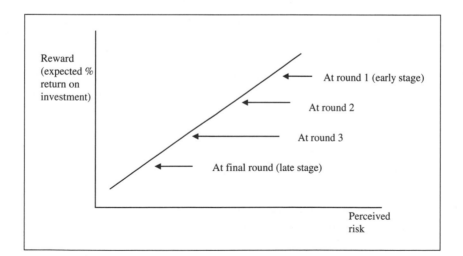

2. ***It helps the investor to effect change in the business.*** If the team is not performing or if prospects are poor, the investor gets a chance to reprice the initial investment in the company. Poor progress indicates that the investor has probably paid too high a price for his or her investment. For investors, more so than repricing the investment, milestone funding allows them to effect change at the executive level in the company. If the company is performing poorly and the investors perceive that the CEO is responsible, it is difficult to remove the CEO, except at the point immediately prior to a new investment. The investors typically comprise a minority of the directors on the board. New funding rounds can provide a point of leverage for effecting change where executive management is resisting change. In between rounds some management teams pay little attention to the suggestions of their investors. This is generally a bad idea.

3. ***It helps to limit the investor's loss in the event of the business failing.*** The returns from early-stage investments are typically binary. The investor can easily lose 100% of his or her capital but can also make a big multiple on the amount invested. Investors investing across a portfolio understand that they can lose their capital only once on an individual investment, but they can make a 10 to 20 times multiple on that investment. If the capital investment has been staged, the investors are able to limit the maximum amount of their loss if it becomes apparent along the way that the company is not likely to succeed.

But most commentators in the venture capital sector rarely note that milestone funding works for entrepreneurs as well as investors. If investors were required to put up all the money in the initial investment tranche, they would expect to own an extraordinarily high percentage, if not all, of the company.

Entrepreneurs play the great game. If the business was to be funded in one tranche from the start by external capital, then why should the entrepreneur get a significant share of the equity? To end up with a good share, the entrepreneur needs to take risk. The essence of risk for

Exhibit 3.9 Why Milestone Funding Works for Entrepreneurs

	Round 1	Round 2	Round 3	Final Round
Amount	$1M	$2M	$5M	$4M
Valuation (postmoney)	$3M	$8M	$30M	$60M
Milestones met (e.g.)	None	Product finished	Ramp-up in customers	Accelerated growth
		Early customers	Stronger team	
Equity with founders	66%	49.5%	41%	38%

an entrepreneur is the absence of the full required amount of capital and the need to prove the merit of investing more capital as the business develops.

The example illustrated in Exhibit 3.9 shows the positive effects on ownership dilution of milestone funding for founders, using the investment tranches set out in Exhibit 3.6.

The valuation of the company in this example has gone up from round to round as the company developed. The effect of this is to reduce the dilution suffered by the founders. They have managed to retain ownership of 38%, with the investors getting 62%. If the entire $12M in capital had been invested in one tranche at the start, at a premoney valuation of $2M (the valuation in round 1), the investors would own 86%—premoney of $2M plus invested capital of $12M gives postmoney of $14M. If you are not familiar with the terms *premoney* and *postmoney*, see Chapter 7.

A 12- to 24-Month Ticking Clock

Every CEO of an early-stage company and his or her investors understand the ticking clock. This is the number of months that remain before the company runs out of money. CEOs probably have two views of how long it will be—an optimistic view assuming a reasonable amount of sales and a cautious view assuming poor sales.

Unless the company is toward the bottom of its J curve and the business plan has sufficient capital to reach operating cash flow breakeven, the company is expected to run out of money at some stage. That point is a moment of truth—has the company met its milestones and enhanced its value? If it hasn't met its milestones, can it still raise some money and will the terms be punitive? Even if it has met its milestones, will it have enough time to raise money? Will opportunistic investors try to take advantage of the ticking clock to impose tough terms? Does the company trust the investors to whom it recently granted exclusivity over the investment to close the investment without "moving the goalposts"—repricing the deal at a late stage?

The investment horizon of early-stage investors tends to be shorter than that of later-stage investors. The business risks are higher, but more importantly, the risk of conflicts between the CEO and executive team are higher—they have yet to prove themselves. Later-stage businesses have less management and business risk, and thus there is less need for potential interventions by people outside the executive team. For this reason, the capital invested by early-stage investors tends to last for shorter time periods than does capital invested in late-stage rounds.

If an investor was to take economic theory to its extreme, he or she should invest in the business in a continuous manner, covering the net operating cash flow deficit each month. This would limit the potential losses in a downside scenario and allow him or her to accelerate investment when the company was outperforming expectations. But the transaction costs of making these investments (legal agreements, due diligence, etc.) would outweigh the possible benefits.

One of the most difficult decisions facing a CEO is the timing of a new fund-raising. For example, a company raised a round of funding 14 months ago and has 8 months of cash left, assuming realistic projections of revenues and costs. However, the company is behind with respect to its planned milestones. The product was delayed, and the pilot customers have been slow to sign up. It will take four to six months to raise a round of investment. The company has a choice: should it start raising a new round of investment now, or should it wait three to four months until the evidence from customers is better?

This is a very common question facing CEOs and CFOs of early-stage companies. The benefits of waiting are clear. The chances of closing an investment round based on good references from customers are improved and any valuation achieved is likely to be higher. On the other hand, the company could run out of money and be forced into liquidation. Alternatively, if the company is close to running out of money, an investor might try to take advantage of the company and impose punitive terms—a very low valuation and stringent control terms. If the company goes for funding now, it might raise money, but the valuation will likely be low.

There is no right answer for the CEO and CFO. Experience and good judgment will be needed for them to navigate through this difficult issue. They also need to have their finger on the pulse of prospective investors: "If we had good references from customers X and Y, would you be interested?" If there is an existing investor in the company, the CEO and CFO should approach him or her about the possibility of bridge financing to cover any short-term cash flow difficulties in the event that the company decides to postpone the fund-raising for a few months.

Timing Is Everything—Buy Low, Sell High

When there is a sale or IPO of a company with a big headline figure, the public seems to attribute untold riches to everyone associated with the company. Investors know that this is not the case—a big exit does not necessarily mean a great investment. It all depends on the time at which the investor invested and the terms under which he or she invested. The value of a company does not go up in a linear or exponential manner. Value increases depend on milestones being reached. If investors invest and good milestones are met, they hope that they have priced their investment well and that subsequent investors will ascribe more value to the stock in the company.

As every investor knows, this is often not the case. The early investor might have invested at too high a valuation or the company might not

Exhibit 3.10 Timing Is Everything

	Round 1 Funding	Round 2 Funding
Amount of funding	$1M	$3M
Valuation (postmoney)	$10M	$6M
% owned by round 1 investor	10%	5%
% owned by round 2 investor	0%	50%

Business sold for $10M
Round 1 investor: −50% ($0.5M)
Round 2 investor: +66% ($5M)

have met its milestones with the capital provided by the early investor. If so, the consequences for the early investor might be severe.

Exhibit 3.10 illustrates such a case. The round 1 investor has paid too high a price ($10M valuation). The round 2 investor paid a post-money valuation of $6M on the $3M investment. While the company has been sold for an amount ($10M) that might have been sufficient to provide a modest return for all investors (total investment of $4M), only the round 2 investor has benefited. The valuation of the round 2 invest-ment was punitive, and the round 1 investor suffered heavy dilution of his or her position.

The key lesson learned here is that an investor in a particular round needs to look ahead and get sufficient comfort that the capital he or she is providing will lead to milestones being met and that those milestones will significantly enhance the value of the company to outside investors.

A Five- to Seven-Year Marathon in Three to Four Stages

Every company has its own unique story that depends on the charac-ters involved, the peculiarities of the market being served, the strength and responses of competitors, the novelty of the product that is developed, and so forth.

However, there tends to be a number of common themes along the time dimension throughout these stories:

1. *It takes at least five to seven years to build a business.* This, intuitively, seems to be the approximate time it takes to develop new technology, build a customer base, achieve cash flow breakeven, and get sufficient market attention from an acquirer or from the public markets. It also matches the personal and family time frame for many entrepreneurs. While successful entrepreneurs in hindsight will proffer positive stories about the joys of building their businesses, for many these five to seven years are tough going, and it would be hard to sustain the energy levels required for a period of much beyond ten years. While some businesses have been an "overnight success" after ten or more years, there might have been a number of years in the middle in which the company made limited progress or went through a down period.

2. *There are three to four common financing stages in the development of a business.* While these are covered in more detail in other books on entrepreneurship, they also match well to funding cycles and rounds of investments. Most companies go through a seed round of investment followed by a series A, B, C, and maybe a D round. Companies with more rounds have generally had a tough period in the middle where it became necessary to recapitalize the company.

3. *The really big hits in a venture capital portfolio tend to be the ones held onto for seven to ten years.* Venture capitalists are always looking for investments that might pay back their entire fund. In a fund portfolio of 20-odd companies, the statistics consistently show that the top three to four investments are the ones that drive the returns. The bottom 40% or so are written off in their entirety, and the next 40% in aggregate return the capital of the fund. The very best give a 10 or 20 times multiple on the amount invested. To achieve this level of multiple generally requires that the investor not exit for a long period of time.

Of course, there have been many investments that have generated a huge return in a much shorter period of time, but these are few and far between.

Five to seven years or more is a long period of time. The entrepreneur needs to ensure that he or she has patient investors onboard. Investors, similarly, need to take a long-term view. It is generally impossible to realize any value from an investment prior to its being acquired or undertaking an IPO.

Gross Margins of 80 to 100%

Investors should generally restrict their investments to companies with products or services with high gross margins, preferably greater than 80%.

The *gross margin* of a product or service is the percentage of a sale that will fall to the bottom line (net profit) of a company. For example, if a store selling home entertainment systems buys a unit for $60 and sells it for $100, the gross margin is 40%.

MINI CASE: CHEMICALS COMPANY
GROSS MARGIN

Consider the example of a chemicals company that has a gross margin on sales of 30%. If it is required to hold three months of sales in inventory, then with annual sales of $60M, it will have average inventory on hand of $10.5M (three months' worth of the total cost of sales for the year of $42M). This will need to be financed. The company will receive some credit from its suppliers, but this will be more than offset by the need to finance receivables due from its customers. If it receives two months of credit from suppliers and has to wait two months to be paid by its customers, then the net investment in working capital will be as follows (this is a simplified view).

Net Investment in Working Capital	
Average investment in inventory:	$10.5M
Average receivables outstanding:	$10.0M (two months of annual sales of $60M)
Average payables outstanding:	$(7.0M) (two months of cost of sales of $42M)
Average investment in working capital:	$13.5M

This company will need to find debt or equity finance of $13.5M to finance its working capital needs. Of this $13.5M, the really critical portion is the $3.5M difference between the inventory and the payables.

For a growing business that does not have a high gross margin, working capital can be a large potential drain on its capital.

Consider the same case but where the gross margin is 90%. With sales of $60M, the cost of sales for the year will be $6M. With the inventory turning every three months, the average level of inventory will be $1.5M and the average accounts payable outstanding will be $1M. While accounts receivable will still be high (at $10M), for every dollar of accounts receivable collected, 90 cents will be earned free and clear and will be available for financing working capital going forward.

High gross margins have another advantage—they allow the company to make mistakes without those mistakes necessarily being very costly. Consider a company developing a new piece of transportation equipment. If the gross margin is 20%, every time the company makes and sells a faulty unit, it needs to make and sell four more to cover the cost of parts and labor of the faulty unit. The cost of materials in the faulty unit is $80, and the profit per good unit sold is $20. If the gross margin is high (at 70% plus), the loss in parts in the faulty unit is quickly made up in an incremental sale.

No Correlation between the Amount of Money Raised and the Company's Success

The best entrepreneurs manage to build their companies on modest amounts of capital. Too many entrepreneurs (and too many early-stage investors) view large new rounds of investment as a mark of success. On the contrary, large capital injections can become a millstone around a company's neck.

The investment agreement will, almost certainly, stipulate that the investors' capital be repaid before anyone else in the company receives any capital. Chapter 8 on term sheets discusses how the investment will generally be made in preferred stock. With a few large rounds of investment, a company will often have raised $40M to $50M or more. All this will need to be repaid first (in most instances).

The hurdle exit price for a company to be seen as successful and for investors to be happy increases dramatically as more capital is taken on. Entrepreneurs shouldn't take on an investor's capital unless they believe that they can, at minimum, return 3 to 5 times the capital to the investor on an exit. While investors might be hoping for a 10 to 20 times multiple on exit, they will not complain with a 3 to 5 times multiple. Anything lower than that will be viewed as a *sideways* deal—one in which the investors received a below par return. Investors in sideways deals become difficult to deal with, and the founders and senior executives of such a company have a habit of losing their jobs and realizing little value on an exit.

A Tension between the "Lemons Ripening Early" and the "Valley of Death"

The worst investment for an investor is the one that fails late in its life. At that point, the investor will typically have invested in multiple funding rounds and will have committed as much in capital to the company as he or she is comfortable investing.

Thankfully, the lemons generally ripen early—the investments with poor prospects often become apparent within one to two years of investment. Anecdotal evidence from discussions among venture capitalists suggests that about half the failures were investments that the investor should not have made to begin with. The market was too small, the executive team was too weak and not open to bringing in first-class people, the channels to market were always likely to be closed or difficult to access. The other half of the failures was caused by poor execution, competitive responses, the market evolving more slowly than expected, and so forth.

Investments that go wrong early are unfortunate for an investor with a broad portfolio, but they are not fatal. Hopefully, the investor has staged the investment against milestones and hasn't fully committed all of his or her capital reserved for the deal. Also, evidence over time from venture capitalists' portfolios suggests that up to 30 to 40% of all investments are outright failures.

But as well as the lemons ripening early, there is another, conflicting, phenomenon that is regularly faced by entrepreneurs and investors. Most companies go through a "valley of death" relatively early in their lives. Product development is slower than expected; it takes longer to capture reference customers than anticipated in the plan; the company loses a key executive; the market evolves slowly; and so on. A crisis of confidence happens among the investors. Some in the investor group are less positive about the prospects than are others. A real debate occurs as to whether to keep the company going or not. Many companies pull through this phase and go on to be large successes.

The hardest part of a venture capitalist's job is figuring out if the company is a lemon or if it is just going through a valley of death. The real moment of truth occurs when the investor is faced with a decision concerning whether or not to write an additional check, against a backdrop of bad news about the company. Is it good money after bad, or is the company just going through a tough period from which it can emerge strongly? Clearly, the founders and the senior executives are not objective players in this game. The individual partner in the venture capital firm and the venture capital firm both need to make a decision.

There are a few influences on this decision that are not often appreciated by entrepreneurs and the wider early-stage community. Venture capitalists, funnily, are often under pressure from their investors (limited partners) to show that they can make tough decisions to cut companies and not throw good money after bad.

On the other hand, the individual partner in the venture capital firm doesn't want to have a negative score against his or her name. A personal failure one year from now is a lot less painful than a personal failure today. And the evidence from the company is always inconclusive. Is the glass half full or half empty? It is easy to read it either way.

Often, the incremental investment decision comes down to a relatively small amount of money. It might, for example, involve a yes or no decision to commit an additional $1M to an investment where $5M has been invested already. Also, explaining a loss of $6M is not a much harder task than explaining a loss of $5M. The $1M might end up being the difference between closing one or two critical reference customers or a large deal that will fund the company to a significant extent going forward.

The natural human instinct is to dig deep and invest a little more to see if the positive news comes through. However, these types of decisions can come up a few times in the course of a company's life. At some stage, the investor will need to say no, and it is better if the investor says no early rather than after all allocated capital has been committed to an individual investment.

A Binary Payoff Profile

Early-stage technology ventures tend to exhibit a winner-take-all profile. The investors can lose 100% of their capital, or the company can be very valuable and the investors can achieve a high multiple on their investment.

The returns on individual investments in venture capital funds show this clearly. As depicted later, in Chapter 5, if a fund makes 24 investments, roughly 10 might be outright failures, 6 might be sideways deals, and the top 8 might be split between modest successes and big hits.

The payoff structure for an early-stage product-focused technology company (e.g., software, medical device, or biotech company) might be as follows:

Percentage of chances of the company having a valuation at exit of:
$0M: 60%
$0–$100M: 20%

$100–$200M:	10%
$200–$250M:	10%

For an early-stage technology company, there are many reasons for an outright failure. In most cases the investor base will have decided to abandon the project midstream. The product might not have worked as expected; a market might not have materialized; and so on. If everything goes according to plan, the maximum exit value will be defined by the size of the market and the company's ability to capture a large share of it. Because there is a tendency toward a winner-take-all attitude in product-based technology sectors, the second most successful company in each sector and the third, and so on down the line tend to be a lot less valuable than the first.

This feature of the ultimate payoff likely being binary plays directly into the valuation techniques used by early-stage venture capital investors. This is covered in Chapter 7.

You would be surprised at the consistency in perspectives in potential exit valuations among different experienced early-stage investors. They will have an intuitive feel about whether the company could be a $100M, a $250M, or a $500M exit, based on the size of the market, the competitive positioning, and so forth.

While product-focused technology companies tend to have binary payoffs, there are some types of businesses in which early-stage investors achieve less skewed returns. These primarily comprise businesses with early cash flow that can reach breakeven fairly quickly.

Take, for example, a start-up radio station. While it will take a few years to achieve breakeven (probably), it should be earning some revenue from the start and build its top line from there. The payoff to the investors will not be binary. On exit, these businesses are valued primarily on prospective revenue and earnings multiples. Revenues and earnings will depend on market share in the target segments and the ability of the station's management to convert its market share to advertising dollars. Success is not an either-or situation—a continuum of outcomes is possible. Also, the options to abandon the venture midstream are less attractive. Consequently, all investors should be onboard and committed from the start to get the company to cash flow breakeven.

PART II

RAISING
THE FINANCE

CHAPTER 4

DETERMINING THE AMOUNT OF CAPITAL TO RAISE AND WHAT TO SPEND IT ON

The basic principle underpinning a new investment round for an early-stage company is that the company should raise enough capital to allow it to reach a set of value-enhancing milestones comfortably.

If too little capital is raised, then failure to reach the milestones could be catastrophic for the company and its early investors. The company could be left in an in-between stage—running out of money and without the evidence to justify a new round of investment. If too much capital is raised, then unnecessary dilution will occur—the company would have been better off raising a smaller amount of capital, achieving value-enhancing milestones, and raising more capital later, presumably at a higher price.

The above dispassionate analysis, however, naively ignores the external investment environment. As the period from 1997 onward shows clearly, the market for investment capital is very cyclical. If the market is very tough and companies are finding it difficult to raise capital, then the company should probably take as much as it can get, assuming the valuation is reasonable. If the valuation is very low, then the company should consider raising less while conserving capital by spending less than it would ideally plan to and hope for a more attractive investing environment later. If the market is very attractive—valuations are very high and capital is abundant—it might be worth taking on an excessive amount of capital and pushing ahead very aggressively. If the company passes up the opportunity, its competitors might absorb the available capital instead. This is a strategic judgment for the CFO and the CEO.

An Established Company—Estimating the Amount of Capital to Raise

The traditional approach to estimating the amount of capital required to fund a business is to build a cash flow statement. A *cash flow statement* is a spreadsheet of revenues and costs translated into an operating cash flow statement with the effects of capital expenditure included. The best split of debt and equity is then calculated. The spreadsheet is built up by month or by quarter as the peak cash requirement can be hidden if only yearly increments are utilized.

The key factors that drive the numbers in the cash flow statement can be isolated; sensitivity analysis then allows the CFO to see the effect of changes in these factors. For example, the revenue growth rate might be a key driver, and it would be important to understand the effect on cash flows of different growth rates, say, 5%, 10%, and 20%.

Cash flow statements based on spreadsheets are crucial for a business with some history and with some predictability in its revenues and costs. In fact, a cash flow spreadsheet overlaid with a tool for assessing the sensitivity of different variables (such as a Monte Carlo simulation capability) would be ideal.

A New Company—Estimating the Amount of Capital to Raise

Cash flow statements are a lot less useful for early-stage businesses than they are for other businesses because the variability in the key factors can be enormous. For example, in an early-stage business, the most important factor might be the elapsed time to first revenues rather than the growth rate in revenues. In fact, some of the factors are binary (e.g., will the product achieve the desired technical specifications? Will the product get regulatory approval?) Binary factors make it hard to model projected cash flows in a meaningful way using a spreadsheet.

For an early-stage company, spreadsheets provide a false level of precision. They are great for understanding the small picture and the interrelationships between the factors. They are poor at giving the investor the big picture on how the capital will be absorbed and how the risk of cash requirements might be a lot higher than expected. That is not to say that all early-stage ventures should not have a one-, three-, and five-year spreadsheet-based bottom-up view of their cash flows. Rather, they also need a top-down view of the activities in their business that absorb capital to allow them to communicate to investors the return on capital that the investor (and the company) might receive for every dollar invested. An analytical decision tree would be a lot better than a spreadsheet, but there are no simple tools available to the early-stage investor.

The first step for the early-stage investor is to disaggregate the different activities in the company that absorb capital. Once these are disaggregated, the management team and the investors then need to gain assurance that the return on investment for investing in each of these activities is high enough. Equity is expensive, and the investor wants 5, 10, or 20 times the capital back—each capital-absorbing activity needs to justify itself against these metrics.

Activities in a New Business That Absorb Capital

There are five primary activities that absorb capital in a new business:

1. *Capital assets.* These are the capital costs required to set up and equip the business. Most are incurred up front to put the company in business, and some are added to over time. They include tangible (fixed) assets, such as equipment and premises, and intangible assets, such as the cost of acquiring patents from third parties.
2. *Product development costs.* These are the costs of feeding the "marching army" and include such things as developing

the product or service prior to it being ready for sale. These costs tend to be fairly straight line on a monthly basis.

3. *Leadership and administration.* These are the costs of coordinating and leading the business. They are also the costs where it is hardest to see a direct positive impact on return on investment, but easiest to see where they negatively affect return on investment if they are missing or deficient. They are also the most discretionary of the five categories of capital being absorbed. The discretion relates to timing—when they start to be incurred.

4. *Working capital.* Every time a sale is captured, it has consequent implications for cash flow—generally negative in the short term and positive in the medium term. Inventories and accounts receivable need to be funded, and accounts payable might be available as a source of funding.

5. *Sales ramp-up financing.* To make sales, a company must invest in resources such as salespeople, literature, and marketing in advance. Each time a salesperson is taken onboard, there is a lag time before this person becomes capable of covering his or her costs and continues on to make a contribution to the company. Distribution networks have their own J curve, and it is critical for the investor to understand the timing of payback on investment in distribution.

The timing of absorption of these five capital-absorbing activities into a typical early-stage technology business is shown in Exhibit 4.1.

As covered in Chapter 3, investors need to understand the shape of the J curve facing them. For the seed investor, if all of his or her capital is absorbed in fixed assets and product development, then there might not be enough to reach commercial milestones and allow the business to raise new rounds of investment. Also, by restructuring the sequence of stepping-stones pursued, it might be possible to reshape the J curve and boost the ratio between capital in (invested capital) and capital out (capital on an exit).

The five absorbers of capital mentioned above are now covered in more detail.

Exhibit 4.1 Capital-Absorbing Activities

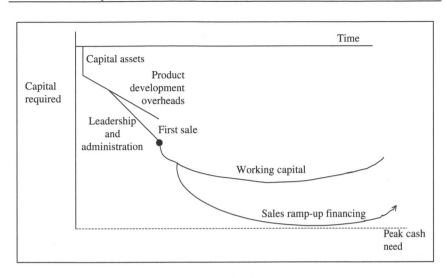

Capital Assets

Capital assets are generally quite predictable. A good entrepreneur should be fairly accurate in estimating the amount of capital expenditure required to establish the business.

The smart CFO will disaggregate the overall fixed assets requirement by time of need—procuring the assets only when required. This requires CFOs to play a major role in challenging expenditures. They might not have a technical background, but they need to push back on the technical team to encourage its members to be creative regarding ways of avoiding or deferring capital expenditure. If the procurement of a piece of equipment can be deferred until after the next round of funding, then, if the price per share in the next round is twice as high as the current round, the cost of equipment will be half as expensive—in terms of dilution and equity given to investors. Entrepreneurs often do not think in this way.

Once the minimum capital assets program is established, the CFO then needs to search for the lowest cost approach for funding the assets.

Leasing and debt can be very attractive if they displace the need for equity. There are a number of companies that provide leasing or "venture debt" to early-stage companies. Often, they look for a high interest rate, plus a small ownership stake—an "equity kicker." The equity kicker is typically an option to buy a modest share of the company at the price of the most recent round of investment.

But the CFO needs to be careful of debt or leasing for three reasons:

1. *Leasing or debt is useful only if it extends the cash flow runway of the company substantially beyond the time period of the existing funds at hand.* For example, take the company with cash on hand to fund the next 18 months of operations that needs to acquire fixed assets worth $1M. If the debt or leasing runs for a period of only two years, then it is probably worth avoiding. Roughly, 75% of the debt taken on will have been repaid at that stage, and the debt or leasing will have had only a minimal impact on extending the cash flow runway of the company. The company will have incurred the interest costs and setup costs associated with the debt or leasing facility, and the ticking clock will not have been pushed further into the future.

2. *If the existing shareholders are extremely likely to fund the next round of the company, then the leasing or debt is probably pointless.* The biggest risk faced by the debt or leasing provider is that the existing shareholders might abandon the company if it fails to achieve its milestones. If the debt or leasing provider is willing to have a balance outstanding beyond the horizon covered by the existing investment round, then it is implicitly or explicitly making the assumption that the existing shareholders will continue to commit capital to the company, at least to the date at which all the debt and leasing is paid back. If the existing shareholders are not willing to walk away from the company at the next funding round, then it is pointless to incur the cost of debt and leasing. Their equity will go into the company only to derisk the situation for the debt provider.

3. *In the event that the shareholders decide not to fund the company at the next funding round, but there will still be a lot*

*of enterprise value (e.g., **in the intellectual property or the fixed** **assets**) at time of closure, then the debt or leasing probably* ***should be avoided.*** Where the debt or leasing still has an exposure beyond the current investment horizon, the assets realized in the event of liquidation might cover this exposure. Any investors familiar with liquidations tend to be leery of realizing much value through the process, given the costs involved and the unexpected liabilities that tend to emerge at time of liquidation.

Debt and leasing companies are generally smart at limiting their exposure and incurring only debt risk—avoiding equity risk (properly, in their view). The goal of the smart CFO is to figure out a way of passing some level of equity risk (the chance of losing some or all of the company's capital) to debt holders—but only to pay them a level of return modestly above the level of debt. If he or she hasn't consciously figured out how to do this, then the debt or leasing provider is probably getting the better of them.

Product Development Costs

Product development costs are often likened to the costs of feeding the "marching army." They are the regular costs incurred each month that are highly predictable. Most investors are quickly able to translate headcount into a cost per month for the company. For example, depending on wage rates in the region, the average fully loaded cost per person per month might be $10,000. The cost of a development team of 15 to 20 can be easily translated into a monthly "burn rate" of $150,000 to $200,000.

Similar to capital assets, it can be hard for the CFO to challenge the size and cost of the product development team. He or she is not typically well placed to judge the amount of resources required to deliver against the product development milestones. The head of engineering will be best placed to judge the subtleties of trade-offs in product development. Can the next generation of the product wait until next year? What impact will waiting have on customers and the company's ability to close sales?

But it is often impossible to have these conversations with heads of engineering. They have severe information asymmetry in their favor. Most CFOs do not have a technical background and lack an intuitive feel for the quantity of resources required to deliver technical milestones. Most importantly, they often don't have a feel for how the technical milestones translate into an enhanced valuation for the company. More resources mean that the head of engineering has a lower risk of underdelivery. But the resources clearly have a cost in capital consumed that needs to be paid in equity dilution.

The best path forward for the CFO in this type of situation is to force the development of alternative stepping-stones and technical milestones and to assess the alternative cost structures of each. More difficult, but no less important, the CFO (with the help of the CEO) needs to make a judgment as to the value enhancement that the alternative stepping-stones imply for the company.

One area for the CFO to examine closely is the time to first revenues. Most companies face a simple trade-off between a good product that demonstrates the concept and the product's potential and a great product that is fully finished, and where the differentiation from competitors is clearly proven and hopefully quantifiable. The technical team might favor the latter, but it might not appreciate that, if any of the costs can be deferred until after the next round of investment, the cost (in terms of equity dilution) might be a lot less.

Leadership and Administration

The expenditures related to leadership and administration are similar to those of product development in that they are straight line. But they are a bit trickier. The caliber of CEO who might be captured when the company is preproduct might be a lot lower than the caliber of one who might come into the company when it has achieved more milestones. CEOs and senior executives are expensive.

Consequently, the board and the investors of the company often have a difficult decision. Do they aim to hire the CEO and the remainder of the senior team very early in the life of the company, incurring the cost and running the risk of underhiring, or do they wait, thereby saving cost and, hopefully, capturing a higher caliber senior executive team? Of course, they will also have the concern that the company will be subject to suboptimal leadership and decision making in the intervening period.

Working Capital

Senior executive teams and investors rarely pay enough attention to working capital requirements in forward-looking cash planning. However, the working capital characteristics of the business are critical. Some businesses are highly consumptive of capital in their working capital cycles, some are fairly neutral, and some are highly cash generative.

In general, working capital cycles are consumptive of capital. Companies need to finance inventories, and there is a time lag before they are paid by customers. This can be offset to some extent by the time lag in payments granted by suppliers.

Consider the following example of a company that makes and sells home entertainment systems for $1,000. The parts cost $500, and the manufacturing, which takes two months, adds another $300 in labor and other costs. The company receives two months of credit from suppliers and grants two months of credit to the retail chains that sell the units. For simplicity, the company sells one unit per month.

As you would expect, the net operating cash flow per month eventually will be $200—as the company sells one unit per month with a profit of $200 per unit.

Exhibit 4.2 presents the expected working capital situation facing the company. Taking into account the time lags mentioned above, the peak working capital requirement is $2,050. If the business were to stay at the same level of sales indefinitely, the working capital need would be a problem only in the early stage of the business.

However, most companies aim to grow their sales. If this company increases its rate of sales by one unit each month (from one in month 1 to two in month 2, etc.), the incremental working capital required each year would be $2,050. As the profit associated with 12 units is $2,400, the working capital requirements would be very onerous. See Exhibit 4.3.

Exhibit 4.2 Home Entertainment Systems Manufacturer—One Sale per Month

	\multicolumn{12}{c}{Months}											
	1	2	3	4	5	6	7	8	9	10	11	12
Working capital for one unit												
• Receive materials	×											
• Pay suppliers			−500									
• Pay manufacturing labor	−150	−150										
• Sell unit				×								
• Receive payment from customer					1,000							
Working capital for one unit	−150	−150	−500	0	1,000							
Unit made in month 1	−150	−150	−500	0	1,000							
Unit made in month 2		−150	−150	−500	0	1,000						
Unit made in month 3			−150	−150	−500	0	1,000					
Unit made in month 4				−150	−150	−500	0	1,000				
Unit made in month 5					−150	−150	−500	0	1,000			
Unit made in month 6						−150	−150	−500	0	1,000		
Unit made in month 7							−150	−150	−500	0	1,000	
Unit made in month 8								−150	−150	−500	0	1,000
Unit made in month 9									−150	−150	−500	0
Unit made in month 10										−150	−150	−500
Unit made in month 11											−150	−150
Unit made in month 12												−150
Monthly cash flow	−150	−300	−800	−800	200	200	200	200	200	200	200	200
Cumulative cash flow	−150	−450	−1,250	−2,050	−1,850	−1,650	−1,450	−1,250	−1,050	−850	−650	−450

Exhibit 4.3 Home Entertainment Systems Manufacturer—Sales Growing by One per Month

	Months											
	1	2	3	4	5	6	7	8	9	10	11	12
Working capital for one unit												
• Receive materials	x											
• Pay suppliers			-500									
• Pay manufacturing labor	-150	-150										
• Sell unit			x									
• Receive payment from customer					1,000							
Working capital for one unit	-150	-150	-500	0	1,000							
One unit made in month 1	-150	-150	-500	0	1,000							
Two units made in month 2		-300	-300	-1,000	0	2,000						
Three units made in month 3			-450	-450	-1,500	0	3,000					
Four units made in month 4				-600	-600	-2,000	0	4,000				
Five units made in month 5					-750	-750	-2,500	0	5,000			
Six units made in month 6						-900	-900	-3,000	0	6,000		
Seven units made in month 7							-1,050	-1,050	-3,500	0	7,000	
Eight units made in month 8								-1,200	-1,200	-4,000	0	8,000
Nine units made in month 9									-1,350	-1,350	-4,500	0
Ten units made in month 10										-1,500	-1,500	-5,000
Eleven units made in month 11											-1,650	-1,650
Twelve units made in month 12												-1,800
Monthly cash flow	-150	-450	-1,250	-2,050	-1,850	-1,650	-1,450	-1,250	-1,050	-850	-650	-450
Cumulative cash flow	-150	-600	-1,850	-3,900	-5,750	-7,400	-8,850	-10,100	-11,150	-12,000	-12,650	-13,100

Exhibit 4.3 of the home entertainment systems manufacturer demonstrates a business with consumptive working capital needs that is growing every month. Instead of the company selling one unit per month, the company's sales grow by one each month. As you can see, instead of a peak capital need of $2,050 as shown in Exhibit 4.2, the capital need is $13,100 in month 12 and will rise slightly higher in year 2 before declining.

Growth can be fatal for a low-margin business if cheap capital is not available. You should note the key aspects of the business that absorb excessive levels of working capital. Manufacturing takes two months, and gross margins are low. Consequently, this type of home entertainment systems business is highly consumptive of capital.

Compare this with a business that is relatively neutral with regard to working capital—a software business. When the product does not need to be coupled with implementation services involving professional staff, the gross margin on the product may be close to 100%. This means that there is no need to finance inventory and no accounts payable. All the revenue is incremental cash flow, and the company can grow limitlessly without any drain on working capital. This is a hugely positive aspect of very high gross margin businesses that makes them attractive to investors.

Negative Working Capital Businesses

Negative working capital businesses are worth extra examination. These businesses, as they grow, generate cash in working capital rather than absorb it. In effect, they are capitalized by their customers. They are paid before they need to pay their suppliers. This makes them highly attractive as the cash flow generated through working capital can be used to finance the broader capital needs of the business and thereby enabling the company to avoid the need for much equity capital.

Such businesses include:

1. *Gift voucher businesses.* A person buys a gift voucher with a specific merchant or through an independent multimerchant scheme. In either case, the voucher is bought up front, and

the cash paid sits on the balance sheet of the shop or the independent gift voucher company. It is only depleted when the voucher is used, which often takes a long time, and in certain instances the vouchers are never redeemed at all.

2. *Loyalty schemes.* A loyalty scheme operator grants points to customers when the customer spends money in a particular shop or on a specific product or service. In effect, the shop or the supplier of the product or service buys the points from the loyalty scheme operator when the customer buys the product or service. It normally takes some time for the customer to "spend" the points earned in the scheme. There can be significant unutilized points, and the cash paid by the shop or supplier of products or services lies on the balance sheet of the loyalty scheme operator, similar to how things work in the gift voucher business.

3. *Some grocery chains.* Some retail chains have the market power to pay suppliers slowly and to turn over the inventory in their stores quickly. If managed very aggressively, they can, on occasion, attain negative working capital positions.

4. *Insurance companies.* Insurance companies—property and casualty and life—charge customers premiums long in advance of paying out claims and expenses. A critical part of their business is to reinvest the cash in the intervening period to make a margin.

Every CFO, particularly those in early-stage businesses, should closely examine the working capital cycles to see where capital can be preserved.

Sales Ramp-Up Financing

Sales ramp-up financing is the most difficult one of the five capital absorbing activities to forecast. This kind of financing depends on the productivity of sales, sales support, and marketing resources. Because the company will have limited or no history of sales, the effort required, the length of the sales cycle, and the pricing to be achieved are difficult to judge.

A good, experienced head of sales should be able to estimate the likely length of the sales cycle, the sales quota a salesperson might carry when fully operational, the length of time it takes for a good salesperson to achieve his or her quota, and so on. But all this depends on reference sales and the length of time it can take to get these is highly unpredictable. The sales ramp-up is the most challenging part of any early-stage business to forecast.

Investors' Views of the Five Capital-Absorbing Activities

Investors want to earn a 5-10-20 times multiple on their capital invested. The return is earned when the business as a whole is sold, or the shareholding of the investor is sold to a third party (e.g., through an initial public offering). It is, of course, impossible to link the multiple ultimately earned back to the specific items of expenditure made in the course of the company's development. It would also be pointless to try to do this.

But, nevertheless, investors (and entrepreneurs) need to ensure that the capital is spent on highly valuable activities. For example, on an exit, capital assets such as premises and equipment will normally sell for a one times multiple or less. The purchaser is not going to want to spend more than the replacement cost to buy physical assets. Consequently, if half of the investment is spent on capital assets and the investor wants to earn a 10 times return on his investment, in a theoretical sense the remaining 50% of the investment will need to earn a 20 times return. While this is not how business valuations work in practice, it serves to highlight the point that capital must be spent on activities that can turn a big multiple.

This sort of thinking drives investors to have the following attitudes toward the expenditure of their investment on the five capital-absorbing activities:

1. *Capital assets.* Investors normally view their money as far too expensive to waste on fixed assets. They look for the entrepreneur to finance capital expenditure creatively, that is, with other

people's money (at a low price). This can include leasing, debt, equipment vendor support, purchasing secondhand, and so on. Simply put, it is very hard to earn a 5-10-20 times return on fixed assets. When the company is ultimately sold, why should the purchaser buy fixed assets at a price higher than their replacement cost? If equity capital needs to be expended on fixed assets then it can create the need for the return on investment on other capital-absorbing activities to be disproportionately higher.

There is one instance when a purchaser might be willing to pay a multiple on the cost of fixed assets. This is when the company has managed to use the acquisition of fixed assets to give itself a monopolistic or oligopolistic position. For example, if a company in the railroad business used its capital to be the first to build a rail line between two cities, such an asset might end up being worth a multiple of its cost. No other company is likely to replicate such a rail line, and the regulatory authorities might prevent any competitor from doing so. The first builder of a television cable system in a region may also get a similar advantage. This applies as well for a retail chain that locks up all the most favorable sites quickly.

The CFO of a business that needs to purchase fixed assets needs to be sure that the purchase of the fixed assets is giving the company a privileged position that will ultimately provide the company with monopoly or oligopoly power. This is discussed more fully in Chapter 6 on business plans.

2. *Product development.* Product development is one area in which investors generally believe they can earn a very high return on capital. If the special skills and insight of the development team can be translated into a high-quality differentiated product, then the investors are likely to be very willing to invest in product development. The sort of questions the investors should ask are: How long will it take to get to the first generation of the product? How long to the first sale? The limit of an investor's patience tends to be about 18 to 30 months—unless the prize is very big (e.g., a new pharmaceutical compound).

3. *Leadership and administration.* A good CEO and senior executive team can be worth their weight in gold. As discussed

earlier, one key question for a board is the timing of the hire of the senior team.

4. *Working capital.* Investors want to avoid having their capital invested in working capital because working capital is seen as a deadweight and will never be worth more than a one times multiple of the capital invested in it. The purchaser of a company will not pay a premium for capital tied up in working capital. The purchaser might even value the working capital at a small discount to its book value.

   The usual maxims apply. Maximize accounts payable, minimize accounts receivable, and minimize inventory. If a negative or neutral working capital position can be achieved, then this can be a huge advantage to the investor. Any business with gross margins of less than 50 to 60% should be avoided—the company can be left holding inventory, and any mistakes in the manufacturing process can be very expensive.

5. *Sales ramp-up financing.* Investors will consider equity spent on capturing early sales to be a good use of equity capital. However, once a repeatable sales model is in place, the investors will aim to substitute equity capital applied to this activity with some other cheaper form of capital.

Investors want a return on their capital. Clearly, they can get a return only if the business as a whole is successful. Consequently, the way the capital in aggregate is invested matters most. But, investors also want their capital to be used productively. Equity capital is best deployed in skills-based activities such as product development, leadership, and winning early sales or in activities that accelerate a company's position where first-mover advantage exists. Cheaper forms of capital should be sought to finance fixed assets, working capital, and repeatable sales. This is not a hard-and-fast rule, but rather a guideline. If a number of fixed assets can be combined to build a market differentiable position (e.g., by preemptively acquiring the "best" retail spots for the rollout of a new retail format), then expenditure of equity capital in this regard may be worthwhile.

In the late 1990s, investors pursued many telecommunications rollout activities such as Internet service providers, cable systems, and broadband rollouts. Regardless of the readiness of the market for these offerings, in hindsight many investors realized that it would be extremely difficult to earn a 5-10-20 times multiple investing in networks and customer premises equipment, particularly when the market was still forming. Most of these markets did not have the potential to build monopolistic or oligopolistic positions. If the market was well formed, then the investors might have been content with a lower 3 to 4 times multiple on the investment, given the lower level of risk.

Businesses with Different Capital-Absorbing Profiles

The four mini cases here illustrate different ways in which capital can be deployed into a business. While the cases are not intended to show attractive and unattractive businesses from an investment perspective, you should be able to see the thought processes with respect to why venture capitalists favor some businesses over others. Remember that the investor's ideal business is one that can create a differentiable position and grow very quickly without consuming excessive amounts of capital.

MINI-CASE: SOFTWARE BUSINESS

Software businesses are skills- and execution-oriented businesses. The early investors' money will be spent primarily on product development. The marching army will typically need to be fed for 18 to 24 months prior to initial revenues. The timing of hire of the top leadership is always a big debating point—the pros and cons are outlined earlier in this chapter.

No fixed assets will be required, other than some IT resources. Sometimes leasing will be available to fund this. Working capital is not a problem, because the gross margin earned on each sale will be close to 100%, assuming that limited implementation services are required.

Sales ramp-up financing will be a significant challenge. The productivity of early sales activities is very low for most early-stage companies, including software companies. The amount of capital to be spent on it is extremely hard to assess.

In summary, all of the investors' money is being spent on activities that can provide a very high level of return. The business can also grow in scale (on both the capital assets and working capital front) without requiring further capital. This is why investors tend to like software businesses as a class.

MINI CASE: BICYCLE COMPONENTS MANUFACTURER

This is a manufacturing business designing and making bicycle components in the United States (at a 50% gross margin) and selling them to Far Eastern bicycle assembly companies.

This will be a very difficult business to finance with venture capital. It will require fixed assets to establish the manufacturing facility. The working capital needs will probably be crippling because the business will need to purchase parts, make the components, and ship the product to the Far East. Only at some stage after that will its Far Eastern customers pay. It will still have product development overhead.

All in all, this is one of the most difficult types of business to finance, and it will be very hard for it to earn a high return on investment.

MINI CASE: LOYALTY SCHEME

This company runs outsourced loyalty schemes for different supermarket companies. Every time a shopper spends $100 in a supermarket, the supermarket pays $1 to the loyalty scheme company for points in the loyalty scheme. In return, the shopper can order gifts or arrange airline flights from the loyalty scheme company, when he or she accrues enough points.

There will be some capital assets to purchase (e.g., systems to network the supermarkets to the loyalty scheme provider). Also, a scheme like this can take a long time to achieve breakeven. Supermarkets need to be signed up, customers need to be enticed to enroll, and customers need to start using their cards at the checkout counter.

But the working capital position of this type of business can be very attractive. As the supermarkets pay the scheme operator up front when points are earned, these payments can sit on the balance sheet of the loyalty scheme provider for a long time.

People take a long time to accrue points prior to cashing them in. Also, many points are ultimately never cashed in. All this benefits the scheme operator, who should be able to use this cash flow to finance the business as it grows.

MINI CASE: WIRELESS BROADBAND ROLLOUT

Capital assets will be a very big part of the financing of this business. The central systems all need to be put in place, and the primary network needs to be built. All this needs to happen before even one customer can be signed up. But there are also capital costs associated with every single customer who signs up. The cost of customer premises equipment and the installation cost of the equipment will rarely be fully covered by the up-front cost paid by the customer. Consequently, every incremental customer (in the early years) will need to be financed by equity.

The investors in this business will be looking ahead to the point where the business can transition from equity financing to debt financing. Normally, this will be determined up front in the legal documents governing the financing. The debt providers will commit to providing certain levels of debt when certain milestones are reached.

One key milestone might be operating cash flow breakeven. At this point, the business will still need to invest in capital assets, but it is generating positive cash flow from operations.

CHAPTER 5

GETTING BEHIND HOW VENTURE CAPITAL FIRMS THINK

Venture capital funds are partnerships, not companies. They are granted a finite 10-year life by investors in the funds. Using this capital, a small group of professionals ferret out investment opportunities in the first three to five years, help to guide them as they grow, and ultimately exit them (normally in years 5 to 10) by selling them to larger companies or by undertaking an initial public offering. The team lives or dies based on its performance; performance is the amount of capital that is returned to the investors and the speed of returning this capital. If the team delivers a good performance to the investors, every three to five years it will normally be able to raise another fund.

Many different types of legal structures have been used to make investments in early-stage ventures. Publicly quoted investment vehicles have been used. Private companies have been tried. Groups of angels have come together. But no structure has matched the durability and flexibility of the venture capital partnership.

Structure of Venture Capital Funds

A venture capital fund is a vehicle for parties interested in investing in high-growth private companies. These parties are gathered together in a fund, bound by a set of commitments for the fund duration.

These binding sets of commitments distinguish them from ad hoc investment groups such as those that might exist within a group of angel investors. Angel investors often come together to support individual companies. But they often have a problem in delivering follow-on investments into the same company. An angel investor who is wealthy in year 1 and willing to invest in speculative early-stage companies might not be so wealthy or so willing in year 5 when the company is on its third round of investment. Other angel investors might have to bear a heavier share of the investment load at that point, and that could lead to tensions that would blow apart the angel investment group. The binding set of commitments between investors in a venture capital fund (typically institutions rather than individuals) overcomes this problem. Investors are compelled legally to invest the contracted amount.

The investors in the fund are called *limited partners* (LP). The venture capital team is called the *general partner* (GP). The GP finds investments, negotiates the deals, monitors the investments (hopefully adding some value along the way), exits the investments, and returns the proceeds to the LPs. See Exhibit 5.1.

Exhibit 5.1 Structure of VC Funds

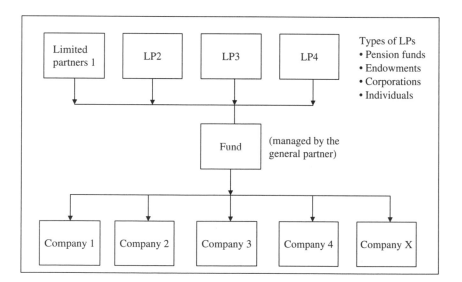

In theory, LPs could make investments in companies directly, bypassing the relatively costly structure of the GP. In practice, finding private companies in which to invest is a complex, time-consuming business requiring a high degree of skill and judgment. Therefore, LPs seek out good teams of GPs and bear the cost of the GP in the expectation that this cost will be more than compensated by the resulting gains.

Other key features of venture capital funds include:

1. ***Ten-year time frame.*** Venture capital funds are, in most cases, set up with a 10-year horizon. The portfolio is built up over the first few years, and good exits generally take about five to seven years or more to come to fruition. The 10-year structure has proven to be a good time frame for entering and exiting a portfolio of investments. A shorter term might mean that the GP would be forced to exit individual investments before they achieved their potential. This would cause the GP and the LPs to leave a lot of value on the table. On the other hand, 10 years is a long commitment for an LP.

   GPs generally have the right to ask for a one- to two-year extension to the ten-year life of the fund. If there are a few investments still in the portfolio for which it would be foolish to rush an exit, most LPs will acquiesce to the GP's request for an extension. The GP always has the option of distributing the stock in the private companies directly to the LPs (in specie), in proportion to their ownership of the fund. As you can imagine, this is not something that LPs generally want. Stock in private companies is not liquid and requires careful oversight.

2. ***Limited partnership.*** Partnerships are tax-efficient vehicles; the capital gains are taxed when they are received by the partner rather than within the fund. If the fund were structured as a company, gains would be taxed within the company and could possibly be subject to double taxation when received by the investor. Also, companies are more complex to wind down—they are set up to live in perpetuity.

   Partnerships, on the other hand, have the risk of unlimited liability. Therefore, investors in the fund position themselves as limited partners—with liability limited to the amount of their investment. To be a limited partner, investors need to divorce themselves from decision making. Consequently, LPs do not make decisions regarding individual investments; they rely on the GP to do this.

The fund will have an advisory committee that will provide oversight of the GP's stewardship of the fund. The advisory committee will include representatives of the LPs. But the advisory committee needs to ensure that it does not get involved in decision making such as go/no-go decisions on individual investments. If it does, LPs run the risk of losing their limited liability status.

3. *Mutually binding commitments.* A fund brings together a coalition of investors. Each of the investors wants to ensure that the GP is tied in closely for the duration of the fund and that there are no conflicts of interest.

The LPs also want to ensure that their fellow investors are tied into the fund for the duration. If investors make a $10M commitment to a fund, it will be drawn down over the first five to six years of the fund. If any of the investors were to renege on their commitment, it would put the sustainability of the whole fund at risk. The partnership agreement will include severe penalties for investors who renege; normally it compels the GP to pursue the reneging party legally to fulfill his or her commitment.

Types of Investors in Venture Capital Funds

Venture capital firms seek investors who have a long-term time frame. Preferably, they will have long-term liabilities that they are aiming to meet with the return from their investment in VC funds and other assets.

The typical investors in a fund are:

1. *Pension funds.* A pension fund with a relatively high ratio of current employees to retirees is an ideal investor in a VC fund.

The total capital in the pension fund grows year after year, and the requirement for short-term liquidity is low. Conversely, if the pension fund has a high ratio of retirees to current employees, it must be careful not to lock too much capital up in illiquid asset classes such as venture capital. That said, venture capital normally constitutes only a relatively small percentage of a pension fund's assets.

2. *Endowments.* Endowments for universities and charitable institutions often have very long-term liabilities and make particularly ideal investors in VC funds. The most successful investors in venture capital over the long run have been endowments; they have been investors in the class for a long time and have maintained their commitment throughout. Investors who entered the sector in the good times have generally done less well.

3. *Balanced fund managers.* In many parts of the world there are investment managers who run balanced funds—managing a mix of equities, bonds, cash, and alternative assets (including venture capital). For example, if a balanced fund manager won a mandate to manage $500M on behalf of a pension fund, the manager would work with the pension fund trustees to figure out the appropriate allocation across different asset classes and then invest the money to correspond with this allocation.

   Balanced fund managers tend not to exist in the United States, where asset managers concentrate on specific asset classes and within each asset class on a particular investment strategy. For example, a public equities asset manager might focus on smaller companies' equities or specific industry sectors. Specialization is the trend, however, and balanced fund managers are increasingly losing their mandates to the specialists.

4. *Funds-of-funds.* Managers of pension funds and other pools of capital might decide not to pick particular venture capital funds themselves. Rather, they might decide to diversify across a lot of VC funds by investing in an intermediate vehicle called a *fund-of-funds*. It aggregates commitments from a number of institutions and then does a lot of due diligence to determine the best VC teams with whom to invest.

5. *Corporations.* Many large companies make commitments to independent venture capital funds. Sometimes the investment is intended as a way of keeping an eye on technology developments within the sectoral focus of the VC fund. On occasion, corporations have established their own VC funds. These include, for example, Intel Capital and Siemens Venture Capital. During the dot-com bubble years of 1997 to 2000, a number of corporations established VC funds, but most of these were subsequently discontinued or wound down.

6. *Individuals.* Wealthy individuals, sometimes through a family office vehicle, make commitments to VC funds. Many funds, however, try to avoid commitments from individuals who have not constituted themselves formally to make investments. A VC fund is a 10-year vehicle, and the financial circumstances of an individual at year 1 can be very different when a drawdown notice comes five years later. As discussed above, if any of the investors in a fund try to renege on their commitment, this can have a very detrimental impact on the entire partnership. Family offices, on the other hand, tend to have more structure and are welcome investors in a fund.

In summary, GPs are looking for investors with a long-term commitment to the asset class. They do not want investors with a short-term horizon who are not fully committed.

One positive secular trend for the industry is the increasing level of allocation to the venture capital asset class. Some of the long-term investors in venture capital funds have achieved high returns and have raised their allocation levels, sometimes having 15% or more of their total assets in the class. Many pension funds that are just entering the asset class might have committed less than 2% of their assets; most observers expect allocation levels in general to rise over time.

Size and Internal Structure of VC Firms

A VC team will consist of a number of partners and probably a number of associates or principals. The partners will own the management company and share in the carried interest (see section below on carry). There is no defined career path for getting into venture capital. Some venture capitalists are former entrepreneurs, some have experience in technology corporate finance, some were analysts focused on the technology sector—there is no winning formula, other than to achieve a good mix of skills and experience in a team.

Many firms focus on investments in their own geographical area although there are a number of funds (Atlas, Benchmark, etc.) that have offices on more than one continent. Many firms have rules of thumb that they won't invest farther than, say, a one-hour flight away from their office. Venture capitalists want to be close to their investments to provide input and to help sort out issues as they arise.

While there are funds that have survived across a few generations, it is not unusual for parts of teams to break away to form new VC firms. Each firm will have a balance between founders, long-standing partners, and young turks. If the young turks do not feel that they are getting a fair share of the economics of the VC firm (part of the management company and a sufficient share in the carry), they might decide to try to raise a separate fund for themselves. Naturally, some partners' investments do better than other partners' investments. The high-performing partners may feel that being part of a separate firm would be an advantage to them.

Regularly, there are industry debates as to whether the sector will become more institutionalized, similar to an international law firm with offices on multiple continents. However, many of the best investors prefer to remain part of small, flexible, entrepreneurial teams. Bureaucracy and formal decision making have the potential to ruin the flexibility and risk taking that are central to good venture capital investing.

How VC Firms Are Compensated

The partners and staff of a venture capital company are rewarded in two ways—through a management fee and through carried interest.

Management Fee

Partners and staff of a venture capital company receive an annual fee— roughly 2% of the total amount of the fund they manage each year.

Over the 10-year life of a fund, the management fee will therefore consume about 20% of the total fund. In the early years of a fund, this fee can appear to be very high, since only 20 to 40% of the fund might have been drawn down and invested. For example, at the end of year 1, if 20% of the fund has been drawn and invested and 2% of the fund has been spent in management fees, the fee as a percentage of the money at work is 10%. Over the life of the fund, this will decline, but it is still higher than the equivalent fee for managing a public equities fund. This is not surprising because the market for private company start-ups is very inefficient. It requires a lot of skill and judgment in making new investments and also a lot of work to help to turn them into successful companies.

Venture capital firms will aim to raise a new fund every three to five years depending on their investing pace. The normal contract underpinning a venture capital fund does not allow the general partner to raise a new fund until a large percentage of the existing fund is *committed*. It is important to note that *committed* is not the same as *invested*. Only 50% or so of the fund might have been invested; another 20 to 30% might be in reserves held back by the GP to support future rounds of investments in existing portfolio companies.

Since VC firms normally have multiple funds under management at the same time, they will earn fees from each of these funds. One important area—conflicts of interest in managing multiple funds—is addressed later in this chapter.

The annual management fees pay the salaries of the investment staff and expenses related to managing the business of the GP. These include, for example, office expenses, travel expenses, and marketing expenses. Where expenses are incurred that clearly relate to making specific investments, these are charged against the fund and are not paid out of the 2% management fee. These include expenses such as due diligence costs and legal costs for closing investments.

Limited partners in venture capital funds keep a close eye on the fees earned by venture capital firms. They would prefer that the partners do not get rich on the fees, but rather that they remain hungry enough to focus on carried interest. This concern has arisen in relation to VC firms that have raised a number of large (e.g., $500M or more) funds.

Limited partners want the comfort of knowing that the individuals in a VC firm will attain personal wealth only if the limited partners benefit first.

Carried Interest ("Carry")

The VC firm managing a fund will be allocated a 20%[1] carried interest in the fund. This means that the firm is entitled to 20% of all the gains, once the LPs have received 100% of the capital of the fund. For example, if a $100M fund has returned $250M from its investments, 20% of $150M (i.e., the gain) will be allocated to the partners in the VC firm—in this case $30M.

There are a few factors to note regarding carried interest:

- *Hurdle rate.* A fund may have a hurdle rate internal rate of return (IRR) (maybe 6% or a Treasury bill rate) before the carried interest becomes payable. Normally, once this hurdle rate has been reached, there is a catch-up clause so that the gain is paid on all gains above the committed capital of the fund—not just the gains above the hurdle rate.
- *Clawbacks.* Some fund agreements allow the general partner to earn carry when the gains from investments exceed the amount of capital drawn. For example, if the general partner had drawn $50M from a $100M fund and had already returned capital of $70M on the early investments, carried interest of 20% of the $20M gain would be payable. This type of arrangement is now unusual because during the dot-com boom, partnerships that paid carried interest in this way became liable for clawback when they didn't manage to return the entire amount of capital ($100M in this case).
- *Division of the carried interest.* One major issue for general partners is the division of the carried interest among the individual partners in the fund. Some funds have a straight-line division of

---

1 Some funds have negotiated up to a 30% carried interest, but 20% is the norm.

the carried interest; others have a tiered structure with senior partners and junior partners getting shares commensurate with their seniority or performance and all other staff receiving a thin slice. Limited partners want to see an equitable split between the long established partners and those who are up and coming.

Partners in a VC fund are primarily motivated by carried interest. For all but the top funds that have very large amounts of money under management, the management fee earned is not enough to generate wealth for the partners.

Valuation of Investments within a VC Portfolio

The rules for valuing investments in a VC portfolio evolve as industry associations, audit oversight groups, and regulatory bodies issue pronouncements.

In general, the companies in a venture capital portfolio should be valued at fair value—*fair value* being the amount for which an asset could be exchanged between knowledgeable, willing parties in an arm's-length transaction.

This is extremely difficult to apply in practice. It is impossible to get an accurate view of the value of companies within a venture capital portfolio until they are exited. All GPs will have investments in their portfolios about which they have a feeling they are going to achieve an excellent exit, but for which there is no justification for revaluing the investment upward.

When an investment is made initially, it is valued at cost. A Series A investment of $1M in Company X in exchange for 33% of the share capital of the company will value that company at $3M. The VC fund will value its shareholding at $1M.

If that company performs more poorly than expected, the fund manager should write down their valuation of the investment. The fund manager will not be too scientific about the write-down. A broad-brush write-down of 25%, 50%, 75%, or 100% is often used. The main purpose of the write-down is to signal the LP that value has been impaired. The extent of the impairment is generally unclear until some future financing or exit event. The "lemons ripen early" in a venture capital portfolio—poor investments are often apparent after 6 to 12 months, whereas good investments often become apparent after a much longer amount of time has elapsed.

If the company performs well, the VC fund will not write up the valuation of the investment in its accounts until some external event occurs. The main basis for a write-up in value of an investment is an external funding round. If a Series B financing round from a third party investor of $2M in Company X above is concluded at a premoney valuation of $6M, the Series A investor should write up the investment from $1M to $2M[2] in the accounts.

In the absence of a financing round led by a third party investor, the venture fund will write up the value of an investment only if valuing it at cost was truly misleading. For example, if the investment had been made three to four years previously and the company was performing extremely well and the value uplift was truly apparent (e.g., increases in EBITDA [earnings before interest, taxes, depreciation, and amortization]), the VC fund should mark up its value, using external benchmarks, but always being conservative.

There are much more complicated rules for valuing stock in the portfolios of private equity and leveraged buyout funds.

To some extent, the value of companies in a venture capital portfolio does not matter much. The LPs are legally committed to meet their obligations. They will receive disbursements from the fund as and when they happen. All that matters is the hard cash result at the end. The valuations in theory provide some guidance regarding how the fund manager is performing along the way. However, there is so much judgment required in valuing investments that managers are often consistently optimistic valuers or consistently cautious valuers. The performance of the consistently cautious valuers versus their peers can be in the lower quartiles while investments are developing, but in the top quartile when the investments are realized. The converse is true for consistently optimistic valuers. The only way to get a true view on the performance of a fund is to wait until the investments have all been realized.

---

2 This valuation may be reduced to take into account the enhanced exit preference position of the Series B investor.

One unfortunate influence on valuations of venture capital portfolios is the need for VC teams to raise new funds. As firms raise new funds every three to five years, the interim performance of the prior fund can be judged only by using subjective valuations of the underlying portfolio companies—although there might be some exits. Consequently, VCs must be vigilant with respect to the temptation to boost internal valuations. Good LPs do their analysis and know at which end of the valuation spectrum each GP lies.

Cash Flows and J Curve at a Fund Level

A commitment to a VC fund is drawn down over time. If an investor makes a $10M commitment to a $100M fund, he or she will expect that $10M to be drawn down over the first five to six years. The GP will make periodic capital calls, roughly every six months, depending on the expectation of the new and existing investments. GPs avoid drawing a lot of cash from LPs that will sit idly before being invested in companies. This is because the fund performance is measured on internal rate of return. The IRR takes into account the dates on which cash is received from LPs and the date disbursements are made to LPs after exits from companies. Cash sitting idly in a VC's bank account is earning a low rate of interest and will drag down the IRR.

For those unfamiliar with IRR, please review the following explanatory note.

INTERNAL RATE OF RETURN

Definition: The internal rate of return (IRR) is the discount rate that results in a net present value of zero for a series of future cash flows. Simplistically, if a person makes an investment of $100 and one year later receives $110 or in two years receives $121 or in three years receives $133.10, then the investor's IRR is 10% in each case.

An IRR is a cutoff rate of return. An investor should avoid an investment if its IRR is less than his or her cost of capital or minimum desired rate of return.

IRR is the flip side of net present value (NPV) and is based on the same principles and the same math. NPV shows the value of a stream of future cash flows discounted back to the present by some percentage that represents the minimum desired rate of return.

IRR, on the other hand, computes a breakeven rate of return. At any discount rate below the IRR, an investment would result in a positive NPV (and should be made). If the appropriate discount rate is above the IRR, then the investment will result in a negative NPV (and should be avoided). It's the breakeven discount rate—the rate at which the value of cash outflows equals the value of cash inflows.

Exhibit 5.2 illustrates a broadly typical pattern of investments and disbursements made by a venture capital fund during its 10-year life.

The fund will make new investments in years 1 to 5. Early-stage investors might reserve 100 to 200% of the initial investment amount for follow-on investments (reserves). These reserves will be drawn

Exhibit 5.2 Funds-In, Funds-Out $100M Fund

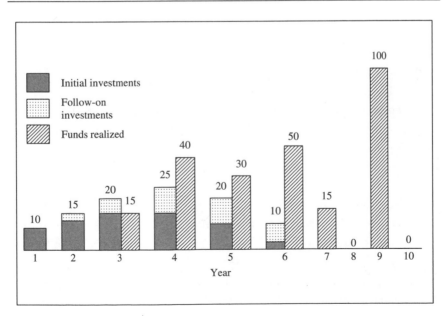

down and applied between years 2 and 7 or 8 on average. These investments will then come to fruition in the latter half of the fund, although, of course, a fund can have some early hits. As investments are exited, the cash received is distributed to the limited partners—cash does not normally get recycled into other investments. Each dollar is invested only once. If stock is received on an exit, it can be sold or distributed directly (in cash) to limited partners. Typically, if the stock amount is small or in a thinly traded public stock, the general partner will aim to liquidate it into cash to avoid hassle for the LP. Stock can be distributed directly (in specie) to an LP only after any lockup[3] period has expired.

The performance of most venture capital funds follows a J curve. The value of the fund almost always goes down in the first few years and, assuming the fund does well, comes back up in later years. There are a few reasons for this:

1. *The lemons ripen early.* Bad investments tend to become apparent early in their life, whereas good investments typically take a few years to show their high performance. Thus, many funds experience net write-downs early in their life.
2. *Valuation rules have a bias toward conservatism.* Good investments will be written up only on a positive external event— such as a new financing round. Poor investments, on the other hand, are written down when the GP believes that there has been an impairment of value. This does not require an outside event. This causes a bias toward conservatism.
3. *Fund expenses drag early performance.* As reviewed in the section above on remuneration of the GP, the management fee as a percentage of capital drawn is high in the early years. This creates a drag on fund performance early in its life.

Experienced, long-term LP investors in the VC asset class understand the J curve. They expect a book write-down in their fund investment in early years, but know that this is not a good indicator for how the fund

---

3 When a company is sold and the shareholders receive stock in a public company, it is often subject to a no-sale lockup for 3 or up to 12 months.

will perform over the long term. They also understand that an investor in this class needs to build up its exposure over time to avoid having an extremely high exposure to funds of one particular vintage year.

Expected Returns on a VC Fund

Investors in a venture capital fund view it as one of a number of different asset classes across which they are diversified. Their portfolio may include equities, bonds, cash, property, and hedge funds.

Investors seek a blend of asset classes that matches their risk profile. Endowments and other investors with very long-term horizons will on balance be more willing to accept higher risk (in return for higher potential reward) and also have less need for liquidity than other kinds of investors. This makes them a good fit with the venture capital asset class.

These investors in venture capital will seek a premium above the expected return of publicly quoted equities. There is a lot of theoretical debate about the premium return above public equities that investors in venture capital funds should aim for—most observers tend to suggest 2 to 5%. The following section covers the reasons for the premium above public equities.

Reasons for Venture Capital Risk Premium above Public Equities

Investors in VC funds demand a premium on the returns they receive from the fund above those returns they receive on public equities. As noted above, most observers of this sector estimate this premium to be 2 to 5%.

There are a few reasons for the premium from the perspective of the LP:

1. *Lack of liquidity.* If an investor makes a commitment of $10M to a $100M fund, he or she has made a 10-year commitment to meet drawdowns of up to $10M throughout this period. Unlike public equities, there is no fully functional secondary market for LP

interests in funds. If investors dislike a public equity, they can sell it for a minor transaction fee. There are some buyers of secondary positions in funds, but they aim to buy these positions at a discount. Funds are subject to a J curve in both book value and market value. But the book value can be a poor guide to the market value of the fund.

2. *Unclear timing of drawdowns and size of commitment to the sector.* An LP with $1 billion under management might decide that it wants a 5% ($50M) exposure to the venture sector. In practice, it is almost impossible to get to an exact target level and to hold it, as cash is being drawn down by VC firms as needed and only returned when investments are realized.

   The LP starts by making commitments to funds—it might make five commitments of $20M to different funds in five consecutive years. The LP should not make all the commitments in one year because the sector is very cyclical and any particular year might prove to be an extremely poor or great year in which to start. The LP has no clear idea when the VC firms might draw the funds. Some might draw them slowly and have investments that yield a return late in the 10-year cycle. Others might invest quickly and generate quick returns. From 1998 to 2000, the investing pace was the fastest on record. From 2001 to 2004, the investing pace was probably the slowest ever.

3. *Distribution of returns on funds.* While investment management funds investing in a particular class of public equities (e.g., large-cap U.S. stocks) can have very different levels of returns, the differences tend to be small in comparison to the differences in returns from VC funds. For VC funds of the same vintage (e.g., established in 2005), the top quartile might end up with returns of 30% IRR, while the bottom quartile might end up with returns of 10% IRR. The best firm might achieve an IRR of 100% or more. A Google, eBay, or Skype in a portfolio can have an unbelievable impact on the IRR.

Investors in funds and GPs tend to talk about multiples on amounts invested rather than IRR. While IRR is the correct measure theoretically, the multiple tends to be a simple, crude way of communicating how well a fund has done. A fund that gives back three or more times the capital committed is viewed as having done very well. Two and a half times would be considered good. Anything under two would be seen as disappointing. A $100M fund that returns anything greater than $200M to $300M to the contributing investors will have done well. This amount is calculated after the fees and carry earned by the GP are factored in.

The relative performance depends on the vintage year of the fund. Consistent investors in the class compare funds set up in the same year. For example, funds set up in 2008 will be compared to one another. This is because funds of a similar vintage will have relatively similar buoyancy in their entry markets (when they are making investments) and exit markets (when they are trying to sell their companies or to undertake an IPO). It would be unfair to compare a fund set up in 1996, which might have made a lot of exits in the dot-com bubble years, with a fund set up in 2000 that faced a number of lean years and a declining sentiment in exit markets.

One reason that people think about multiples is that the GP typically earns carry on all gains above the point at which the capital is returned.[4] Thus, there is a big emphasis on getting 100% of the capital back to the investors as quickly as is feasible.

The appropriateness of the 2.5/3 multiple metric can be seen in Exhibit 5.3. The vertical axis shows the multiple of capital returned to the LP. The horizontal axis shows the length of time the average dollar was invested by the LP—while the fund is a 10-year fund, drawdowns are made over time and capital is returned to LPs when an individual investment is exited. For example, if the average dollar is invested by the LP for seven years and the multiple returned is 3.5, then the LP earned a 20% annualized return on his or her investment.

For a fund invested in early-stage technology, the average length of time between an amount being drawn down by the general partner and being returned after liquidity investments is often five to seven years. While it was shortened in the dot-com boom of 1998–2000, experienced investors understand that it takes five to seven years for a typical good investment to come to fruition.

---

4 Assuming no hurdle rate.

Exhibit 5.3 Relationship between Multiple of Capital, Length of Time, and IRR—Fund Level

	Number of Years Average $ Is Invested			
Multiple of Capital Returned	5	6	7	8
1.5	8%	7%	6%	5%
2.0	15%	12%	10%	9%
2.5	20%	16%	14%	12%
3.0	25%	20%	17%	15%
3.5	28%	23%	20%	17%
4.0	36%	26%	22%	19%

Expected Returns on Individual Investments in a VC Fund

If the expected return on a venture capital portfolio is 2 to 5% above the expected return on public equities, entrepreneurs might question why venture capitalists seem to be seeking much higher returns on individual investments. In practice, this argument arises when VCs push for low valuations on their investments and larger percentage ownership positions in companies than the entrepreneurs would like.

To understand this, it is important to understand the mathematical dynamics of a portfolio of venture capital investments. The following example reviews a $100M fund that aims to return two and a half to three times the capital on the fund to its LPs.

TO RETURN THREE TIMES THE CAPITAL TO LPS

Capital back on all investments	$350M
Carry earned by general partner	$50M*
Capital distributed to LPs	$300M = 3 times return on the fund
Total fund	$100M

Management fees over 10 years	$20M
Capital invested in companies	$80M
Expected complete write-offs	$26M (say one-third of amount invested)
Capital to be earned on all investments	$350M
Capital earned on complete write-offs	$0 (amount invested, say, $20M—one-quarter of $80M)
Capital earned on "sideways" deals[†]	$40M (amount invested, $20M—one-quarter of $80M)
Required capital to be earned on good deals	$310M
Amount invested in good deals	$40M (half of amount invested)
Multiple required to be made on good investments	7.7

To Return Two and a Half Times the Capital to LPs

Capital back on all investments	$287.5M
Carry earned by general partner	$37.5M
Capital distributed to LPs	$250M =2.5 times return on the fund
Total fund	$100M
Management fees over 10 years	$20M
Capital invested in companies	$80M
Capital to be earned on all investments	$287.5M
Capital earned on complete write-offs	$0 (amount invested, say, $20M—one-quarter of $80M)

Capital earned on "sideways" deals	$40M (amount invested $20M—one-quarter of $80M)
Required capital to be earned on good deals	$247.5M
Amount invested in good deals	$40M (half of amount invested)
Multiple required to be made on good investments	6.2

---

* 20% of the gain on the fund ($250M gain = $350M minus $100M) equals $50M.
† Sideways deals might be ones in which the VC fund gets back on average twice the capital invested.

Based on the analysis provided in the box, if the fund is to return two and a half or three times the capital subscribed to its LPs, the good investments need to yield a 6 to 7 multiple. Exhibit 5.4 illustrates that a 6 to 7 times multiple will require an IRR on individual investments of 35 to 38% (assuming each company takes six years on average to reach an exit).

Exhibit 5.4 Relationship between Multiple of Capital, Length of Time, and IRR—Level of Individual Investment

	Number of Years Average $ Is Invested			
Multiple of Capital Returned	**5**	**6**	**7**	**8**
5.0	38%	31%	26%	22%
6.0	43%	35%	29%	25%
7.0	48%	38%	32%	28%
8.0	52%	41%	35%	30%

Venture capital investors generally say that they will invest in a company only where they can see a way to earning a 10 times or higher multiple on the investment. Clearly, if the fund needs to earn a 6 to 7 times multiple on good investments to provide a 2.5 or 3 times multiple to its LPs, then some of these investments will be above the 6 to 7 level and some will be below.

It's All about Big Winners

The distribution of capital returned from investments across a venture capital portfolio is striking because of the extreme differences from company to company. Consider the example of the fund shown in Exhibit 5.5.

The fund was $100M and made 25 investments, which is a reasonable spread of investments. Of the fund that was invested, 85% was invested in the 25 companies—the remaining 15% went to pay fees. The fund generated exits worth 300% of the capital committed.

Exhibit 5.5 Distribution of Capital Invested and Capital Returned Across a Portfolio

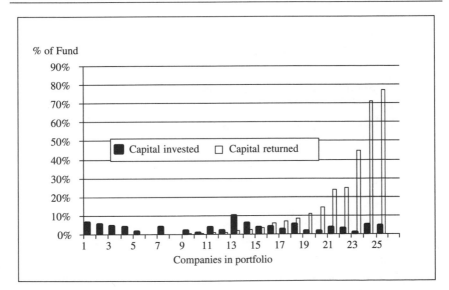

The 10 worst investments are shown at the left of the exhibit (companies 1 to 10); these lost their entire invested capital. Of the next nine investments (companies 11 to 19), the firm made sufficient gains to pay back the capital committed to these investments as well as to cover the losses on the first 10 investments. On the next three investments (companies 20 to 22), the fund made sufficient gains to repay the capital of the fund and to generate a small IRR—roughly equivalent to the returns likely seen on Treasury bonds. Returns at this level would not be enough to encourage the LP to make a commitment to the fund, but at least they would have received their capital back plus a small premium. It is important to note that a good VC firm should be able to return the capital on the fund without getting any big hits.

It is only when the three big hits (companies 23 to 25) are added in that the fund provided a venture capital level of return of 3.0 times the capital or more with a midteens or higher IRR.

This distribution of returns is not unusual. Empirical evidence on fund returns shows that big hits are the difference between the highest-performing venture capital firms and the average ones. A big hit might be defined as one that repays one-third, half, all, or even a multiple of the fund. No VC investor should make an investment unless he or she believes that it could be a big hit for the fund.

Portfolio Construction

VCs are opportunistic investors who look for good investments wherever they can find them. Each investment is considered on its own merits. But there are occasions when portfolio considerations come into the investment process regarding individual investments.

The dimensions of a portfolio that a VC fund takes into account are the following:

1. *Number of investments.* Industry observers tend to use heuristics (rules of thumb) such as, *One-third will be complete write-offs, one-third will be sideways, and one-third will be big hits.* While not particularly accurate, it illustrates the point that if one is really

relying on one-third of the investments to provide all of the gains, there had better be enough investments in the top third. Most funds aim to have 15 to 25 investments in a portfolio, and experience has shown that the higher end of this range provides a good degree of diversification.

2. *Sector.* There is an ongoing debate in the sector as to whether funds should cover multiple sectors or focus on one. An ongoing debate at industry conferences revolves around IT only, life sciences only, or mixed funds. Since IT and life sciences tend to operate on different cycles, it is hard to judge the better strategy. Clearly, it is easier for a firm to build expertise in a narrow domain area such as wireless, optical components, communications equipment, and enterprise software. But each of these subsectors has its own cycle and is subject to different levels of maturity. Software has historically been a high-growth sector that has provided good returns for investors. But, it now appears to be developing into a mature investment sector with investment dynamics like highly mature sectors such as automobiles or chemicals. If this is true, it will prove to yield poor investment returns to venture capitalists looking for big multiple exits.

3. *Geography.* One dimension that VCs tend to ignore is geography. They want to make investments locally, preferably in the same city. Diversification across geography in practice tends to provide limited or no diversification to investors in global markets such as technology. Rarely is one region doing very well while another one suffers. Each region is subject to the same exit markets. VCs aim to add value to investments, and this generally requires them to have easy physical access to the investments.

4. *Stage of investing.* Some investors see themselves as early-stage investors and some as late-stage investors while some aim to balance their investing across stages. For the ones who balance themselves across stages, one maxim often heard is, "Invest one-third of the fund in safe investments that will provide a three times return reasonably quickly." Thus, the chance of repaying 100% of the capital—an important benchmark for all funds—is high.

Experienced investors are good at diversifying their portfolios. They understand the risk profile of each investment and balance the risks accordingly. Even though a fund may invest in early-stage technology companies, some of these investments will have a lower risk profile than others. To the extent that all investments are relatively high risk, the good investor will make a lot of them.

Sorting Out Conflicts of Interest

The relationship between a limited partner which provides the capital and the general partner which manages the fund is like any principal-agent relationship. Rules are required to align the interests of the GP with the goals of the LP that is providing the capital. In theory, the compensation structure (a fee plus carry) in a venture capital fund should closely align the interests of the fund manager and the investors. However, investors are tied in to the fund very tightly for 10 years—if they were not, the interests of all of the other investors in the fund might be damaged. In return, the actions of the manager of the fund need to be governed tightly in legal contracts. This is reinforced by the fact that the oversight and control normally provided by a board of directors is not in place because of the rules governing partnerships with limited partners.

A large number of clauses in the partnership agreement exist to align these interests:

- The GP is obliged to provide a small percentage, maybe 1%, of the capital of the fund. When the fund is a large fund ($300M–500M), this can be a material proportion of the liquid net worth of some GPs.
- The GP earns a management fee, but this is generally not enough to provide more than a reasonable salary. To garner some wealth, the GP needs to earn carry, and this requires a return of the entire fund.
- Fees earned on investments or fees for acting as a director of portfolio companies are normally for the benefit of the fund rather than the GP.

- GPs are motivated to make high-risk investments because they need to return large amounts of capital to LPs in order to earn carry. This generally suits the risk profile of LPs.
- GPs are restricted regarding the amount of money that can be invested in any one company—maybe 10 to 15% of the fund. This prevents the GP from pursuing an excessively risky strategy.
- Debt can be used only under restricted circumstances in order to avoid leveraging the risk on an individual investment or across a portfolio.
- Profits and realized gains are distributed rather than retained and reinvested.
- When a GP has multiple funds under management, the conflicts of interest are more pronounced. If a GP is allowed to cross-invest funds (e.g., the Series A round on Company X is done by one fund, and the Series B round is handled by another fund under management), then rules need to be put in place. The danger to an LP is that the Series B round is done to bail out a failing investment of the first fund or that the Series B round is done at an artificially low price per share, thus providing an advantage to the second fund. The legal agreements governing funds normally allow cross-investments only where the market price for the Series B round has been set by a third party investor and where the advisory committee for each fund has approved the investment. Good GPs almost never cross-invest funds. They provide sufficient reserves against each investment in a fund to allow them to protect their investments.
- GPs cannot make personal investments in portfolio companies, unless perhaps they are investing a similar proportion in every portfolio company. This ensures that the GP will not invest fund capital to protect a personal position.
- GPs cannot sell their carried interest to a third party. GPs are only allowed to have limited commercial interests outside of the fund.

CHAPTER 6

CREATING A WINNING BUSINESS PLAN

There are many books that discuss the ways to write a business plan. But most miss the point. A business plan aimed at attracting investors needs to prove the following: "The team and assets to be committed to the business can plausibly achieve sustainable *market power* in a market large enough to justify the investment." It is as simple and as difficult as that.

While economists might say that market power is demonstrated by the ability to earn a return on investment well above the cost of the capital committed to the business, in a business context it is simpler. Market power is the power of the bully—it allows the company to extract a disproportionately high return on capital and cast a deep footprint on its industry. There are many levers for achieving a high return on capital. Pricing power is one; it allows a company to charge more for its product than anyone else and to earn a very high (greater than 70%) gross margin on each sale. Scale is another lever; it allows the company to achieve a lower manufacturing cost than others, or it helps the company to capture more power over its suppliers. The many possible levers for exercising market power are covered in more detail below.

Without market power the product or service is a commodity. Commodity businesses find it very hard to earn a high return on investment over any sustained period of time.

Most professional investors such as venture capitalists need to articulate and document their investment thesis—the reason(s) for investing in the business. Thus the business plan should be a carefully constructed set of arguments underpinning the investment thesis that the entrepreneur wants to put forward to the investor. Every good investment thesis has at its core how the company will capture market power, how long the window of opportunity for exploiting it is, and how the market power will be monetized. Every fact, assertion, or hypothesis included in the entrepreneur's business plan should be crafted in support of the investment thesis. Most business plans get lost in long narrative functional descriptions of the market, the products, the team, and so forth. All these elements, of course, need to be in a plan, but a business plan should not be a review of the business. Like a novel, a plan needs to tell a story, not just convey facts.

Market Power—the Key Ingredient Missing in Most Business Plans

Of business plans developed, 99% do not ruthlessly cover how the company will achieve and sustain market power. In fact, most entrepreneurs don't recognize that market power is the Holy Grail.

The primary thought that a business plan needs to communicate to a prospective investor is the manner in which the business will capture, defend, and exploit market power. It will need to be defended strongly because every competitor is chasing this elusive ingredient.

Market power is the only way for a business to earn a supernormal profit. It is the driver behind the market value of the company greatly exceeding the book value of the invested capital—being the only way in which investors can earn a return on their investment worth the risk. If there is no market power, the market value of the company will gravitate over time to the book value of the invested capital, and the return on investment will decline. If the market power is fleeting, a supernormal return will exist only in the short term.

Evidence to Include in the Business Plan

Entrepreneurs need to prove six specific propositions to prospective investors of the plan. If these six are proven, the investors should have no reason to reject the plan.

The first three set the foundation for the absolute potential value of the *opportunity* for all shareholders (founders and investors). These three should prove the investment thesis—why the business is worthy of investment:

1. Potential for accelerated growth in a big, accessible market
2. An achievable position of market power—a sustainable, differentiated product or service proposition
3. Capable, ambitious, trustworthy management

The second three propositions should prove that the opportunity will be a good *deal* for the investors. If these three are not proven, the business might turn out to be a good one, but the investors will not get a decent return on their capital. These three are covered in more detail in other chapters in this book:

4. Plausible, value-enhancing stepping-stones
5. Realistic valuation to allow the investor to earn a sizable multiple
6. Promising exit possibilities

The *opportunity* (investment thesis) and the *deal* must be right. The first three are now examined in more detail.

1. Potential for Accelerated Growth in a Big, Accessible Market

The first case to make is that the company can grow quickly to a large size and that it can be successful in bringing its proposition to market.

A Big, but Not Too Big, Market

The market size needs to be big enough to justify the level of investment. (See the mini case.)

MINI CASE: COMPANY DEVELOPING A NEW TYPE OF LASER

If the total available market for a new laser is $50M per annum, then the amount of investment required to support the company through its life had better not exceed about $5M. Using very crude rules of thumb:

- The company might capture 50% of the market if it is extremely successful.
- The value on exit might be two to four times sales, depending on the gross and net margins earned. This means that the company might be worth $50M to $100M on exit, at best.
- If the investor owns half the company, then the maximum proceeds on the sale of the company would be $25M to $50M.

This is a potentially fine result, if the capital committed is $5M (or preferably $2M to $3M), but this is an unattractive result if the capital committed is $10M, given the likely risks involved.

There should be a minimum proportionate relationship between the ultimate potential value of the company and the investment required for it to capture this value. For example, many observers of the semiconductor industry suggest that it takes $25M to $70M to build a new semiconductor design company pursuing a business model in which manufacturing (fabrication) of the product is outsourced to a third party. If this is the case, then the minimum market size for the product probably needs to be $250M to $700M or more for the basic investment economics to make sense.

These can be hard lessons for investors to learn because it takes a full investment cycle of a fund for these rules of thumb to become apparent. Many investors have invested in a company and learned five to eight years later that they could never have made enough money from the project, irrespective of the quality of management execution, because of the limited size of the market.

Consequently, the market needs to be big enough. Most venture capital companies will not consider an investment unless the potential exit price is $200M to $300M or more. Remember, investors are rightly looking for home runs rather than singles and doubles. But, on the other hand, the market size should not be too big.

If the potential market is truly enormous and it is well signaled to the industry and the investment community that the opportunity is arising, then investors need to consider the investment opportunity very cautiously. For example, in 2007 there was much discussion about interactive programming and Web and mobile television. The market for such a development is likely to be enormous. But it is clearly signaled to the marketplace. The vast majority of commentators are expecting it to become a reality for the mass-market consumer at some stage.

A start-up might have a chance of capturing part of this market but, no doubt, the incumbent platform television companies, the broadcasters, and many other start-ups are eyeing the prize as well. Large evolving markets that are well signaled to the investment communities are generally to be avoided. While the prize for the winners will be significant, the weight of capital pursuing the opportunity through different investment vehicles might drown the prospects for a good return on capital by one specific company.

Investors like large markets that are not well signaled—where the deep domain knowledge of the entrepreneur and the founding team provide them with insights to the evolution of large markets that are apparent to very few in the industry.

Company Growth to Come from Market Growth Rather Than Market Share Gains

Similar to the market being big, but not too big, investors want markets that are, ideally, in their early development stage—not so early that customers are not yet willing to consider the product, but not so late that there are established competitors with good revenues that will need to be displaced. Investors are looking for markets that are right on the cusp of takeoff.

All experienced investors have a story of where they invested too early and the company needed to wait for the market to happen—most companies die in the meantime. While some investors will make seed investments in the hope that the market will happen, if the company is to attract significant capital at a good valuation, the early signs of market development must be in place.

In the business plan presentation, the entrepreneur needs to be able to line up some prospects to whom the investor can talk. While the company might not yet have a product, it should be working to stimulate the market with conversations such as, "If we were to deliver product X or service X, how attractive would that be to you?" This sort of feedback is very useful to investors and can highlight the impending advent of the market and validate the company's proposition. If the company or the investor cannot find prospects interested in the future product or able to see the benefits, then the market might be too early.

Investors are often criticized for not supporting very early-stage companies where the market potential might be enormous but where basic research still needs to be completed. This is often the case with college-based research. The investor response to these types of opportunities is often to suggest that the technology be matured further in the college and commercialized later.

On the other hand, investors tend to want to avoid opportunities that involve taking market share from established competitors in more mature markets. Customer inertia and a direct onslaught from competitors can be debilitating for early-stage companies.

Clearly then, the investor looks for opportunities in the middle—the market is developing (or about to develop), but is not too developed.

Capability of Being Number 1 (or Maybe Number 2) in the Market

A start-up's ability to be number 1 or 2 in the market is linked to its ability to attain market power. If the business plan does not articulate a path to becoming number 1 in a market, then it cannot make the case for the company to be able to exercise market power. The number 3 or 4 player in a market has no market power.

Investors will discard plans that talk about capturing 1 to 3% of $2 billion markets—even though this might suggest an attractive level of sales. The path to dominate the market must exist. Without dominance, a very high (supernormal) return on capital is difficult to achieve.

Identifiable Access Route to Customers

It seems an obvious point, but having an identifiable access route to customers is often overlooked. The company needs to be able to access customers and close sales in a cost-effective manner.

An electronics component manufacturer might want to forward integrate (start developing the products that its customers previously made) to become a subsystem or module manufacturer and sell its product to system level or application companies. This move might shift the company to a much higher price point and to a less competitive part of the industry value chain. But, in practice, it might be impossible to achieve. The company might have no relationships at the system level (even though its components had previously been incorporated into these systems, via subsystem manufacturers). Also, the company's previous customers, the subsystems manufacturers, might try to block such a move—seeing it as cannibalization of their business.

Direct sales are probably the primary initial access approach to customers. But direct selling as a technique tends not to be scalable beyond a certain point because of the increasing need for salespeople. For example, many budding enterprise software companies find it impossible to scale much beyond $2M to $4M in sales using a direct sales model. At that point they often need to move to indirect channels, such as resellers and systems integrators, and this can be very challenging. Many companies hit a glass ceiling at this point.

The business plan needs to address not just how the early sales will be closed but how the sales model will scale over time. Examples of companies in adjacent spaces can be very useful for illustrating how this might work.

In addition to a long-term access route to customers, the plan needs to outline how the early customer engagement is going to happen. Most technology customers need references from early customers. Even though the product might not be finished, the early-stage company needs to get prospects lined up who are willing to take and try the product, even at a highly discounted price point. Clearly, industry leaders admired by their peers make the ideal reference customers.

One technique used by many early-stage companies is to try to get a foothold in the door of customers by making a very minor sale to a customer to try to prove the proposition. Good salespeople know that a manager in a customer company might spend $500,000 just to prove that the $50,000 spent on a demonstration product was not a mistake.

2. Achievable Position of Market Power

Simply put, the product or service must be a lot better than the competition, and based on this superiority, the company must find some way of extracting a premium for it. The evidence required here normally fits into three categories—the product or service must provide huge value to customers relative to the offerings of competitors, the company must have a sustainable, defensible position to allow the market power to be exploited for some time, and it must usually yield very high gross margins.

Huge Value to Customers Relative to the Competition

Customers are lazy and apathetic. They like the familiar and the risk-free. They might be intrigued by new possibilities, but if the new product or service will cost a lot of money, they will probably stick to what they know or they will do what others expect or want them to do. How can new companies break through this wall of inertia?

The first step in breaking down this inertia is to have an irresistible customer value proposition. Investors will use clichés or questions to get to the nub of the proposition:

- The product needs to be 10 times better than the alternatives along some dimension.
- What's the secret sauce?
- Is this at the top of the customer's list of problems?

While these are clearly exaggerated for effect, they express the appropriate sentiment. It is not good enough for the product to save customers some money; it needs to save them a lot or make them a lot. It is not good enough to be better than the competition; the product or service needs to be clearly superior, the benefits being so apparent and compelling that they cannot be ignored.

Investors tend not to like value propositions that involve a product being a bit better along multiple dimensions. For example, a software product is sometimes a little cheaper than the alternatives, but it also offers better information for decision making and streamlines complicated business processes. These multiple benefits are difficult to communicate and lack a killer punch. It is far easier to convey a value proposition to a customer when the product is demonstrably superior along one dimension. The best value proposition might be one in which the product can solve a problem that the customer cannot solve using anything else.

Don't forget that the status quo in any company will have many supporters. The purchasing person might already have procured a competitor's product. He or she might be playing golf at fancy golf courses with the competitor's salesperson every quarter. The IT department might be too lazy or too busy to handle another software supplier. The CFO might have imposed a blanket ban on capital expenditure (even if it is value enhancing). The person running operations might not want the pain of achieving the cost savings facilitated by the company's product—cost savings often require staff to be laid off. The businessperson in the line organization might have promoted a competitor's product internally—your product might reveal that this decision was a mistake.

The only way to cut through the apathy and the blockers is to get a champion, and a champion will be possible only if the product is extremely compelling—not just a bit better than the status quo.

The value proposition must be capable of being articulated at multiple levels—the one-sentence version, the two-minute elevator pitch, and the return on investment (ROI) analysis. There are many good examples of simple statement value propositions. Attendees at venture capital conferences will be very familiar with elevator pitches. The challenge in these two-minute pitches is to avoid describing the business and to focus instead on the company's superlative value proposition to customers and why the company is better placed than the competition to deliver this value.

But entrepreneurs rarely go as far as to put together ROI spreadsheets.

The investor needs to believe, intuitively, in the superiority of the product or service. But, to clinch the investor's and the customer's support, it is often necessary to prove, deductively, the tangible superiority of the product or service. The ROI spreadsheet can help here.

A good ROI spreadsheet will allow prospective customers to input data describing their own parameters of their own business in order to figure out the specific financial benefits of the product to them. Of course, they also need to believe that the product or service can actually deliver on the stated benefits.

Many entrepreneurs are good at articulating benefits in a general sense but are less skilled in helping the customer to build a compelling financial case. Often, entrepreneurs can convince line businesspeople in a corporation of the merits of their product or service. Businesspeople "in the line" of a corporation know their business well. As well as understanding the hard economic benefits, they intuitively understand many of the main gains that manifest themselves in soft benefits such as improved customer satisfaction and faster decision making.

But soft benefits are useful only if they lead to hard financial gains at some stage. This link needs to be made explicit, and the key decision makers throughout the customer organization need to believe the link.

Often, the sale fails when line businesspeople need to convince the gatekeeper departments—IT, purchasing, and finance, for example—that fulfill a challenge function. The main goal of IT, purchasing, and finance in many companies seems to involve stopping the line organization from doing what it wants to do or second-guessing the line's decisions.

A sharp ROI spreadsheet, bought into by all the business users, can be a compelling device for getting these gatekeeper departments over the line. The ROI spreadsheet needs to transform the soft benefits into financial numbers, no matter how difficult this may be.

The types of line items to include in an ROI spreadsheet of a new parts inventory management and automatic ordering system for a car dealership might be as follows:

- Elimination or pinpointing of shrinkage of parts stock.
- Reduction in underbilling of customers for parts used on their cars.
- Reduced staff in the parts-handling division.
- Cost saved by holding less inventory, resulting from proper calculation of minimum appropriate inventory levels.
- Cost of mechanic time saved by having the right parts always available.
- Cost of front office staff time saved by having to deal with customers only once (because the right parts are always available).
- Margin associated with increased sales of new cars resulting from higher customer satisfaction. The customer loyalty rate is raised from 80 to 85%.

The goal of the ROI spreadsheet is to force all parties in the sale process to be much more explicit about the economic benefits of the company's product.

Sustainable, Defensible Position to Allow Market Power to Be Exploited

With a hugely superior product or service in hand, the plan needs to outline how this superiority can be exploited on a sustained basis. There are many ways to sustain and defend market power.

- *Patents* give a company a legal monopoly. Patents are critical for businesses producing medical devices, therapeutic drugs, semiconductor designs, and so on.
- *Know-how,* while not having the legal defensibility of patents, can also be potent. If no one else knows what makes up your superior product or can emulate the production process, you can

create a privileged position in the market. For many software companies, the key differentiator is know-how. Software patents, to the extent that they are allowed, provide limited comfort. Often, the entrepreneurs behind a software company have some unique insights into business processes and are able to design software that streamlines processes or that produces information for decision making that was not previously available.

- ***First-to-market strategies*** allow companies to block competitors out of customer relationships. In an ideal world, the company experiences increasing returns to scale—the bigger it gets, the bigger the percentage chance it has of getting the next customer and ultimately dominating the market. In the networked world, after the arrival of the Internet, it is apparent that in many market sectors one firm dominates all others. There is a tendency toward standardization. This can be seen in operating systems, browsers, routers, and so on. This winner-take-all trend allows the winner to extract enormous amounts of value.
- ***Natural monopolies*** are similar to first-to-market strategies, but they might be based on a position created with fixed assets. They include electricity distribution, fixed line telecom, gas distribution, and the like.
- A ***step change reduction in cost*** can give a company a head start so that it is difficult for competitors to catch up. The low-cost airline that drops prices to rock bottom on a particular point-to-point route is often trying to wipe out all other competitors on the same route in order to then charge and earn a premium (off of a very low cost base). If competitors come back in again, prices can be quickly reduced to punish the new entrant.

There are many other ways of sustaining market power. A new retail concept (e.g., a chain of coffee shops) might gather all the most appropriate locations before competitors react. A business in which market power looks impossible to achieve (e.g., book retailing before the advent of the Internet) might be transformed into a business where sustainable market power in the new Internet channel can be achieved through a first-to-market strategy.

Think of any successful business that has earned a high return on its invested capital for some time. If you look carefully, you will see that it has market power of some sort.

Very High Gross Margins

To some extent, high gross margins are a natural consequence of market power. If it is not possible to earn high gross margins (greater than 70%), then the investor will legitimately start questioning whether there is truly a superlative value proposition for customers and whether the company can exert market power.

Clearly there are some businesses that can earn a high return on capital from a low cost strategy—witness the success of the low-cost airlines. But, from the perspective of the early-stage investor, most attractive businesses will have high price/high gross margin strategies. These businesses are much more highly valued in general.

3. Capable, Ambitious, Trustworthy Management

It goes without saying that the quality of management execution has a very strong impact on the success or failure of a company. In an ideal world, every team would be full of individuals who have prior successful entrepreneurial records. They will have been through the ups and downs and will be far more surefooted in the environment of an early-stage company than a strong manager from a large corporate environment. Prior successful entrepreneurs are not always available, however. Investors therefore look for the following characteristics in the people with whom they invest:

- *Balanced team.* The team needs to be balanced with a mix of technical, sales, marketing, etc., skills. While the preponderance of skills at the start of a new venture is often rightly technical, they will need to be supplemented quickly. The CEO might be part of the team at the start of the venture. Often, he or she will be hired over time when the company has gathered enough proof that the opportunity exists. This allows a very high quality individual to be brought on board. Investors don't want to back an individual—they want to back a team.

- *Deep domain knowledge.* Nothing gives an investor more comfort than a team that understands its domain deeply—not just the macrolevel trends, but also the microlevel facts. The only way to give investors comfort on this is to truly possess the knowledge and insight.
- *Prior experiences and record.* Needless to say, all investors want to back entrepreneurs who have been successful before. A great highly relevant résumé is a good place to start in convincing an investor of the merits of an investment opportunity.
- *Ambition, not oriented to lifestyle.* One concern investors always have is that the company will be run for the benefit of the founders and management rather than the shareholders. While legal agreements go some way toward resolving conflicts of interest, investors need to get comfortable with the style and motives of the entrepreneurs. Also, they need to believe that the company will never be turned into a lifestyle business—run for current compensation and status of the founders and management rather than to create a capital gain.

In summary, the three factors covered thus far define the absolute size of the *opportunity:*

1. Potential for accelerated growth in a big accessible market
2. Achievable position of market power—a sustainable, differentiated product or service proposition
3. Capable, ambitious, trustworthy management

Only when the investor gets comfort in the attractiveness of the *opportunity* is it worth moving on to talk about the attractiveness of the *deal.*

4. Plausible, Value-Enhancing Stepping-Stones

Each investor needs to believe that his or her investment will allow the company to reach new stepping-stones that will enable the company to raise further funding at a higher price per share. This aspect of early-stage businesses is covered in detail in Chapter 3, "The Unique Cash Flow and Risk Dynamics of Early-Stage Ventures."

The business plan needs to outline the milestones that can be reached in the investment round sought in the business plan and how these milestones will boost the value of the company. Most entrepreneurs don't do this explicitly. They should.

Entrepreneurs tend to outline the broad milestones for the business. They rarely zero in on the specific milestones that will be reached with the investment funds sought. They also rarely outline the alternative sets of milestones that were considered before deciding on the chosen set of milestones. Most investors would relish such a discussion; investors' thought processes regarding what milestones constitute value enhancement might differ from those of the entrepreneur.

5. Realistic Valuation

Investors need to be assured that, if the company is successful, they stand a good chance of making a big multiple on their investment. Thus, the business plan needs to pull together the evidence suggested in Chapter 7. This should include the ultimate potential value comparables and the next round comparables.

6. Promising Exit Possibilities

To be worthy of external investment, a business should always be able to realize its potential without being part of a larger company. To exit the investment, the investor must have some belief that an initial public offering might be possible. Of course, the investor and the entrepreneur will have an opinion as to the types of companies or specific companies that would make good owners for the business (and be willing to pay a high price for it).

PART III

VALUING THE EARLY-STAGE VENTURE

CHAPTER 7

VALUING EARLY-STAGE COMPANIES

Valuation of early-stage companies is a black art to those not involved on an ongoing basis with funding early-stage companies. None of the traditional valuation techniques—discounted cash flow analysis, payback formulas, and so on—seem to be relevant. Everyone involved recognizes that these highly analytical approaches require so many assumptions that they eventually become meaningless—there are simply too many moving variables. Also, the outcomes for many variables can be binary—success or failure. A market might take off, or it might not. A product might reach a particular specification, or it might not. Regulators might approve the product, or they might not.

A relevant question might not be whether the market growth rate will be 5% or 10%, or 20%. It might be whether the market will ultimately be $50M, $200M, or $500M. But, while decrying analytical valuation techniques, the fact remains that every company will need to be valued at some point. If an investor wants to invest, the valuation will determine the percentage of ownership of the business he or she will receive. Valuation, while difficult, is critical.

To some extent, there are analogies between real estate and early-stage company valuation. The only way in which real estate agents are able to come up with valuations for a house is through tacit knowledge regarding the neighborhood and the special features of the particular house. They use no meaningful analytical tools, yet they can often give a highly accurate view of the price at which a house will sell.

Venture capitalists and other investors are like real estate agents—they know their market. And, if they have been in the sector on a sustained basis over the ups and downs of a cycle, they will have their own view of the appropriate valuation for the company and the top price they might be willing to pay.

Clearly, some mental process is going on that allows the venture capitalist to form an opinion of the appropriate valuation. This chapter attempts to analyze this mental process. No venture capitalist follows the exact process presented here, but he or she should recognize the essence of the thought process.

Traditional Valuation Methods—Why They Don't Work for Early-Stage Ventures

Any person familiar with a modicum of corporate finance theory will know that the theoretical value of a business is the net present value (NPV) of future cash flows from the business discounted at the cost of capital applicable to the company—see the section below on discounted cash flow for an explanation of the mechanics of calculating NPV. This theory holds for early-stage businesses—their value equals the NPV of the future cash flows discounted at the cost of capital applicable to the company. But this is not how it is done.

This chapter does not cover in detail the ins and outs of different corporate finance techniques used to value businesses. This topic is covered well in many textbooks. Rather, it highlights the impracticalities in these techniques when they are applied to early-stage companies (particularly those in the technology sector).

This chapter then goes on to sketch out the thought processes that venture capitalists and other investors go through (implicitly or explicitly) when they have to value an early-stage business. Knowledge of these processes will help entrepreneurs to understand how venture capitalists operate and may help them to achieve better valuations for their business. It will be apparent why venture capitalists reject long-term cash flow projections out of hand as a basis for negotiating valuations. Indeed, venture capitalists will view entrepreneurs who put forward a discounted cash flow–based valuation as naive and lacking commercial instincts—this is not the impression entrepreneurs wish to make with investors.

First, a quick review of the traditional techniques for valuing businesses.

Discounted Cash Flow (DCF) Method

The DCF method involves the following simplified steps:

1. Project the future revenues and costs of the company year by year.
2. Convert these revenues and costs into a year-by-year net operating cash flow schedule that takes into account the timing of receipt of revenues and payment of costs.
3. Assume the net operating cash flows are paid out in dividends (it is more accurate to use actual projected dividends).
4. Project the timing of capital expenditures.
5. Use items two and three above to create a projected year-by-year cash flow schedule for the company.
6. Estimate the cost of capital applicable to the business.
7. Discount the year-by-year cash flows using the cost of capital applicable to the business.

This sort of analysis is fairly straightforward for established companies. Companies that have been up and running for some time have a history of revenues and costs. Also, the size of the market they are pursuing can generally be estimated, and assumptions about current and future market share can be made. Capital expenditures can be somewhat predictable. Also, people valuing the company can look to similar companies for an estimate of the cost of capital.

The basic challenge in valuing these companies tends to involve rigorous analytical modeling and the development of plausible scenarios. Will sales increase by 5% per annum or by 10%? Will the company's market share cap out at 10% or 15% of the market? Will the gross margin improve from 35% to 38% as volumes increase? By running these different scenarios, an analyst can develop a valuation range that might make sense for the company.

With the range established by the sensitivity analysis, the buyer and seller can have a meaningful discussion about the valuation to place on the business. The seller might have a bullish view that sales will grow by 15%, and the buyer might offer the view that he or she expects sales to grow by 10%. At least then the buyer and seller can have a deeper discussion about growth expectations to try to bridge their differences.

This sort of analysis is not possible with early-stage companies. Or, to be more accurate, it is possible, but it tends to yield nonsense. There are far too many moving variables that have a huge possible range associated with them or that are even binary. The market size might end up being tiny, or if events evolve as the company hopes, it might end up being huge. Even if the market is huge, will the company be a winner in the market? Technology markets tend to exhibit a winner-take-all feature. If the company is very successful, it can end up as a mini monopoly either because of intellectual property protection (no one else can make the same product) or because of the inherent dynamic toward standardization of technology. In a networked world, it makes sense for equipment and protocols to be standardized. If a company can position itself as a standards-setter, the benefits can be enormous.

Because of this possible variation in outcomes, DCF as a valuation technique does not make practical sense. Investors tend to find that DCF tends to grossly overestimate the value of the company. DCF works well only when the range of possible outcomes is bounded. Also, DCF implicitly assumes that the company will be successful. Inherent in any early-stage project is the high possibility of outright failure.

Where an entrepreneur has developed a view of the value of his or her business using DCF, it is pointless for the investor to engage in a discussion about the key drivers of that DCF analysis. Even by cutting down the optimistic assumptions fairly aggressively and by ratcheting up the cost of capital, it would still not get the valuation of the company down to the appropriate level that reflects the degree of risk and possibility of abandonment inherent in early-stage projects.

The bottom line is that early-stage technology companies tend to be binary—they succeed or they don't. If they succeed, they are very valuable; if they don't, they tend to have little or no value. The valuation technique needs to take this into account.

Price/Earnings (P/E) Ratios

P/E ratios are a simple valuation metric used to compare different companies and to develop a comparative valuation. However, early-stage companies normally lose money, thereby making P/E ratios impossible to calculate. It is, of course, possible to project earnings forward over time and use a future earnings figure as the denominator. But this suffers from the same forecasting challenges faced by DCF. In addition, modestly sized technology companies are losing money in most cases at the time they are sold. In fact, somewhat counterintuitively, losing money is often a way of maximizing the value of the company at the point of sale; this can be the case when the company is making a valid, heavy investment in distribution.

Price-to-Sales Ratios

Since early-stage companies are normally losing money, occasionally valuations are made using comparative price-to-sales ratios. However, this completely fails to take into account the gross margin on sales for the different companies, the different growth rate in sales, the relative size of the markets, and any capital investment that might be required to support the sales.

Where the company has been up and running for a few years with an established revenue line, price-to-sales ratios are sometimes used.

Are Valuations of Technology Companies Crazy?

Outsiders to the early-stage technology sector often view the valuations ascribed to the companies as excessive. Compared to companies in other well-known sectors such as consumer products, utilities, and chemicals, the valuations appear very high relative to the underlying performance. Furthermore, the high level of valuations seems to be inconsistent with the high losses often incurred by younger technology companies. What is going on?

The short answer is that early-stage technology companies are different—or at least they can be different. Forgetting about corporate finance theory for a minute, there are three simple factors that suggest that these types of companies have the potential to provide very high returns on investment:

1. *Fast growth.* Given the level of innovation typically inherent in new technology, companies with intellectual property (or some other type of market power) often have the potential to grow very fast globally. By definition, the product or service will be new to the market and will be meeting customer needs that have been unfulfilled or poorly addressed historically. Furthermore, most traditional businesses are constrained by geographical factors (e.g., the weight of the product, differing preferences from country to country, and jurisdiction-specific regulation). Technology companies do not often face these constraints, particularly if they can avoid a direct selling distribution model and instead use third-party channels or the Internet.

2. *High gross margins.* Businesses in many commoditized sectors of the economy work against comparatively low gross margins. By contrast, technology companies earn margins of 70% plus and often up to 100%. This provides huge advantages—low or small inventories need to be financed, and mistakes in production have a limited impact on costs.

3. *Low capital intensity—the ability to grow using a low capital base.* The true promise of a technology company (only occasionally realized!) is the ability to grow the size of the company without commensurate growth in the capital base. Thus, the return on investment for the investors can be extremely high. This is unlike companies that have to finance capital equipment or inventories and working capital where every increase of a dollar in sales requires an increase in the invested capital. A steel mill or a car company might need to invest $1 to $2 in capital for every

$1 in sales that it achieves. As investors are looking for home runs rather than modest multiples on their investment, this promise of low capital intensity is very attractive.

The question then arises concerning how corporate finance theory factors in the effects of these positive drivers.

Corporate Finance Theory—Technology Company Valuation

Investors in an early-stage business want to earn a good multiple on their investment. As covered in Chapter 5 on venture capital companies, early-stage investors probably shouldn't make an investment unless they have the possibility of making a 10 to 20 times return on their investment. They want (and need) huge productivity on their capital, given the attrition rate of investments.

Corporate finance theory encapsulates the productivity of capital in the market-to-book ratio.

Market means the market value of the company (or the value of a share of stock in the business). *Book* means the invested capital on the balance sheet of the business (or the invested capital per share of stock). Thus, the market-to-book ratio shows how effectively the capital invested in a business has been used. If a ratio is, say, 3:1, then every dollar originally invested in the business now has (or is worth) a value of $3.

This is the true measure of the productivity of capital in any business. The higher the market-to-book ratio, the better the value of an investment in that business. This is the multiple with which the investor is concerned.

Under corporate finance theory, the market-to-book ratio of a company is calculated using the following formula:

Market-to-book ratio = (Return on capital [ROC] – the growth rate
in earnings)/(Cost of capital [COC]
– the growth rate in earnings)

Market-to-book ratio = (ROC – g)/(COC – g), each expressed
in percentages

This formula allows the early-stage investor to judge whether the desired multiple on the investment is possible or likely to be achieved.

The simple definition of ROC is the amount of profit the business earns each year divided by the capital invested in the business. Normally, the formula needs to be adjusted to take into account the cost of debt, but it is not required in early-stage companies because of the absence of debt. The growth rate is the expected growth rate in the profits[1] of the business in perpetuity. Clearly, no business can grow at a high rate in perpetuity; therefore, the assumed growth rate needs to represent a blend of a higher rate of growth over the short or medium term and a lower rate of growth over the long term. The COC represents the expected cost of the money to be committed to the business, adjusted for the risk level associated with the business. For a business with no risk, its COC would be the Treasury bond rate. Clearly, it is a lot more difficult to estimate the COC for an early-stage business.

Exhibit 7.1 shows how the market-to-book ratio for a particular business (with an assumed COC of 10%) varies depending on the ROC and the growth rate.

Exhibit 7.1 Market-to-Book Ratios for a Business with COC of 10%

Return on Capital	Growth Rate				
	5%	6%	7%	8%	9%
10%	1.0	1.0	1.0	1.0	1.0
12%	1.4	1.5	1.7	2.0	3.0
14%	1.8	2.0	2.3	3.0	5.0
16%	2.2	2.5	3.0	4.0	7.0
18%	2.6	3.0	3.7	5.0	9.0
20%	3.0	3.5	4.3	6.0	11.0
25%	4.0	4.8	6.0	8.5	16.0
30%	5.0	6.0	7.7	11.0	21.0

---

1 For technology companies, profits are normally quite close to operating cash flow. Capital expenditure is normally very limited, and inventories are not a major concern when gross margins are high.

There are a few points worth noting. When the cost of capital associated with an investment in a business is 10% and the ROC is 10%, then logically the value of that business can only be worth the same as invested capital, irrespective of the growth rate. Investors will get back from the business only their minimum return. If the money costs 10% and the investors receive 10% in return, they have not created any value for themselves. At its simplest, if investors borrow $100 at a 10% interest rate and receive $110 back at the end of the year, they are no better or worse off.

When the ROC increases progressively above the COC, the increase in the market-to-book ratio is very steep. For example, if the ROC increases from 10% to just 12% (when the growth rate is 5%), the value of $1 invested in the business rises from $1 to $1.40. Similarly, an increase in the growth rate, when the ROC is above the COC, leverages up the market-to-book ratio quite dramatically.

Investors want to earn a 5-10-20 times multiple on their investment. Therefore, they need to be targeting businesses with the potential to be in the bottom right part of this matrix—businesses with a high *return on capital* (relative to the cost of capital) and a high *growth rate*.

The return on capital is derived from two factors:

$$ROC = Profits/Capital\ invested$$

If both sides of this formula are divided by sales, then

$$ROC = (Profit/Sales)/(Capital\ invested/Sales)$$

Profit/sales equals the net margin (expressed as a percentage). It is derived from the gross margin of the business and the fixed overhead of the business. Thus, the higher the gross margin, the higher the ROC—all other factors being equal.

Capital invested/sales equals the capital intensity of the business. The *capital intensity* of the business identifies the incremental amount of capital required as sales increase. For example, to increase sales by $1 in a steel mill might require $1 or more in capital, because investment will be required in fixed assets, accounts receivable, and inventory. Most technology businesses have a very low capital intensity.

In summary, if disaggregated, the market-to-book ratio of a business depends on three primary factors:

1. Growth rate (the higher the better)
2. Gross margin (the higher the better)
3. Capital intensity (the lower the better)

These three factors make technology-based businesses much more attractive than most other types of businesses. As these three factors become more and more attractive, the effect on the market-to-book ratio is extremely potent. This is why investors like technology businesses.

After reading this section, you might have the impression that this is how venture capitalists analyze the multiple they are aiming for with a specific investment. It is not. This section merely shows that there are strong corporate finance theory foundations for the high attractiveness of early-stage technology businesses.

Triangulation Process of Venture Capitalists

There is no simple analytical technique for valuing early-stage companies. In theory, one could estimate the three key factors mentioned above. In practice, it is hard to develop a firm view on them.

Funnily enough, different venture capitalists will typically come up with broadly similar valuations for a company. Consequently, behind a seemingly arbitrary valuation exercise lies a mental process that is rarely articulated. This section attempts to put some science and methodology to it.

In essence, venture capitalists triangulate on a proposed valuation in the following way:

1. They identify the maximum valuation they should consider based on their view of future valuations of the company.
2. They identify the floor valuation based on the expected competition from other investors.
3. They keep to the bottom end of this range, if possible, depending on the expectations and readiness of the entrepreneur.

The most important of these is the venture capitalists' *view of future valuations*.

View of Future Valuations to Identify Maximum Valuation

Consider the typical valuation challenge.

Three to four individuals leave a large software company with plans to develop a new software product—for example, a new way of transferring messages from cell phones to fixed line phones. They need $2M to fund the development of the product for about 18 months. They and the investor need to agree on the percentage of ownership of the business to be allocated in return for the investment.

The primary way that professional investors value such an early-stage company is by taking a view of the likely future valuations of the company at different points in its development and discounting those future valuations to develop a view of the appropriate valuation of the company today. The discount factor is the multiple they hope to achieve—normally 10 to 20 times for a risky start-up.

To be more specific, investors tend to take a *bifocal* view of future valuations of the company. They look at the *plausible potential value* of the company at the expected time of exit/sale, and they look at the *likely next round value* of the company. This gives them a long-term and short-term view of the later valuation.

They then take a view of the valuation today that should give them a good *step-up* or *multiple* on their investment with respect to both of those future valuations. They will be aiming for a step-up in both the next round and at time of exit. This bifocal view is shown in Exhibit 7.2.

Plausible Potential Value at Exit

Investors tend to be reasonably good at estimating the plausible potential value of the company in the event that it achieves its goals. For example, investors can make a quick judgment as to whether, if the company is successful, it could be a $500M company or a $200M company or a $50M company. Among experienced investors, there is a surprising level of consistency in the plausible potential value that each would put on a company.

Exhibit 7.2 Bifocal View on Later Valuations

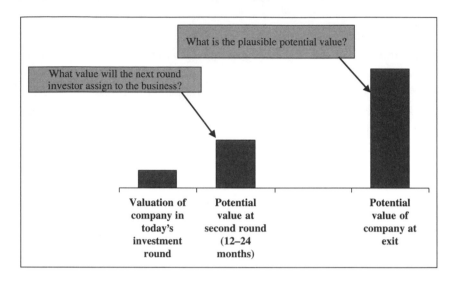

One reason for this is that there are lots of analogous companies, publicly quoted on the stock exchanges around the world, or private companies within the portfolios of investors. While, of course, the technology and the customer benefits of each company will be different, a seasoned view of the likely size of the future market, the strength of differentiation of the product versus the alternatives open to prospective customers and the skills and experience of the management team will allow someone familiar with early-stage investing to develop a view concerning the scale of the plausible opportunity.

For example, if the company is selling a new type of foreign exchange trading system, there will be other companies doing something broadly similar. Even if there isn't, one can make a broad-brush estimate of the likely market size (by looking at the number of potential customers and the achievable price per customer) and the possible market share. Most important, the investor will be able to take a view of this opportunity compared to the history of opportunities that he or she has previously seen—similar to the real estate analogy earlier.

Investors should invest in a company only if it has the potential to live and develop independently of other companies in the long run.

If a company can get to market and succeed only by being part of a larger company, then it might not be possible to extract full value at exit. The acid test for this condition is that it is plausible that the company could undertake an initial public offering (IPO). In being independent in the long run, the only way for an investor to realize good value on his or her investment is in selling stock in a public company. Most investments in a venture capitalist's portfolio will end up achieving an exit by being sold to a larger company rather than by undertaking an IPO. But the investment should not have been undertaken to begin with unless, at that point, the investor believed an IPO might be possible.

Since all investments should have the potential to undertake an IPO, this facilitates the investor in developing a view of the plausible potential value of the company on a stand-alone basis by examining the following types of factors:

- Valuations of comparable publicly quoted companies and/or comparable mergers and acquisitions (M&A) transactions
- The size of the market
- Long-run growth rates in the sector
- Typical gross margins earned by similar companies
- Capital intensity of similar companies

But, since most successful investments achieve an exit by being sold to another, larger, company, the following types of factors should also be examined:

- The importance of the product (or other assets of the company) to other companies
- The level of differentiation between the company's product or service and that of the competition
- The likely number of potential acquirers—to ensure there will be plenty of "demand tension" at the time of sale
- The difficulty of the problem solved by the technology of the company

The section at the end of this chapter reviews why large companies buy small companies and how they develop a view on their value to them.

With all the above factors considered together, the investor should be able to develop an informed view of the plausible potential value of the company. For the early-stage investor, precision in estimating the plausible potential value is not necessary. You will see from the section on multiples below that early-stage investors will be using expected multiples of 10 to 20. Whether the forecasted plausible potential value of a company is $150M or $175M matters little when this value is to be divided by 20. The difference in valuation is $7.5M versus $8.75M.

For later-stage investors, precision in estimating the plausible potential value is much more important. The multiple they are expecting on their investment is far lower; thus the need for accuracy is higher.

For an early-stage investor, the implications of the plausible potential value being at the following levels might be as follows:

- Less than $50M: too small; not worth making an investment.
- $50M to $100M: small; worth making an investment only if the capital needs of the company over its life will be less than $5M to $8M. Don't forget that the investors will not own 100% of the company.
- $100M to $250M: good size.
- Greater than $250M: large.

Late-stage investors will conduct a lot more analysis to develop a precise view of the market size and the plausible potential value at exit than will early-stage investors. They are looking for a smaller multiple and thus have less margin for error. However, they have the advantage of much more accurate information than does the early-stage investor. They will know the run rate of sales and have a clearer estimate of the market size. They will know from the history of the company how well the management team is likely to execute the business plan.

Likely Value at the Next Round

While the plausible potential value can be quite subjective, the likely value at the next round is far more tangible.

While it might be extremely difficult to value the plausible potential value of the earlier example of the software company that devised a new way of transferring messages from cell phones to fixed line phones, it would be a lot easier to determine the value of the company if the product were finished and the company had made one or two reference sales. Any investor in a market will have a very good feel for valuations of companies that have achieved tangible commercial milestones. As the risks are taken away and the fog clears, the size of the opportunity becomes more apparent.

Given the commercial, technical, and other risks, the investor in today's round should invest only if he or she will get a 100% or more step-up on the valuation (price per share) that will likely be achieved in the next round. This step-up compensates for the risks, but it also compensates for the fact that the rights associated with the shares issued in the new round will be senior to those issued in today's round. (More on this in the chapters on term sheets.)

Probably the most fruitful line of discussion for an entrepreneur trying to boost the value of his or her company in an investment round is to make a strong case that if the company executes most or all of its business plan for the next 12–18 months, the value of the company will be significantly higher than it is today. It should be possible to find examples of companies in other sectors that are just a bit ahead of the company in terms of its development.

Discounting Back Subsequent Valuations Using Multiples

Once the investor has a view on the plausible potential exit value and the likely next round value, he or she needs to convert that to a valuation to put on the company today.

In Chapter 5 on venture capital companies, you will see that the venture capital company needs to earn a 6 to 7 times multiple on the good investments in order to provide good returns to the limited partners who have invested in the fund. Since most companies do not tend to reach their potential and because venture capital investors are hoping for home runs on each of their investments, they will look for a premium on the 6 to 7 times multiple. In discussions with early-stage venture capitalists, you will frequently hear them say that they want to have "a chance of making a 10 to 20 times multiple on an investment." They know that this will rarely happen but, if the investment has a possibility of making a 10 to 20 times multiple, it has a better chance of making a 6 to 7 times multiple. Also, the venture capitalist always wants to keep alive the dream of hitting a home run on an investment.

Later-stage investors deal with lower levels of risk. The vast majority of the companies in which they invest will yield some value—they will have few outright losses. Thus, in order to give a good return on the fund of two and a half to three times the capital to the limited partners, they only need to earn 3 to 5 times the capital on individual good investments.

Typical multiples used by investors at different stages are shown in Exhibit 7.3. Clearly, there are no hard and fast rules. But each investor will make an informed opinion of each investment and, implicitly or explicitly, use a multiple to work back to the maximum valuation to pay for the company today.

Exhibit 7.3 Working Back from Ultimate Potential Value

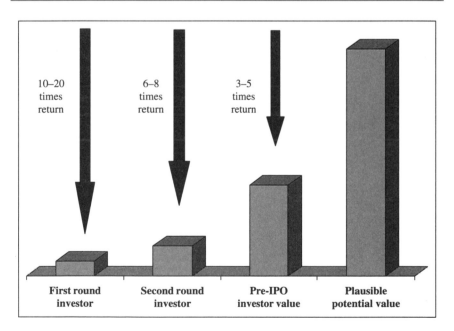

The pre-IPO investor might be content with a possible 3 to 5 times multiple on his or her investment, while the earlier investors will be targeting a much higher multiple.

Consider the following two mini cases—the first sets a maximum valuation for an early-stage company, and the second sets a maximum valuation for a late-stage company.

MINI CASE: START-UP MEDICAL COMPANY

An investor is considering an investment in a start-up medical device company. The potential annual market for the device is $500M based on an analysis of the number of people having the medical condition requiring the device, the likely penetration of the device into that market group, and the expected selling price of the device achieved by the developer.

The investor considers it plausible that the company might end up capturing 20% of the market ($100M in sales). At $100M in sales the company might make $30M in profit. Companies with comparables devices (e.g., similar gross margin) tend to sell for 3 to 4 times revenue or 15 to 20 times the annual profit. Based on this simple analysis, the investor might conclude that the plausible potential value of this company at exit might be $300M to $500M.

Since early-stage investors want a 10 to 20 times multiple on their investment, they might be willing to pay a maximum valuation of between $15M and $20M.

The investor will also look ahead to the milestones in the next round and gain assurance that the valuation at that point, assuming the milestones are achieved, will be at least 100% higher than the valuation the investor is to pay.

MINI CASE: SETTING A MAXIMUM VALUATION ON A LATE-STAGE COMPANY

Instead of being a start-up, the company is well developed. It has sales of $30M and is at breakeven. It needs investment to take it to an exit.

Consider the same facts on exit as those in the previous mini case—a plausible potential exit value of $300M to $500M. Here, the investor has a much lower level of risk. The risks of product development and early customer references are gone. The market needs to continue to open up, and the management team needs to continue to execute very well. But, these are factors for which the investor should be able to conduct insightful due diligence.

In such a case, the investor might be aiming for a 3 to 4 times multiple of its investment. This would lead to a maximum valuation today of $75M to $125M.

Any person with a good finance theory background will point to holes in this three-stage analysis. The *plausible potential exit value* is subjective and cannot be supported by rigorous analysis. The *next round value* is highly judgmental, but the active investor should have his or her finger on the pulse of the venture capital market. There is a high level of consistency in the valuations in midstage companies put forward by professional investors. They have a good feel for what the market will bear. Finally, the *multiple* can be very crude. Clearly, whenever you divide any plausible potential exit value by 10 or 20, you will end up with a relatively modest valuation. But this reflects reality. Early-stage investors take enormous risks, and most companies fail outright or fail to achieve anything like their early promise.

If you look closely, you will see that the method contains broad consistencies with the DCF approach. Since no dividends are typically paid, the plausible potential exit value is analogous to a terminal value some number of years out. The multiple is similar to a compounded high discount rate. But trying to force a DCF mindset onto this venture capital valuation approach would be futile. Investors think of multiples rather than rates of return[2] when they are looking at individual investments.

In reality, a multiple can be converted quickly to an internal rate of return. Assuming an average company is in a portfolio for six years, multiples equal the rates of return shown in Exhibit 7.4.

---

2 Investors think about internal rates of return generally only at a portfolio level.

Exhibit 7.4 Converting IRR into an Equivalent Multiple

Internal Rate of Return	Equivalent Multiple Over Six Years
10%	1.8
20%	3.0
30%	4.8
40%	7.5
50%	11.4

As discussed earlier, the early investor is looking for a multiple of 6 to 7 and preferably 10 to 20. This equates to 40 to 50% or higher. To investors in traditional established companies, these rates of return sound extraordinarily high. They would question why they should be so high.

Consideration of Perceived Competition from Other Investors to Determine Floor Valuation

While the view on subsequent valuations will set the maximum price that the investor might be willing to pay, the perceived level of competition from other investors will determine the minimum (or floor) valuation that the company will receive.

Simply put, if there is a lot of perceived competition for the deal, the company should be able to extract a valuation from the investor close to the maximum valuation. The goal of the entrepreneur in an investment round with a lot of perceived competition is to ensure investors gain a clear (high) view of the plausible potential exit value for the company.

The CEO and CFO must always convey a sense of competition and demand tension to the prospective investors. If the company is bringing together a syndicate, management must strive to keep investors separate and avoid having them talk to one another until as late in the process as possible. Better still, the identity of each competing investor should be kept confidential. Do not let them collude to keep the valuation down. Where there is no competition in reality, the CEO and CFO must create the impression of competition. If the investor gets the feeling that he or she is the only investor pursuing the deal, then there is a danger that the deal will slow and it will be hard to achieve close to the maximum valuation.

Assessment of Expectations and Readiness of Entrepreneur to Pinpoint Valuation to Offer

When the team does not have a prior entreprencurial record or when there are apparent gaps in the team, the valuation of the company is likely to be substantially less than it would be if the team had a first-class record of entrepreneurial achievement. While this will already have been factored into the plausible potential value outlined in prior sections, it also tends to come in as a factor in its own right.

Early-stage investors in an incomplete or inexperienced team will tend to position themselves as founders and, thus, will be expecting cheap founders' stock to form part of their position in the company. This reflects the fact that the investors will commit a large amount of time and effort to closing the gaps in the team. In practice, rather than giving the investors founders' (ordinary) stock, they will receive a relatively large position at a low price per share.

How the Company Can Maximize Its Valuation

The first thing the CEO and CFO must do is recognize that venture capital investors do not use the traditional valuation techniques. Investors will want to see that the company has good financial projections for the next few years, with plenty of detail for years 1 and 2 in particular. But these projections will be used for budgeting—they won't be used for company valuation.

If the CEO and CFO understand the venture capital valuation approach, they will have the chance to influence the valuation placed on the company. Their goal in negotiations is as follows:

1. Make a strong case for a high ultimate potential exit value for the company.

2. Maximize the plausible potential exit value by giving the investor few reasons for believing that the company is not set up to achieve the ultimate potential exit value. If there are gaps in the team, these can be bridged not necessarily by hiring people up front, but by identifying people who will come onboard, subject to the funding closing. Sometimes, great people will not come onboard until there is sufficient capital committed to the company.

3. Understand the valuations of slightly later-stage companies and identify the commercial and technical gaps between the company and them. The company's business plan can be tightly focused on closing these gaps.

4. Make sure the investor perceives competition in the deal.

Why Big Companies Buy Small Companies

Big companies buy small companies because small companies are better at innovation than big companies are. Organizational lethargy, slow decision making, structured work environments, hamstrung pay and rewards packages, and many other factors make it hard for large companies to be as nimble as small companies. It is hard to inject a venture capital mindset into large companies. They do not want to be seen as trying something and then abandoning new ventures midstream if they are not working out as expected. The careers of up-and-coming managers tend not to have any outright failures in their history. Capital in large companies is treated less preciously than it is in small companies and venture capital firms—they have a lot more of it. Large companies, to the extent that they innovate at all, are good at incremental improvements to products and services; breakthroughs of the type likely to create enormous value are rare.

The world of innovation has become one in which small companies develop new products and services, gather early customers (at a high cost), and then sell the business to large companies who use their manufacturing and distribution muscle to turn them into large profitable businesses.

Most forms of technology businesses fit this pattern—software, medical devices, biopharmaceuticals, semiconductors, and so on. But, many traditional businesses fit this model as well. Food and drinks companies often buy smaller, regional food and drink product companies and then roll their offerings out globally.

Value of Small Companies Compared to Large Companies

Other than folly or hubris (common causes of acquisitions!), the large company is seeking to capture one of the three following sources of value by buying a small company: hard stand-alone economic benefits, distribution multiplication and economics, and strategic value. (See Exhibit 7.5.) These elements are additive. If sellers want to maximize the value captured, they must get the acquirer to recognize and value these three elements. The acquirer will be most willing to pay for the hard economics first, will then consider adding a premium for distribution multiplication and economics, and finally may consider adding a premium for strategic value. The acquirer will volunteer neither of the two premiums. These are the two elements for which the seller must negotiate hard with good evidential support.

Exhibit 7.5 Elements of Acquisition Value

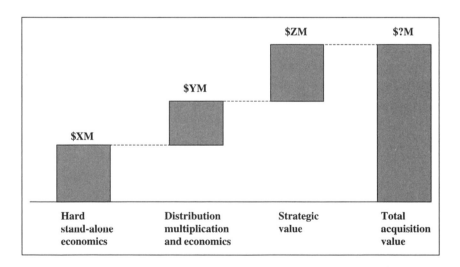

Hard Stand-Alone Economic Benefits

The large company should be willing to pay a fair price for the good revenues and good profits of the smaller companies. If the large company is a public company, its valuation might be high relative to the comparative price to be paid for the revenues and profits of the small company, thus making acquisition more attractive. The large company can capture the earnings of the small company and gross them up in market value at a higher price/earnings ratio than the multiple of earnings paid for the small company. When markets are depressed and the mergers and acquisition (M&A) cycle is at a low ebb, companies will typically be bought for good valuations only when the hard economics make the deal attractive.

The hard economic value is the easiest of the three categories to agree with the acquirer. There should be some comparables available based on revenue multiples, earnings multiples, valuations of similar stage private or public companies, and so on. If there are profits, it should be possible to undertake a discounted cash flow analysis.

But the sellers should not settle for a valuation based solely on hard economic benefits unless they are compelled to sell.

Distribution Multiplication and Distribution Economics

Small technology companies generally lose money. But you need to look at the reasons behind their losses. First, the revenues are much lower than their potential—the market for the new innovation might be at the bottom point of an S curve and about to head into a period of accelerated growth. Second, the company is probably spending much more on product development (as a percentage of revenues) than a more developed company would. Third, and more importantly, the cost of distribution for an early-stage company can be exorbitant, as a percentage of revenues or on a per sale basis.

Compare the two income statements in Exhibit 7.6—one for a small company and one for a large company.

Exhibit 7.6 Income Statements for a Small and a Large Company

	Small Company		Large Company	
	$M	%	$M	%
Revenues	10	100	200	100
Product development	(4)	(40)	(40)	(20)
Central administration	(2)	(20)	(40)	(20)
Sales and distribution	(6)	(60)	(60)	(30)
Net profit (loss)	(2)	(20)	80	40

The small company is weighted down by the cost of distribution. This is the biggest challenge for most small companies. They can often develop a world-class product, but they struggle in bringing it to market. Where markets are fragmented (e.g., selling software to the Fortune 1000), the cost structure to distribute to such a market is probably expensive if the product is complicated and cannot be sold over the Web. A large company with established channels to market has an enormous advantage. It has relationships with customers. It has a sales force and is already incurring the cost of distribution on a fragmented basis and is (probably) making money doing this.

Therefore, if a large software company takes over a small software company, the larger company has two huge advantages to bring to bear. It can multiply the distribution footprint for the product to access far more customers, and it can push the product through its channel on a zero or low incremental cost basis.

There are many good examples of large technology companies taking over small companies and multiplying their sales levels very quickly by opening up their distribution channels. Many people tend to forget that the distribution cost is marginal to the acquirer.

If, for example, the large company could multiply the sales level of the small company by three, by pushing the product through its own channels, a fairly high acquisition price can quickly be justified based on the economics set out in Exhibit 7.7.

The CEO of the company being sold needs to be armed with this analysis and should aim to extract some of these gains from the acquirer.

Exhibit 7.7 Incremental Value of Small Company to Acquirer

	Small Company	
	$M	%
Revenue	30	100
Product development	(4)	(13)
Central administration	0	0
Sales and distribution	0	0
Net profit (loss)	26	87

Strategic Value

After the distribution economics are added to the hard stand-alone economic benefits, the vendor needs to try to capture some of the strategic value the acquirer is aiming to gain.

Strategic value is the most nebulous of the three sources of value. It is also the one that can really juice the valuation to a high level. The ideal scenario facing a small company, which is trying to capture some of the acquirer's strategic value, is as follows:

- The market segment for the small company's product has opened up and a clear growth trajectory is well signaled.
- The product contains intellectual property that would be hard to work around or would take a long time to replicate. The acquirer does not have the option to build her or his own version of the product.
- The product has the potential to displace sales of the acquirer or has the potential to accelerate sales of the acquirer's product.
- If the product were to be acquired by a competitor of the potential acquirer, the acquirer would be seriously disadvantaged.

These are the arguments that the vendor and his or her advisors need to make. The evidence also needs to be compelling. The only real way for the vendor to capture some of this value is to create some competitive tension between potential acquirers.

PART IV

NEGOTIATING THE DEAL: TERM SHEETS

CHAPTER 8

AGREEING ON A TERM SHEET WITH A VENTURE CAPITALIST

Investors invest in companies in the hope that the companies will become successful and valuable. After a decision in principle by investors to invest in a company, they normally put forward a term sheet that outlines the way in which the investors want the investment to be made. The most important term in a term sheet is the percentage ownership of the company granted to the investors in return for their investment.

Percentage Ownership of the Company Granted to the Investor

The level of ownership assigned to an investor is a function of the amount of the investment and the valuation (postmoney) of the company agreed to by the investor and the entrepreneur. If the investor puts up an investment of $1M and the postmoney valuation is $4M (premoney is $3M), the investor will own 25% of the company.

The explanatory note reviews pre- and postmoney valuations.

PRE- AND POSTMONEY VALUATIONS

The *premoney valuation* ascribed to a company is the valuation of the company excluding the capital about to be invested by the investor. The *postmoney valuation* is the valuation of the company including the capital to be invested. The premoney valuation of the company is the postmoney valuation of the company minus the capital to be invested.

For example, if investor A wishes to invest $2M and requests 20% of the company in return, the implied postmoney valuation is $10M, and the premoney valuation is $8M. In essence, the value being ascribed to the company prior to the investment is $8M, and this value is boosted by $2M with the cash injection. If there are 80,000 shares in issue prior to the new investment, the value of each share is $100, and the new investor would receive 20,000 shares for a $2M investment.

A year later, if investor B offers to invest $4M for 20% of the company, the postmoney valuation is $20M (premoney of $16M). Since there are 100,000 shares in issue prior to investor B's investment, the new price per share is $160. Investor A has achieved a step-up in the value of her shares of 60% (from $100 to $160) in the space of a year. Note that the value creation in the intervening year is $6M—the difference between the postmoney valuation on the first round and the premoney valuation on the second round. The earlier investment of $2M has been absorbed into the company and is reflected in the premoney valuation of the second round.

Alternatively, if investor B offers to invest $1M at a $6M postmoney valuation (premoney of $5M), then the price per share is $50, and the book value of investor A's investment has been impaired by 50%.

The investor normally proposes the creation of a pool of stock options for retaining and motivating key management (or an expansion of an existing stock option pool, if the preexisting pool is viewed as too small). One important issue, prior to sorting out the relative shareholdings of each of the parties, is whether the option pool is to be created (or expanded) before or after the investment by the investor. If the new investor is to receive 20% of the company, will this shareholding be diluted subsequently when the stock option pool is created? Will the 20% be diluted to 18% if a 10% option pool is created, or will the other pre-existing stockholders suffer all the dilution when the pool is put in place?

TIP TO ENTREPRENEUR

Propose that the stock option pool be put in place after the investment—this will reduce the dilution experienced by the preexisting shareholders.

If this proposal is not accepted, suggest that only part of the pool be put in place before the investment; the remainder can be put in place if the first part of the pool does not prove large enough. One way to make the case for this is to establish the list of individuals to be recruited over the next 18 months or so—the investment horizon of the incoming investor—and the number of options to be granted to each. You should then be able to argue that this is an appropriate number of options to put in place now. If the pool needs to be expanded later, all stockholders, including the new investor, can bear a share of the required dilution.

All term sheets should include a capitalization table that summarizes the ownership position of all parties. A capitalization table flushes out any inconsistencies and ambiguities regarding shareholdings.

Exhibit 8.1 is a simplified capitalization table for a company issuing a Series B round of shares. Investor B's term sheet proposed a 25% shareholding and a 12% option pool; the option pool is to be created prior to investor B investing. Note that to end up with a 12% option pool after the dilution of 25% associated with the new investment, the option pool will need to begin at 16% of the preinvestment shareholding structure.

One way to work out the capital structure simply, given the conditions laid down by the Series B investor, is to dilute the preexisting shareholders by 37% and then allocate 25% to investor B and 12% into the pool.

Exhibit 8.1 Capitalization Table for Company X

	Initial Stock Position	Initial Ownership	Stock Option Pool Created	Ownership Preinvestment	Series B Stock Issued	Fully Diluted Ownership Postinvestment	Issued Stock Position
Founders/executives							
J. Smith	10,000	16.7%	10,000	14.0%	10,000	10.5%	11.9%
M. Jones	15,000	25.0%	15,000	21.0%	15,000	15.8%	17.9%
A. Davis	15,000	25.0%	15,000	21.0%	15,000	15.8%	17.9%
Investor A	20,000	33.3%	20,000	28.0%	20,000	21.0%	23.9%
Investor B	0	0.0%	0	0.0%	23,810	25.0%	28.4%
Option pool	0	0.0%	11,429	16.0%	11,429	12.0%	0.0%
Total stock	60,000	100.0%	71,429	100.0%	95,238	100.0%	100.0%

Round B premoney valuation of $7.5M; postmoney valuation of $10M

Amount Invested in Series B Round		Price per Share
Investor A	$0.5M	$25
Investor B	$2.5M	$105

Options, until they are exercised by the person to whom they have been granted, are considered unissued. This leads to two definitions of share capital—*issued*, which excludes unexercised options, and *fully diluted*, which treats all options as if they are issued and exercised. If the option pool is created (or expanded) after the investor invests, the dilutive effects of the pool are spread over the entire shareholder base, rather than just over the shareholders in situ prior to the funding round.

On the sale of the company, only the issued stock (including exercised options) is sold to the acquirer. Options that remain unexercised at the time of sale of the company are not included in the calculation of the proceeds each unit of stock will receive. For example, if a shareholder owned 20% of the issued stock, equaling 18% of the fully diluted stock (10% of the share capital structure remaining in unexercised options), he or she would receive 20% of the proceeds. However, the acquirer might take a deduction from the headline acquisition price for unissued options on the grounds that these options will be required to reward the employees and management of the acquired company after purchase.

What Each Side Tries to Achieve in a Term Sheet

The term sheet is a skeleton of the impending contract between the company, the founders, key management, and the investors. It establishes the terms under which the investor proposes to invest. The flesh comes later in the detailed legal documents. If the term sheet is clear and precise, there should be few surprises later when the first draft of the investment agreement emerges from the lawyers.

Investors aim to achieve the following objectives in a term sheet:

1. Maximize their upside in the event of an exit.
2. Protect their investment if the company ends up performing poorly. This is achieved through provisions that allow them to get a larger percentage of the ultimate prize than would be determined by looking solely at their ownership percentage.
3. Retain vetoes over certain corporate actions that could affect the investor's position.

4. Be able to force the company to pursue a liquidity event (e.g., a sale of the company) after the investors have been involved for a considerable period of time.

5. Ensure the founders and key managers are locked into the company (as long as they continue to be an asset to the company) and align their interests with those of the investor.

Entrepreneurs aim to get the following in the term sheet:

1. Garner sufficient capital for the business to reach the next stepping-stone, while giving away as little of the prize as possible.

2. Give up as few levers of control over the company's actions as possible.

3. Protect the personal position of the entrepreneur, in the event that the investor perceives the entrepreneur to be surplus to the company's requirements at some point.

Each side rarely achieves all its objectives, unless the balance of power in the negotiation is one-sided. If there is a severe shortage of capital in the market or if the business is doing poorly, the investor can generally drive the terms. If the business has stellar prospects or there is strong competition between investors to win the deal, the company and the entrepreneur can drive the terms.

The best term sheets dynamically allocate control between the entrepreneur and the investors. If a business is doing well, the controls and protections allocated to the investors should not be required. If the business is doing poorly, in particular if this is the result of perceived underperformance by the entrepreneur, the investors should have the power to solve the problems.

Note that the term sheet is not a binding contract for the investor to invest in the company on the terms outlined. It merely sets out the proposed high-level terms that will govern the relationship. Both parties can decide to walk away at any point prior to the finalization and signing of the detailed legal documents; one of the parties might be forced to bear due diligence and legal fees incurred to that point, if that party is the one to walk away. The only section of a term sheet that is generally binding legally is the exclusivity clause. Under the exclusivity clause, management and founders are obliged not to talk to any other prospective investor for the six to eight weeks (or more) granted under exclusivity. Failure to respect this clause could give the investor grounds for legal action.

Why It Isn't Like Investing in a Public Company

An investor in publicly quoted companies typically invests in common stock. Each unit of common stock is exactly the same and has the same rights. Sometimes more complex preferred stock structures are used by public companies, but this is a fairly rare occurrence.

Public companies are subject to many rules and regulations that are aimed at protecting the interests of each common stockholder. The company publishes a lot of information about its activities; this transparency gives comfort to the investor. Also, the stock generally has a liquid market. If an investor does not like the company's strategy or its management, he or she can sell the stock. The owners of common stock are all treated the same, and they should not need the additional protections often granted to preferred stockholders.

Private companies are very different. Once it is invested, the capital is tied up and, in the absence of good shareholder protections, the investor can be subject to the whims of management and the board. The company might decide to change radically the strategy of the business. Executive compensation might be multiplied to enrich management. The company might issue more stock with rights and privileges that damage the value of the preexisting shareholders—without the preexisting shareholders having the right to protect their investment.

Therefore professional investors in private companies buy preferred stock. The preferred stock will have rights and privileges attached that protect and enhance the investors' position. There is a dazzling array of options open to preferred stockholders concerning the rights and privileges they might seek. The array of options is limited only by the creativity of the investors and their lawyers.

In general, however, venture capitalists seek rights and privileges attached to the preferred stock that achieve three basic goals:

1. Skew the *investment returns* to favor the preferred stockholder over the ordinary stockholder. The returns are skewed aggressively if the company exit value is much lower than projected.
2. Allocate a disproportionate level of *control* to the preferred stockholders to help them to protect their investment.
3. Ensure *aligned interests* between the preferred stockholder and the founders or key managers.

These three essentials—skewed returns, disproportionate controls, and aligned interests—can be put in place by the creation of a class of preferred stock. They are much more complex to put in place if the investor owns common stock. In a public company, common stockholders can register their objections to their treatment by selling their stock and obtaining a fair market price. This is not possible in private companies.

The specific rights and privileges sought by venture capital investors to achieve these three essentials have evolved over the past few decades. Today, with some minor regional preferences, the terms sought by venture capitalists on the West and East Coasts and overseas tend to mirror each other. Innovations and good practices spread from deal to deal through lawyers, investors, and entrepreneurs.

If entrepreneurs are to be successful in their negotiations with venture capitalists, they need to be fully conversant with these terms, their implications, and the psychology behind them. That is the goal of the next three chapters.

A sample term sheet is included as Appendix B. You will see from it that most of the terms fall into the three categories outlined above.

CHAPTER 9

TERMS FOR SPLITTING THE REWARDS

When all of a company's stock is common stock, each unit of stock is assigned exactly the same monetary amount (or stock in the acquiring company) when there is a sale or merger. For example, if a company is sold for $100M in cash and there are 10M units of common stock in issue, the holders of the stock will receive $10 for each unit. In early-stage ventures, each unit of stock does not necessarily receive the same value.

The most important term in a term sheet is the percentage of ownership allocated to the investors, based on the valuation of the company. The next most important terms are those that skew the returns in favor of the investors. Some entrepreneurs are so concerned with the valuation that they pay insufficient attention to the exit preferences, the dividends, options, milestones, and so on. Investors do not make this mistake. They are always fully aware of where their capital lies in the "pancake stack" of exit preferences and the potential value of the "kickers" (terms that boost the return to the investor) and protections. When a company has raised a lot of capital over multiple rounds of investment, the position in the stack is vital. Many investments go sideways and are sold for not much more than the capital invested in the business. Entrepreneurs tend to be enthralled by the possibility of selling the company for a very high amount—at which point the terms for skewing the returns become unimportant. They should pay more attention to the distribution of returns between the preferred and common stockholders at lower value exits.

Investors try to skew the distribution of value between different groups of stockholders for two reasons—first, to ensure that they get a disproportionate amount of the value created by the business and, second, to motivate the founders to not sell the company too early.

There are five primary methods for investors to skew the returns:

1. Exit preferences, linked to the type of preferred stock
2. Staging of investment against milestones
3. Options to invest more money at a defined price per share
4. Preferred dividends
5. Antidilution

1. Exit Preferences, Linked to the Type of Preferred Stock

One big concern for all investors is an early exit that benefits the entrepreneur but damages the investor.

Consider the situation in which an investor invests $3M in January in a start-up company for 30% of the common stock. If the entrepreneur were to sell the company in March for $5M (against the wishes of the investor), the entrepreneur would receive $3.5M, and the investor would receive $1.5M. This is clearly unacceptable to the investor. The investor has made the investment in the hope of getting a 5-10-20 times return on his or her investment. Instead, the value of the investment has been cut in half in a few months, while the entrepreneur has made a sizable gain.

If the investor had an exit preference, this problem would not have occurred. With an exit preference, the investor gets his or her capital back first and then potentially shares in any remaining proceeds from the sale. The formula for the sharing of the remaining proceeds depends on the terms negotiated regarding the preferred stock. The different types of sharing formulas are covered in more detail in the section on types of preferred stock later in this chapter.

Using the example above, with an exit preference the investor would have received the $3M in capital back first and then shared in the remaining $2M of proceeds (probably receiving 30%—another $600,000). The entrepreneur would be far less keen to pursue an early exit with such a provision in place.

The exit preference fulfills two purposes:

1. *Protection for investor in case he or she paid too much for the shares.* In all negotiations, the entrepreneur makes the case that the company will be very valuable at exit and that the investor should settle for a lower percentage shareholding today. The investor always wants a higher percentage because the exit valuation is likely to be less than the entrepreneur expects. One way to bridge this gap in expectations is to include an exit preference. The effect of the exit preference is that it gives the investor a higher percentage of the proceeds in the event that an exit is at a low value and a lesser percentage in the event of a high-value exit.
2. *Motivation for the entrepreneur not to sell out early at a low valuation.* As shown above, in the absence of an exit preference, the entrepreneur might sell the company early at a low valuation that hurts the investor.

Instances When Exit Preferences Might Be Activated

The following types of corporate events normally activate an exit preference clause.

Liquidation of the Business

When a company is liquidated, whether by a decision of the board or under pressure from creditors, exit preferences may come into play. For example, if after liquidating the assets (e.g., selling inventory, capital assets and intellectual property, collecting receivables) and paying off its liabilities, the company has cash available, this cash will be paid to the preferred stockholders first as part of the exit preference. Only when the exit preference of the preferred stockholders has been satisfied will the common stockholders receive anything.

Sale of the Business for Cash

The purchase price will be allocated first to the preferred stockholders with exit preferences, and the remainder will be shared between the preferred and common stockholders depending on the agreed formula.

Sale of the Business in Exchange for Stock in the Acquiring Company

The stock in the new entity will be allocated first to satisfy the exit preferences, and the remainder will be shared depending on the sharing formula. The situation can vary, however, depending on whether the acquiring company is a public or a private company.

When the acquirer is public, it has a fixed market value per share, which in most cases can be converted to cash. Where the acquirer is a private company, the situation can be far more complicated and contentious.

When one private company buys another for stock, the most important point to be negotiated is the percentage share of the acquiring company that the acquiree's stockholders will receive. But since the ascribed value of both the acquiring company and the acquiree are hypothetical rather than market-based, this can lead to severe disputes between the preferred and the common stockholders of the acquiree.

Consider the example in Exhibit 9.1 where it is agreed that the stockholders in the acquiree will receive 25% of the acquiring company. The preferred stockholders in the acquiree have a $3M exit preference.

In the first case the value placed on each company is fairly low. The exit preference leads to the preferred stockholders in the acquiree receiving all the available stock in the acquirer company. In the second case, when the value placed on the two companies is high, the common stockholders in the acquiree company benefit.

The arbitrary ascribing of value in the two companies determines the allocation of value between the preferred and ordinary stockholders in the acquiree company. This conflict is very hard to resolve without arbitration of the value by independent corporate finance advisors.

Exhibit 9.1 Impact of Valuation on the Split of Proceeds among Stockholders of Acquiree Company

Low Value Placed on Each Company	High Value Placed on Each Company
Value ascribed to each company:	Value ascribed to each company:
Acquirer: $9M (75% of combined entity)	Acquirer: $21M (75% of combined entity)
Acquiree: $3M (25%)	Acquiree: $7M (25%)
Allocation of stock in acquirer to stockholders of acquiree:	Allocation of stock in acquirer to stockholders of acquiree:*
• Preferred: 100% ($3M)	• Preferred: 60% ($4.2M)
• Common: 0% ($0)	• Common: 40% ($2.8M)

* Assuming that the preferred stock is participating preferred stock (see later section for explanation) and the preferred stock has a 30% ownership position in the acquiree. Value to be allocated to preferred stockholders is $3M (exit preference) plus 30% of the remaining $4M in value ($1.2M), giving a total value of $4.2M.

Merger of the Business

When two private companies merge, the same problems arise with regard to liquidation preferences as with the sale of a private company to another private company. In fact, the problem can be doubled, because both sides will typically have exit preferences for their investors.

Initial Public Offering

Most term sheets provide for the elimination of exit preferences in the event of an IPO. The preferred stock will be converted automatically into common stock. Preferred stockholders allow this because the value of a company on an IPO is normally quite high and the preferred shareholders are likely to have received a good return on their investment. As early preferred stockholders in a company bear the risk that their investment might be heavily diluted by later preferred shareholders, the terms under which an IPO is qualified (where the preferred stockholders can be forced to convert without getting the benefit of an exit preference) are normally established in the term sheet. For example, in the legal agreements, the definition of a qualifying IPO (under which the preferred stockholders are automatically converted) might say "for an initial public offering where the value of the company is greater than

$70M and where the new money raised is greater than $20M." Qualifying the IPO means that the automatic conversion should take place only under circumstances that suit the preferred stockholder.

New Equity Investment in the Company Where the New Investor Owns a Highly Significant Shareholding

The term sheet might include a provision to trigger the exit preference clause if a new investor buys a large share of the company—typically 50 to 75% or more. In this case the value of the residual percentage shareholdings of the preferred and common stockholders might be reallocated taking into account the exit preference clause.

For example, if a new investor buys 75% of a company for $15M, the entire remaining shareholding (preferred and common) would be valued at $5M. If the existing investor has an exit preference on his or her investment of $10M, then all the existing stock should be allocated to the existing preferred stockholder thus wiping out the position of the common stockholders. In such a case, the preferred stockholders are treating the acquisition of a large shareholding as a "creeping acquisition" of the whole company by a third party. If the price per share at which the creeping acquisition starts is low, then the preferred stockholders want to capture most of the value through their exit preference.

Variants of Exit Preferences Sometimes Seen

Most term sheets contain exit preferences. The most common form of exit preference is for preferred shareholders to get 100% of their capital back first and then to share in the remaining proceeds. In the venture capital business, this is known as a 1X (or one times) exit or liquidation preference.

Multiple Exit Preferences

When the balance of power, at the time of negotiating the deal, is with the investor, he or she might demand a multiple exit preference. The investor might insist on 200% (2X), 300% (3X), or more of his or her investment back before the common stockholders share in any of the proceeds. In 2001 and 2002, when investment capital for early-stage ventures was very scarce, some investors even asked for 5X preferences. Only companies in extremely desperate circumstances would accept investment on such penal terms.

In most cases, these types of aggressive terms prove counterproductive; management teams lose their economic incentive to make the company succeed. If the company progresses and it is possible to sell it, management might be unenthusiastic about the sale because it may receive no value. Sometimes, where exit preferences are onerous, the deal between management and the investors will be recast to provide some value to management and to motivate it to pursue a transaction. Management might be "carved out" from the exit preference. For example, if the investor invested $3M with a 4X exit preference, he or she would expect to receive the first $12M of the proceeds on a sale. If a possible sale of the company for $10M arose, management might approach the investor to carve out, say, $1M of the proceeds.

Layered Exit Preferences

A venture capital backed company will likely raise at least three rounds of investment on its way to a trade sale or an IPO. Different venture capitalists often lead each round of investment, leading to Series A preferred stock being allocated to the first group of investors, Series B preferred stock to the second, Series C preferred stock to the third, and so on. The best way to view these layers of preferred stock is to compare them to a pile of pancakes; those on top are eaten first. The most recent investors reign supreme. Most legal agreements provide for the latest investor to have the most senior preference. Then the preference of the second most recent investor is satisfied, and so forth, until all preferences have been fulfilled. Then the common and preferred stockholders share in the residual proceeds.

The following situation is not unusual. A company raises a lot of money (say, $30M from Series A and B stockholders) but is performing poorly. A further $10M investment is required to turn the company around and make it ready to be sold. The A and B stockholders can put up only a small share of the round (say, $2M). This puts the Series

C stockholder in a difficult position. If the company is sold for $50M, the Series C stockholders will receive the first $10M, and the A and B stockholders will get the next $30M. The Series A, B, and C stockholders and the common stockholders will share the last $10M. This is not a good structure for attracting Series C investors.

To solve this, the Series C investors might insist that the Series A and B stockholders waive their right to an exit preference. If this is agreed to, on a sale, the Series C investors will get their preference, and the remaining proceeds will be shared among the holders of the Series A, B, and C investors and the common stockholders depending on their relative ownership positions.

The sharing formula will need to be agreed upon and depends on the type of preferred stock owned by each class of investor.

Types of Preferred Stock

Preferred stock is the instrument through which investors get their exit preferences. While there are an infinite number of permutations and combinations of preferred stock, there are three core types—redeemable preferred (nonconverting), convertible preferred, and participating preferred.

Redeemable Preferred Stock

Redeemable preferred stock is like a loan to the company. For example, assume an investor invested $3M in redeemable preferred stock with a 10% coupon rate.[1] If the company is sold in three years for $10M, the preferred stockholder will receive $3.9M, and the remaining $6.1M will be shared among the common stockholders. (See Exhibit 9.2.)

If the company is sold for less than $3.9M, all the proceeds go to the preferred stockholder.

---

1 Assume for simplicity that it is not compounded.

Exhibit 9.2 Redeemable Preferred Stock

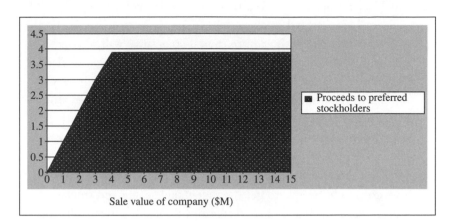

For most early-stage ventures, investors will not be happy with redeemable preferred stock; they want a share in the ultimate prize in the event that the company is sold at a high valuation.

Redeemable preferred stock used in isolation is rare. It tends to be used in three situations:

1. *Late-stage ventures.* It occasionally makes sense in late-stage ventures where a positive exit is virtually guaranteed or where the company has turned the corner from losses and is generating positive cash flow every month. This might suggest to the investors that they put their money in via redeemable preferred stock with a high coupon rate (say 30%). In effect, the investor might be "guaranteed" his or her capital back plus a high but capped return. In practice, companies in this type of position can typically go for debt financing at a much more modest coupon level.

2. *In conjunction with common stock.* In an early-stage venture the buyer of redeemable preferred stock will almost always want common stock as well. This provides the investors with two types of return—a return of capital (the redeemable preferred stock) similar in effect to an exit preference and a potential capital gain

on the common stock. Typically the price paid on the common stock is extremely low, given that the investor is investing in redeemable preferred stock as well.

People familiar with venture capital structures will see that the profile of returns to the investor of this combination of two instruments (redeemable preferred plus common stock) is very similar to the profile generated by a participating preferred stock structure (covered later in this chapter). The potential return profile of a participating preferred instrument is discussed below. One advantage of a combination redeemable preferred/common stock structure over a participating preferred structure is that the investor might be able to get the redeemable preferred stock repaid (redeemed) at an early stage and then share in the ultimate upside through the common stock later. If an investor owns a participating preferred alone, he or she couldn't get an early return of the capital invested; dividends might solve some of this problem, but they are probably paid to all stockholders, not just the investors. If the stock were to be redeemed, the investor would lose his or her rights to share in an exit.

As an alternative to a redeemable preferred/common stock structure, investors might prefer to combine a loan with common stock; this should yield the same return profile. However, using a loan rather than redeemable preferred stock damages the balance sheet of the company; the loan is considered to be a liability, whereas the redeemable preferred stock is seen as share capital. New accounting rules sometimes demand that preferred stock be shown as a liability.

3. *If the investor owns "too much" of the company.* Sometimes, management of a company has been aggressively diluted in its ownership position—perhaps down to 20% of the company. When the existing investors have agreed to invest a final amount of money prior to an exit and they do not want to dilute management ownership further, they might use a redeemable preferred structure. Management will continue to own 20%; investors will receive an additional top slice of exit preference out of the proceeds of a sale.

Convertible Redeemable Preferred Stock

Convertible redeemable preferred stock can be either converted into common stock or redeemed; the option[2] to convert or redeem will generally rest with the investor. Typically the option to convert will be exercised only when an exit of the company takes place—when the company is sold, goes public, or fails (goes into liquidation).

The investor will decide to convert his convertible redeemable stock into common stock when the value he would receive on an exit (if he held common stock) exceeds the price per share he would realize if he does not convert and relies instead on an exit preference.

The best way to understand this is to consider an example similar to the redeemable preferred stock above.

The investor invested $3M for 30% in convertible redeemable preferred stock. If the company were sold for $3M, the investor would redeem (or rely on her exit preference) rather than convert her stock. If she redeemed her stock or relied on the exit preference, she would receive all of the $3M, as the preferred stock ranks higher than the common stock. If she converted, she would own 30% of the company; 30% of the $3M proceeds equaling $900,000; she would be better off redeeming rather than converting. In fact, the investor would then be indifferent to the sale price of the company between a range of $3M and $10M (because she would still redeem or rely on the exit preference rather than convert and receive just $3M). Only if the sale price went above $10M would she convert and own 30% of the company (30% of $10M is $3M).

The typical return profile for an investor when he or she owns convertible redeemable preferred stock is shown in Exhibit 9.3.

As any entrepreneur will quickly spot, the investor is indifferent to a sales price between $3.1M and $10M, whereas the entrepreneur would get $0.1M rather than $7M. The incentives are misaligned.

---

2 The investor can be forced to convert if the company is to undertake a "qualifying" IPO or if the investor decides not to invest in a down round when a "pay-to-play" clause is triggered. More on pay-to-play and down rounds later in this chapter.

Exhibit 9.3 Convertible Preferred Stock

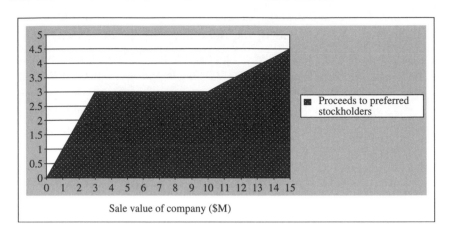

Proceeds to preferred stockholders

Sale value of company ($M)

When the investor has a lot of decision rights in the company, this can cause conflict. If an offer for $3.5M for the company came in, the investor might be happy to take it.

On an IPO, the convertible redeemable preferred stockholder is generally forced to convert to common stock. However, there will typically be restrictions built in so that the stockholders are not forced to convert into common stock, unless it is valuable.

Participating Preferred Stock

Participating preferred stock offers the best of both worlds from the investors' perspective. When a company is sold, the investors get their capital back first, and then they get to share in all proceeds above the returned capital. This is sometimes called a *double dip*; the investors are dipping into the proceeds twice, first to get their capital back and, second, to share in any remaining proceeds.

Consider the example above where the investor bought 30% for $3M in participating preferred stock. If the sale price is less than or equal to $3M, the investor gets all the proceeds. If the company is sold for $10M, the investor gets $3M back plus 30% of the remaining

$7M—a total return to the investor of $5.1M ($4.9M to the common stockholders). Exhibit 9.4 shows a profile of the proceeds under different exit prices.

In the current environment, most investments in early-stage ventures are made with instruments that resemble participating preferred stock in the profile of the returns they provide to investors.

A variant of participating preferred stock is capped participating preferred stock, which is exactly the same as participating preferred stock with one exception. A formula is agreed upon that sets a trigger point at which the stock ceases to provide a return like participating preferred stock and starts to act like convertible preferred stock. The formula might say that the stock participates up to three or five times the price per unit of stock that the investor paid.

Consider the situation in which the investor owned 30% of a company and paid $3M (owning 3M shares at $1 each out of the 10M outstanding after the investment). He or she has participating preferred stock capped at three times the price per share. Consequently, the participating cap is $3 per share.

If the company is sold for $3M, the investor gets all the proceeds— the price per share realized by the preferred stockholder is $1. If the company is sold for $16M, the investor gets $3M plus 30% of

Exhibit 9.4 Participating Preferred Stock

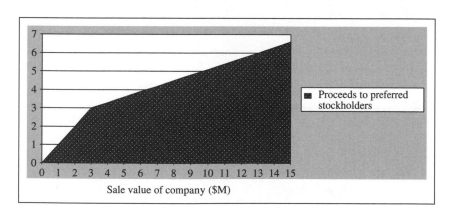

Sale value of company ($M)

Exhibit 9.5 Capped Participating Preferred Stock

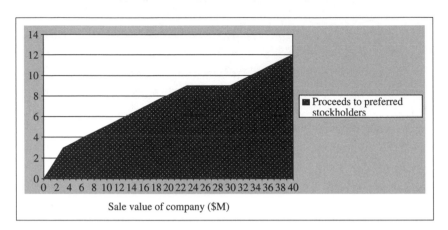

Sale value of company ($M)

the remaining $13M—which results in $6.9M or $2.30 per share. The cap is reached at a sales price of $23M. At $23M, the investor receives $3M in preference and 30% of the remaining $20M in proceeds ($6M). This totals $9M—three times the capital invested and three times the price per share.

Note that the investor's proceeds are flat between an exit price range of $23M to $30M; 30% of $30M is $9M. The investor will receive $3 per share in this range. When the exit price exceeds $30M, the investor will receive a straight 30% of the proceeds. For example, at an exit price of $36M the investor would receive $10.8M (30%) or $3.60 per share. (See Exhibit 9.5.)

Entrepreneurs need to model analytically the split of proceeds between the investors and the common stockholders to ensure that they understand fully how it works.

ENTREPRENEUR TIP

If investors are insisting on a participating preferred instrument, it may be possible to negotiate with them to get them to agree to a capped participating preferred. The primary purpose behind a participating preferred instrument is to juice the return to investors in a low-value exit. Clearly, if when selling the company, investors are to receive three to five times their investment, the entrepreneur might be able to make the argument that it is no longer a low-value exit.

2. Staging of Investment against Milestones

If exit preferences are the primary way in which investors skew the returns in their favor, a second way is to invest a portion of the capital up front and to have the remaining amount of the investment be invested automatically at a fixed price per share, if agreed-upon milestones are met. Typical milestones might include: pilot programs under way with target customers, revenue levels, and executive team gaps filled. This mitigates the investors' risk and, in effect, gives them the option to withdraw capital from the deal if it is not going well.

This staging of the investment gives the Series A investors two advantages if the company does not meet its milestones. They can abandon the investment; in practice, there is a high chance that the company will then fail because it will have limited time to raise new capital, and other investors will see that the company has a history of not meeting its milestones. The investors will only have lost their initial tranche of capital. Alternatively, the investors can seek to renegotiate the price on the second portion of their investment—reducing their average valuation.

ENTREPRENEUR TIP

If the Series A investor insists on investing in two tranches, make sure that you are extremely confident of meeting the milestones. Running out of capital might result in the whole deal being renegotiated with the entrepreneur in a very weak position.

3. Options to Invest More Money at a Defined Price per Share

Sometimes, if it is impossible to agree on a straight valuation, an option to invest more money at a defined price per share can act as a concession from the entrepreneur to get the investors over the line. For example, consider a company attempting to raise $4M where the entrepreneur and the investors are deadlocked about agreeing on a valuation; the entrepreneur believes that the company is worth $12M, and the investors believe it to be worth $8M. One way to bridge this gap might be for the investors to invest $4M at a valuation of $11M, but to receive an option to invest a further, say, $2M at $15M within the next 24 months.

ENTREPRENEUR TIP

Avoid options to invest more money. All options have value, and entrepreneurs can often underestimate the value of the option granted. It is better to negotiate harder to bridge the gap or to agree to a dynamic price mechanism (see below).

Also, always set a time period for the option. Whether the entrepreneur's view of the valuation ($12M) or the investors' view is correct will become clear within the next 12 to 18 months, as the company approaches a future round of investment. The time period for exercising the option should not run beyond this point.

A dynamic price mechanism sets the valuation in the future rather than today. Often the differing proposed valuations are derived from differing views of the company's ability to reach targets. In the example above, the investors might believe that next year's sales will be as low as $2M, while the entrepreneur believes they will be $4M.

If it proves impossible to close this valuation gap, the following dynamic price mechanism might work. The investors get a 25% shareholding (equating to a $12M premoney valuation), but have the potential to get up to 33% (equating to an $8M valuation) if sales are as low as $2M. This can be worked out on a sliding scale.

While dynamic price mechanisms are seductive and allow the entrepreneur and investors to avoid the pain of agreeing on a valuation, they never seem to work as well as expected in practice. The incentives are misaligned. In the example above, the entrepreneur will be focused single-mindedly on achieving the $4M sales target. He or she might divert valuable resources from product development and drive up recruitment of salespeople too aggressively.

Most investors have found through experience that it is better to go through the tough process of agreeing on a firm valuation today, rather than create a set of misaligned incentives.

4. Preferred Dividends

Sometimes investors will propose that a coupon be paid on the preferred stock—often 8 to 12% per annum. For example, if the investors put up $5M with a 10% coupon, $500,000 would accrue each year. Unlike interest, the dividends are not typically compounded, but they accumulate over time to be paid out on an exit rather than each year. In effect, if structured this way, they add to the exit preference of the investors. If an exit happened after five years, the first $7.5M (rather than $5M) would go to the investors.

ENTREPRENEUR TIP

Dividends do not tend to be important to investors; the coupon rate might be easier to negotiate out of the term sheet than other matters which are more important to the investors.
Avoid a high coupon rate on early-stage Series A investment rounds. If the Series A investors are not granted a coupon, it will be easier to negotiate out any coupon on term sheets for later Series B or C rounds. As the amount of capital invested in Series

B and C rounds are typically many times that of the A round, avoiding a coupon on the A round can be in the best interests of the A investors—any accumulating dividends on B and C shares will probably need to be paid before the A investors receive their exit preference.

5. Antidilution

Many ventures, including ones that ultimately achieve attractive exits, go through a tough period and have problems raising capital. The price per unit of stock can fall from round to round of investment. Chapter 3 describes the valley of death commonly faced by nascent companies. It is not unusual for a company to raise an initial Series A round of capital at, say, $1 per share, a Series B round at, say, $0.50 and to be sold for $10 per share or more.

How are the Series A investors to be affected by the fall in the price per share from the A to the B round? Do they suffer the same dilution as the common stockholders, or do they receive some compensation for the fact that they bought their Series A stock at too high a price?

To account for the possibility of such a fall in price per share, investors sometimes introduce a mechanism called *antidilution*, which, as the name suggests, protects them from dilution under certain conditions.

To those not familiar with the financing of early-stage ventures, antidilution and pay-to-play can sound like arcane legalities. They are not. Any entrepreneur or investor who has been through a few financing rounds and experienced difficulties along the way knows that antidilution and pay-to-play clauses can have a profound impact on the capital structure of the company and on the behavior of different classes of investors.

Antidilution and pay-to-play clauses might be complicated, but how they work and the behaviors they encourage must be understood.

How Antidilution Works

Antidilution is a protection given to investors to mitigate the impact of a later round of investment at a low price per share. With antidilution, if the company raises a round of investment at a price per share less than the price per share paid by the existing investors, then the earlier investors' price per share is reset (reduced)—they are issued bonus stock (essentially free). Alternatively, the rate of conversion of preferred stock into common stock might be adjusted. For example, if the initial rate of conversion is 1:1 (one unit of preferred stock converts into one unit of common stock), this might be changed to 1:1.5. Either way, the earlier investor ends up with a higher percentage of ownership of the company than he or she would have had in the absence of antidilution protection.

Antidilution rights contain an implicit promise from an entrepreneur to investors at the time they invest, along the following lines:

The price per unit of stock that you are paying in this round is a fair price and should increase from the date of your investment. If the next round of funding is at a lower price per unit than you have paid, the founders and any other existing shareholders at the time of your investment will, in effect, transfer some of their ownership position to you to compensate you for the overvaluation of the company at the time of your investment.

The extent of the transfer of ownership will depend on the way in which the antidilution clause is constructed. There are three primary antidilution formulas that are presented in the next section.

To many entrepreneurs, antidilution seems unfair. If the investor makes an offer to invest in a company at a particular price per unit of stock (and the associated implied valuation), then he or she should be willing to face the downside risk of a decline in the price in subsequent rounds. Investing is not intended to be a one-sided bet. But the reality in the world of early-stage funding is that an investor can press for antidilution if capital is scarce in the market. Many investors look for it.

For many investors, antidilution is a protection against paying an excessive price in the investment round. The investors clearly don't understand as much about the prospects for the company as the founders do. If the founders believe that the valuation of the company should be $20M, then why are they objecting to antidilution? It comes into play only if the valuation proves to be too high.

But antidilution is much more than a compensation mechanism in the event of modest declines in the stock price over time. It provides investors with a powerful weapon to be drawn from the holster when rounds of investment on tough terms are being considered. The entrepreneur and a new investor considering making an investment in the company tend to view the existing investors as a legacy problem if they are tapped out—have no more capital to invest in the company. This is not surprising. The existing investors might own 30 to 40% or more of the company and have little further to contribute to the company's development financially. Clearly, being viewed as a legacy problem is a tag that the earlier investors want to avoid.

MINI CASE: DOWN ROUND EXAMPLES

Example A

Investor A owns 40% of the company after investing $4M (4M shares at $1 each) a year ago; the founders own the remaining 60%. The company has done reasonably well over the past year. It requires new investment, and investor A has no more capital. Investor B has presented a proposal to the entrepreneur. The new investor will buy 25% of the company for $1M and will create an option pool for the founders comprising 35% of the company.

Exhibit 9.6 shows the impact of this proposal on the different parties.

As you can see, this proposal allows the founders to avoid dilution in the current round (ownership going from 60 to 59%, including the pool). The impact of the 60% dilution (25% to the investor and 35% allocated to the pool) falls disproportionately on investor A. The 25% given to investor B has, in effect, been carved out of investor A's shareholding.

Exhibit 9.6 Impact of Proposal

	Before Proposal of Investor B	After Proposal of Investor B
Founders	60%	24%
Option pool	0%	35%
Investor A	40%	16%
Investor B	0%	25%

Example B

If example A does not seem too punitive to you, rerun the numbers where the new investor gets 35% and an option pool of 65% is created for the benefit of the founders. This information is illustrated in Exhibit 9.7.

Here, investor A has been wiped out while the founders have preserved their position. Existing investors are always rightly cautious of management getting too cozy with a new investor and striking a deal that damages their interests.

Exhibit 9.7 Impact of More Severe Proposal

	Before Proposal of Investor B	After New Proposal
Founders	60%	0%
Option pool	0%	65%
Investor A	40%	0%
Investor B	0%	35%

Collusion between management and a new investor is rare. More common is the situation in which there are multiple investors in a company and one of them is tapped out or is unwilling to invest more capital. The other investors may try to craft a punitive financing round, with or without the input of management, to penalize the investor not participating in the round by dramatically reducing his or her ownership.

This is why early investors in a company normally put antidilution provisions in place. If a round of investment happens at a low price, the early investor will be issued bonus stock to protect his or her position. The extent to which the investor is protected depends on the form of the antidilution clause.

Alternative Antidilution Approaches

There are three basic types of antidilution provisions, with minor variants on each:

1. Full ratchet antidilution
2. Narrow-band weighted average antidilution
3. Broad-band weighted average antidilution

These three vary in the level of protection they grant to the incumbent investor and conversely in the level of dilution they impose on the founders and any earlier investors who do not have the benefit of antidilution. Full ratchet has the most severe impact, and broad band the least severe impact.

Because formulas for these approaches are quite complicated in their application, they are perhaps best explained through examples. See the following mini case.

MINI CASE: ANTIDILUTION PROVISIONS AND IMPACTS

Investor 1 acquires 25% of the stock of Creditica for $2.5M (2.5M shares at $1 each). The founders own 60%, and 15% is allocated to an option pool. The company needs more capital, and only new investor 2 is willing to invest ($1M for 20%). Clearly, the price per unit of stock that investor 2 is willing to pay is less than that paid by investor 1. Therefore, any antidilution clause negotiated by investor 1 will now be triggered.

Full Ratchet

Full ratchet has the most dramatic impact on the situation. A full ratchet clause reprices the shares of investor 1 at the price per share paid by investor 2, assuming the price per share paid by investor 2 is less than that paid by investor 1.

You will note that investor 2 has not nominated a price per unit of stock; he has demanded a specific share in the company. This is for a good reason. With a ratchet in place, the capitalization table will be in flux, with bonus shares being issued to investor 1, who has the benefit of the ratchet.

On first pass, it appears that the price per share to be paid by investor 2 will be 40 cents. Since there are 10M shares outstanding before the investment, to own 20%, investor 2 will need to be issued 2.5M shares, leading to total shares outstanding of 12.5M. With an investment of $1M, the 2.5M shares will cost 40 cents each. You will see how the issuance of these new shares to investor 2 affects the capitalization table in Exhibit 9.8 in the set of columns titled "Issue of Stock to Investor 2." Note that these calculations ignore the effect of the full ratchet antidilution.

Exhibit 9.8 Shareholdings under Full Ratchet Antidilution

	First Round		Issue of Stock to Investor 2			Initial bonus: Investor 1			Second Bonus: Investor 1			Third Bonus: Investor 1		
	Number of Shares	Percent Owned	New Shares Issued	Total Owned	Percent Owned	New Shares Issued	Total Owned	Percent Owned	New Shares Issued	Total Owned	Percent Owned	New Shares Issued	Total Owned	Percent Owned
Common stock	6,000,000	60%		6,000,000	48%		6,000,000	35%		6,000,000	30%		6,000,000	27%
Option pool	1,500,000	15%		1,500,000	12%		1,500,000	9%		1,500,000	7%		1,500,000	7%
Series A preferred	2,500,000	25%		2,500,000	20%	3,750,000	6,250,000	36%	2,343,750	8,593,750	43%	1,464,844	10,058,594	46%
Total position of pre-round B stockholders	10,000,000			10,000,000	80%	3,750,000	13,750,000	80%	2,343,750	16,093,750	80%	1,464,844	17,558,594	80%
Series B preferred		0%	2,500,000	2,500,000	20%	937,500	3,437,500	20%	585,938	4,023,437	20%	366,211	4,389,648	20%
Total position of post-round B stockholders	10,000,000	100%	2,500,000	12,500,000	100%	4,687,500	17,187,500	100%	2,929,688	20,117,188	100%	1,831,055	21,948,242	100%
Price per share—both investors	1.00		0.40			0.29			0.25			0.23		
Amount invested	2,500,000		1,000,000											

Investor 1 will be issued bonus shares, since the price per share to investor 2, at 40 cents, is less than the price per share paid by investor 1 ($1). Investor 1's holding of stock will be reset as follows: Originally, she invested $2.5M and received 2.5M shares (at $1 each). Since the new price is 40 cents, her total holding after round 2 should be 6.25M shares ($2.5M invested at a price of 40 cents). Investor 1 will be issued 3.75M bonus shares (6.25M less the original 2.5M shares).

You might have noticed that issuing a bonus stock to investor 1 is creating circular logic. The new low price per share (40 cents) to investor 2 triggers the issue of bonus shares to investor 1. This increases the effective number of shares in issue at the point investor 2 is investing. In this iteration, the number of preexisting shares has increased from 10M to 13.75M. Since investor 2 has specified that he wants to own 20% of the company, he needs to be issued 3.4375M shares rather than the 2.5M shares calculated initially. The price per share will need to be 29.1 cents ($1M divided by 3.4375M shares). The bonus shares to be issued to investor 1 will need to be reset again—the price per share to investor 2 is 29.1 cents rather than 40 cents.

When this circular logic is followed through to its conclusion, the final position is that investor 2 will own 20% (as he has demanded) and investor 1 will own 50%. This makes mathematical sense because the full ratchet clause states that investors 1 and 2 will be treated as having paid exactly the same price per share. Since investor 2 will own 20% having invested $1M, by definition investor 1 must own 50% having invested $2.5M.

If investor 2 had merely stipulated a price per share that he was willing to pay, then the above circularity would be avoided. Investor 1 would simply have been issued bonus shares to take her price per share down to the new level.

Narrow-Band Weighted Average Antidilution

Under narrow-band weighted average antidilution, the price per share at which investor 1's investment will be repriced is the weighted average of the price per share at which investor 1's original shares were issued and the price per share at which the new shares to investor 2 are issued. They will be weighted according to the ratio of shares originally issued to investor 1 and the new shares to investor 2.

Exhibit 9.9 Shareholdings Under Narrow-Band Weighted Average Antidilution

	First Round		Issue of Stock to Investor 2			Initial bonus: Investor 1			Second Bonus: Investor 1			Third Bonus: Investor 1		
	Number of Shares	Percent Owned	New Shares Issued	Total Owned	Percent Owned	New Shares Issued	Total Owned	Percent Owned	New Shares Issued	Total Owned	Percent Owned	New Shares Issued	Total Owned	Percent Owned
Common stock	6,000,000	60%		6,000,000	48%		6,000,000	43%		6,000,000	43%		6,000,000	42%
Option pool	1,500,000	15%		1,500,000	12%		1,500,000	11%		1,500,000	11%		1,500,000	11%
Series A preferred	2,500,000	25%		2,500,000	20%	1,071,429	3,571,429	26%	191,327	3,762,755	27%	34,165	3,796,921	27%
Total position of pre-round B stockholders	10,000,000	100%		10,000,000	80%	1,071,429	11,071,429	80%	191,327	11,262,755	80%	34,165	11,296,921	80%
Series B preferred		0%	2,500,000	2,500,000	20%	267,857	2,767,857	20%	47,832	2,815,688	20%	8,541	2,824,230	20%
Total position of post-round B stockholders	10,000,000	100%	2,500,000	12,500,000	100%	1,339,286	13,839,286	100%	239,158	14,078,444	100%	42,707	14,121,151	100%
Price per share—investor 1	1.00		0.70			0.66			0.66			0.66		
Price per share—investor 2	0.40		0.40			0.36			0.36			0.35		
Amount invested	2,500,000		1,000,000											

You can already see that the impact will be less dramatic than the full ratchet. Instead of investor 1's price per share falling all the way to the level of investor 2's, it will be reduced to some price between the two. The extent to which it falls will be related to the quantity of shares issued to each. If a lot of shares were issued initially to investor 1 relative to the number of shares issued to investor 2, the price per share would be at the upper end of the range and the number of bonus shares would be limited.

The rationale for weighting the price is that if round B was a relatively small-sized investment round and round A was relatively large, it would be harsh for the money originally invested in round A to be repriced all the way down to the lower round B price.

The calculations underlying the narrow-band weighted average formula are shown in Exhibit 9.9 with the first few rounds of circular logic worked through. Investor 2 ends up with 20%, and investor 1 ends up with 27%.

Broad-Band Weighted Average Antidilution

This is quite similar to the narrow-band weighted average formula except that it has a slightly gentler impact on the equity owned by founders.

In the narrow-band formula, the revised price per share for investor 1 is calculated as weighted between investor 1's and investor 2's price per share—weighted according to the number of shares issued to investor 1 and investor 2. In the broad-band formula the revised price per share for investor 1 is calculated as weighted between investor 1's and investor 2's price per share—weighted according to the number of total shares in issue after investor 1's investment and the number of shares issued to investor 2. You will notice that many more shares will consequently be weighted at investor 1's (higher) price than under the narrow-band formula. The revised price per share for investor 1 will be higher in the broad-band than in the narrow-band option. This results in fewer bonus shares being issued to investor 1 and less dilution for the founders, leaving investor 2 with 20% and investor 1 with 25%. See Exhibit 9.10.

Exhibit 9.11 shows the investor 1 shareholding percentage following the application of different ratchet formulas.

Because all the incremental shareholding gained by investor 1 comes from the shareholders other than investors 1 and 2 (typically the founders and senior management), the ratchet formulas are very important.

Exhibit 9.10 Shareholdings Under Broad-Band Weighted Average Antidilution

	First Round		Issue of Stock to Investor 2			Initial bonus: Investor 1			Second Bonus: Investor 1			Third Bonus: Investor 1		
	Number of Shares	Percent Owned	New Shares Issued	Total Owned	Percent Owned	New Shares Issued	Total Owned	Percent Owned	New Shares Issued	Total Owned	Percent Owned	New Shares Issued	Total Owned	Percent Owned
Common stock	6,000,000	60%		6,000,000	48%		6,000,000	46%		6,000,000	44%		6,000,000	44%
Option pool	1,500,000	15%		1,500,000	12%		1,500,000	12%		1,500,000	11%		1,500,000	11%
Series A preferred	2,500,000	25%		2,500,000	20%	340,909	2,840,909	22%	451,705	3,292,614	24%	56,463	3,349,077	25%
Total position of pre—round B stockholders	10,000,000			10,000,000	80%	340,909	10,340,909	80%	451,705	10,792,614	80%	56,463	10,849,077	80%
Series B preferred		0%	2,500,000	2,500,000	20%	85,227	2,585,227	20%	112,926	2,698,153	20%	14,116	2,712,269	20%
Total position of post—round B stockholders	10,000,000	100%	2,500,000	12,500,000	100%	426,136	12,926,136	100%	564,631	13,490,767	100%	70,579	13,561,346	100%
Price per share—investors 1	1.00		0.88			0.76			0.75			0.74		
Price per share—investors 2	0.40		0.40			0.39			0.37			0.37		
Amount invested	2,500,000		1,000,000											

Exhibit 9.11 Impact of Each Ratchet Formula

Ratchet Formula	Percent Owned by Investor 1
Full ratchet	50%
Narrow-band weighted average	27%
Broad-band weighted average	25%
No ratchet	20%

The outcomes under the formulas will be much closer to one another if the quantity of capital raised in the second round is high relative to the amount of capital raised in the first round—because more weight would be given to the lower second round price. The narrow band and the broad band would end up giving investor 1 a shareholding closer to the 50% achieved under the full ratchet.

Problems with Ratchets

Every investor who has been involved in a company in which a ratchet clause has been activated will testify to the problems that they cause. While they appear to be a fair protection for an investor, they can end up being very divisive. The problems can be categorized into the three areas discussed below.

1. Excessively Penal Impact on Founders and Management

Under the full ratchet example discussed in the mini case, the ownership of founders and management (including share options) falls from 75% after round A to 30% after round B. If the premoney valuation demanded by investor 2 had been $2M rather than $4M ($1M for 20%—postmoney valuation of $5M, premoney of $4M), then the founders would have been wiped out. Investor 2 would have owned 33%, and the bonus shares to investor 1 would have taken up all the other ownership (and more!).

Many founders have found that antidilution formulas have had devastating consequences, even where the decline in valuation does not seem to be particularly dramatic. It seems to have a far more potent impact than they expected at the time of signing the initial investment agreement.

Clearly, a ratchet formula that takes all or most of the ownership away from the founders and management will be unacceptable to investor 2. If truth be told, the founders and management would prefer that investor 1 only owned a modest share and that the founders and management owned a stake sufficiently large to motivate their performance.

Where new investors foresee that their investment will trigger antidilution for the existing investors, with a consequent severe effect on management, they might specify the specific percentage they want to own and the minimum percentage that management must own; for example, a new investor will own 40%, and management must own at least 30% (say). This circumvents the operation of the antidilution formula. In some cases, the new investor might demand that the old investors waive their right to exercise the antidilution clause completely. If there is no other new investor willing to invest, then the old investors might be forced to accede to this request.

As you will see, if there are multiple existing investors, all with antidilution rights, it may be extremely difficult to get all of them to waive their rights.

2. Poor Wording of Formulas

There is no universal legal phraseology for different types of ratchets. A clause that looks clear at the time of investor 1's investment can turn out to be very ambiguous when it is disentangled at the time of investor 2's investment. This can lead to contentious discussions among three sets of lawyers—those for investor 1, those for investor 2, and those for the company.

3. Small Issues of Stock at Low Prices

When the new investment round is very small—say, $500,000 in the above example—or when stock is issued for purposes other than to raise capital (e.g., issuing low-priced stock from the option pool or an allocation of stock to a strategic partner), then clearly it would be wrong for antidilution to be triggered. The value of the stock has not necessarily fallen. Normally, the clauses governing antidilution will waive the activation of the clause in these types of unusual situations.

The situation that can cause the most problems is when minority investors use antidilution rights as a blocking mechanism. Consider the following circumstances. Three investors each invest $1M in a company at a $2M premoney valuation. Each owns 20%. Each also has been given full ratchet antidilution rights.

If the company's commercial milestones have not been met before the next round, the company is in a tricky position. The existence of the antidilution formula practically encourages the existing investors not to participate in the upcoming required round of funding. If they do not invest and the price per share falls, they will be issued bonus stock. The antidilution formula protects them from dilution.

If two of the three investors are willing to invest another $1.5M each ($3M in total) to rescue the company, they might be aiming for a target capitalization table in which each of the two of them owns 30% and the founders own most of the remaining stock. But, with the antidilution formula, the third recalcitrant investor can sit tight knowing that his or her shareholding will get a free ride by benefiting from the fall in the stock price. This situation will probably put an end to the willingness of the other two investors to invest, and the company will be stymied. This is not an unusual situation.

Similarly, if a new investor were willing to invest but requested that the existing investors invest in the new round to demonstrate their ongoing belief in the prospects for the company, then the antidilution formula can cause problems. It encourages one or more of the existing investors to aim for a free ride in the round by not investing and relying on the antidilution as a weapon. In theory, the three investors should get together to work out a cooperative solution. Where one of the investors simply cannot invest, because of lack of capital, the company may again be stymied.

The party whose interests may end up in extreme conflict with the rest of the shareholders has been given an effective veto over the company's survival.

TIP

The company should try to avoid giving antidilution protection to an investor who is unable to invest much more capital in the company.

When a company grants antidilution protection to a group of investors, it should aim to have it accompanied by a pay-to-play clause.

Pay-to-Play Clauses

Coupling a pay-to-play clause with antidilution can be an elegant solution to aligning the incentives of the existing investors in a business. It gets around the potential problem of an antidilution clause creating barriers to participation in an investment round by existing investors.

A *pay-to-play clause* states that investors will be entitled to exercise their antidilution rights only if they invest their pro rata share of the upcoming investment round.

Consider the example above in which the three existing investors each owns 20% of the company. If one of them does not contribute 20% of the upcoming round of $3M ($600,000), he or she will not be eligible to exercise his or her antidilution rights. This means that the investor who does not play will suffer severe dilution while the others will be getting their bonus stock. Even worse, many pay-to-play clauses have a further sting in the tail if the investor does not play for a share of the investment round; the investor's preferred stock may be converted to common stock, and the investor may lose exit preferences and other superior rights associated with the preferred stock.

Such a pay-to-play formula encourages all existing investors to participate in an upcoming round of funding, where the price per unit of stock is a lower price than the prior round. Only by playing can they get the benefit of antidilution and protect their position.

The pay-to-play clause often contains a few modifications. Small investors might make a good case to not have to play for their full pro rata share because of their limited capital. They might negotiate that they get their antidilution rights (or a portion of them) if they play for, say, at least half of their pro rata amount.

Again, these formulas are quite complicated and often prove to have been sloppily drafted when they are examined by nitpicking lawyers in the cold light of day a few years after they were written.

Following is an example of an antidilution clause with a pay-to-play provision.

If while any of the Series A Preferred Stock remains in issue there is any issue or allotment of any stock (or options to acquire stock) at a subscription price payable which is less than the Series A Original Issue Price (other than stock issued in respect of the Stock Option plan) the Company shall forthwith serve written notice of such occurrence on each holder of Series A Preferred Stock of an entitlement to elect pursuant to this Article, whereupon:

1. Each holder of Series A Preferred Stock that elects to subscribe at the New Price for 50% or more of the new stock to which it is entitled to subscribe for by virtue of its pre-emption rights under Article X shall thereupon be deemed to have served a conversion notice[3] in respect only of such Series A Preferred Stock with respect to which an election to subscribe has not been made (being zero in the case of a 100% election) and such stock shall forthwith be converted into

---

3 This clause provides for the conversion of some of the preferred stock into less valuable common stock, if the investor does not play for its full allocation in the round.

Common Stock. With regard to that stock for which there has been an election to subscribe at the New Price, the holder thereof may elect either to receive bonus issues of additional Series A Preferred Stock at no cost ("Bonus Stock") concurrently with such issue or allotment of New Stock, so as to result in each such holder of Series A Preferred Stock having paid, in subscribing for its entire holding of Series A Preferred Stock (excluding the new shares if it is Series A Preferred Stock) on average a price per unit of Series A Preferred Stock equal to the New Price; and

2. *Each holder of Series A Preferred Shares that elects to subscribe at the New Price for less than 50% of the New Stock to which it is entitled to subscribe for by virtue of its pre-emption rights or that elects to subscribe for no such stock or who shall fail within 21 days of receipt of written notice to make any form of election shall thereupon be deemed to have served a conversion notice in respect of all Series A Preferred Stock then held and all such stock shall forthwith be converted into common stock.*

The provisions of this Article shall not be of application with regard to any issues or allotments of Series A Preferred Stock as may occur in any rolling period of 12 months (whether by a single issue and allotment or a series of issues and allotments) at a subscription price payable in aggregate therefore that does not exceed [$500,000].

In effect, with provisions such as the ones above, if investors play for more than 50% of their preemption rights, they can exercise their antidilution rights on the proportion for which they played. For example, if investors took up 75% of their preemption rights attached to its Series A stock, they get to reset the high price paid in the Series A round down to the low price paid in the Series B round on 75% of the Series A stock that they hold. They will receive bonus stock or a better conversion rate for converting preferred into common stock. If the investors took up less than 50% of their preemption rights, they cannot exercise any antidilution rights.

Washout Financing Rounds—Down (and Out!) Rounds

In exceptional cases, it will be necessary for investors to undertake a washout financing. In such a financing, the entire shareholding structure of the company is recast along the lines desired by an investor who is investing fresh cash in the company. All the existing shareholdings are eliminated.

Consider the following situation.

Creditica has performed poorly since its establishment. Since the first round of investment in mid-2008, the company has failed to achieve its milestones. Management has proven unable to finish product development; it has ended up in a vicious cycle of adding more and more features to attract customers. The existing investors have decided not to invest in the company anymore. A new investor willing to invest $2M has been found, but this new investor has the following conditions:

1. The premoney valuation will be $1,000 (not $1M!).
2. A new CEO skilled in managing complex product development projects will be brought in. She will be allocated stock options representing over 10% of the company stock.
3. The existing management team, excluding the existing CEO (who will depart from the business), will be allocated 20% of the company in options.
4. All prior liquidation preferences will be wiped out. Only the new investor will have a liquidation preference of $2M.

In this case, the new money will buy 100% of the company, and the new investor will create an option pool of 30% to be allocated to the new CEO and the team as noted above.

If there were 1M shares in issue prior to the new investment, then each of them would be valued at one-tenth of a cent each; 2 billion shares will be issued to the new investor—drowning the ownership of the prior investors and management. Following a massive stock issue like this, the company will probably do a reverse split of the stock. The company might replace every 1,000 units of stock in issue with one new unit.

You might ask why the existing investors would agree to a devastating outcome like this. There are a few reasons. This is probably the only chance for the company to stay in business and avoid liquidation. While the existing investors will receive no proceeds under a liquidation (and no proceeds under the new share capital structure), there are no economic benefits to them in withholding their consent. More importantly, if any of the existing investors are directors of the company, they have a fiduciary duty to the creditors of the company and will not want to be seen to be rejecting an offer of fresh capital into the company.

Washout financing similar to that described above sounds extreme, but this kind of thing happens from time to time. If a company has three existing shareholders and only two will support the company going forward, the two committed investors might decide to undertake washout financing to wipe out and capture the shareholding position of the recalcitrant investor. Management might then be given new stock options that represent a good ownership position.

CHAPTER 10

ALLOCATING CONTROL BETWEEN FOUNDERS/MANAGEMENT AND INVESTORS

In any public company there should be a good corporate governance structure in place that allocates the decision rights between the executive team, the board, and the stockholders. The executive team should be able to make ongoing decisions in the ordinary course of business, the board should approve bigger decisions, and the most important decisions (e.g., major acquisitions) should need the approval of the stockholders.

In a private company, a similar tiered governance structure is required; however, there will be a set of decision rights specifically reserved for the preferred stockholders. Furthermore, the structure of the board will be delineated in the agreement governing the preferred stockholder's investment in the company. The preferred stockholders will almost always have the right to one or more board seats.

Restricted Transactions/Protective Covenants

Any investment agreement will contain a long list of restricted transactions—the topics over which the preferred stockholders will have a veto. The entrepreneur often misinterprets these restrictions as potential impediments to his or her approach to managing the business. In reality, the vast majority of the restricted transactions are intended as protections for the investors. They should not interfere with the entrepreneur implementing the business plan presented to the investors at the time of the investment.

The typical restricted transactions contained in an investment agreement and the reasons why investors want a veto over them are outlined below. The term sheet will probably list a subset of them.

1. *Except for the issue of validly created options over stock pursuant to the agreed option pool, create or issue or agree to create or issue any equity or loan capital or give or agree to give any option in respect of any equity or loan capital, or purchase or redeem its own stock.* Investors want a veto over future investment rounds taking place. If the company legitimately needs investment, the investors won't exercise the veto. They want to protect against inappropriate dilution, for example where the entrepreneur colludes with new investors to the detriment of the existing investors. The term sheet should identify the number of options over stock or the percentage of fully diluted share capital of the company to be allocated to the stock option pool. Normally the remuneration committee of the board of directors, rather than the preferred stockholders, will approve the allocation of options to individuals.

2. *Consolidate, subdivide, or alter any of the rights attaching to any of its issued stock or capitalize any reserves or redeem or buy back any stock or otherwise reorganize its equity capital in any way or create any new class of stock.* Similar to item 1, the investor will want to ensure that the class of stock in which he or she has invested (and the relative set of rights of the stock) will be protected and not changed without his or her consent.

3. *Alter the Articles of Association in any way.* The Articles act as the "constitution" for the company. Any changes should need the consent of the investors.

4. *Register any transfer of stock other than in accordance with the Investment Agreement and the Articles.* Investors will be concerned if founders try to sell their stock. If the founders sell out, they might not be motivated to drive the company forward fully and create capital value. Investors might also want to avoid having certain parties as stockholders in the company.

5. *Enter into any contract or transaction whereby the business would be controlled otherwise than by the board of directors.* The board of directors will be structured carefully in the term sheet and the legal agreements. The investors will not want this arrangement upset by having the board bypassed in any unintended manner.

6. *Enter into any scheme of arrangement with its creditors or take steps to effect a voluntary liquidation.* The investors' position will probably be damaged if any such scheme is entered into without their consent.

7. *Create, agree to create, or suffer to exist any charge, mortgage, lien, or other encumbrance on or over the whole or any part of its present or future undertaking or assets (including Intellectual Property).* Any security on the assets of the company will give the loan providers a higher claim on the assets (including the intellectual property) of the company than the preferred stockholders.

8. *Enter into any merger, liquidation, dissolution, or acquisition of the Company or sale of substantially all of its assets.* These are highly material events in the development of the company that can positively or negatively affect the position of the investors.

9. *Make, give, enter into, or incur a guarantee, indemnity, undertaking other material commitment on capital account or unusual liability outside the ordinary course of business.* The legal agreements should give the management the ability to run the business "within the ordinary course of business." Decisions outside these bounds are rightly reserved either for the board or for the preferred stockholders or even the stockholder base as a whole.

10. *Establish a retirement, death, or disability benefit scheme.* Retirement, death, or disability benefit schemes can be very costly. Also, management has a personal interest in the creation of these schemes and rightly should not have the discretion to put them in place without higher approval.

11. *Dispose of any stock or otherwise reduce the percentage shareholding held by it in any companies nor whether by one*

transaction or by a number of transactions (whether related or not and whether at one time or over a period of time) sell, transfer, license, or otherwise dispose of the whole or any substantial or material part of its assets (including fixed assets) or undertaking. Again, these are highly material decisions, and it is not surprising that the preferred stockholders would like a say in them.

12. *Pass any resolution of its members in general meeting the effect of which would be to alter in any material way the nature of such company and/or its business as envisaged by this Agreement.* The investors invested in a specific business plan. If management decides to change the business plan radically (e.g., change the markets being pursued), this changes the risk profile for investors.

13. *Enter into any partnership or joint venture other than in the ordinary course of business.* Again, highly material decisions.

14. *Employ any person at an annual basic salary of in excess of $120,000.* Investors will want to be consulted on senior management hires because they are backing a specific team to make the business a success. On the other hand, it is important not to set the threshold too low and involve the investors in routine or midmanagement hires.

15. *Appoint or remove any chairman, director, or other senior executive.* This is self-explanatory.

16. *Transfer, assign, license, or otherwise dispose of any Intellectual Property rights of the Company and its Subsidiaries to any third party or accept a license of Intellectual Property rights from any third party other than in the ordinary course of business.* Intellectual property might prove to be the core salable asset of the company.

Naturally, all entrepreneurs will aim to keep the list of restricted transactions as short as possible. The list tends to be long, but most of the items on it are not particularly contentious. However, entrepreneurs do not typically focus on the two aspects of restricted transactions, which require close attention.

Who Has the Vetoes?

If one investor undertakes the round of investment, that investor will likely hold the vetoes.

Where there are multiple investors, it is more complicated. Consider the following: Two investors participate in a round of investment for $3M. One leads the investment and puts in $2.25M, and the other puts in $0.75M. This is not uncommon. If the investment agreement states that, "The company must seek the approval of the investors" before undertaking any of the list of restricted transactions, this company could end up in trouble. "The investors" refers to each of them unless specifically defined in another way. This means that the minor investor will have very broad-ranging powers to veto company activities.

This danger can be best illustrated by looking at the dynamics of a subsequent round of investment. As all investors know, company fortunes can deteriorate and the capital in the company can be depleted before any real milestones have been reached. In such a case, it might be necessary to undertake a round of investment, primarily from existing investors, at a low valuation in order to attract the required new capital. If the smaller investor in the above round is unwilling or unable to invest in the new round of investment, he or she will have a blocking veto on the transaction. This can create a very damaging stalemate. A low price on the round might be needed to entice investment, and this is likely to be highly dilutive; the small investor clearly won't like this. The small investor might withhold consent and insist on a higher price. The larger investor will be in a tough position; he or she has more capital already invested in the company and therefore has more to lose.

Lead investors in a round where there are multiple investors should aim to bind the vetoes to themselves solely. There are a few ways of doing this—by saying that restricted transactions require the approval of either:

1. The holders of $X\%$ or more of the preferred stockholders, where $X\%$ is less than the holding of the lead investor and greater than the combined holding of the smaller investors.

2. The lead investor, whose name is explicitly stated in the agreement as holding the vetoes (perhaps plus one of the smaller investors).

ENTREPRENEUR TIP

Entrepreneurs tend to focus on the vetoes that are put in place and stand back from the discussion of, "Who gets the vetoes?" They often view this discussion as power politics between the various investors. This is a mistake. Entrepreneurs should seek common cause with the lead investor to limit the number of vetoes.

Clearly, there are many permutations and combinations for structuring vetoes. The principle of having few (preferably one) entities with vetoes stands.

ENTREPRENEUR TIP

The most troublesome person to have a veto is the small investor who is unable or unwilling to invest more capital in the company. Every venture capitalist and many entrepreneurs can proffer a war story of a company where highly fraught discussions have taken place with small investors with blocking vetoes. See the section below "Conflict between Role as a Director and Representative of Investor" for an example of how this might play out.

What Notification of Approval Is Required?

Many investment agreements provide for written approval by a representative of the investor company. This approval process can become cumbersome, particularly if the list of vetoes is long and defined broadly.

ENTREPRENEUR TIP

When there is a corporate investor or corporate venture capitalist involved, it is important to set a time limit in which they must respond positively or negatively to requests for approvals of restricted transactions. These types of organizations can be notoriously slow in decision making and very insensitive to the speed of decision making required in a small, agile company. If they don't respond within the desired time period, approval may be deemed to have been given, if this is provided for the legal agreements.

When Series A investors make an investment, the vetoes will be allocated to some combination of them. When a Series B investor makes a subsequent investment, the structure of the vetoes will need to be reset. It would be unworkable in practice to have a set of nested vetoes whereby the Series B investors approve a restricted transaction followed by the Series A investors. The same principle of as few vetoes as possible holds.

In the normal course of events, the latest and greatest investors—those in Series B—should reign supreme and hold the vetoes. Typically they have invested the most money at the highest price per share. In practice, the structure of the vetoes depends on the unique capitalization table of the company and the relative power that the B investors have at the time of their investment. For example, were there a lot of competing investors at the time of B's term sheet? Exhibit 10.1 covers three hypothetical companies and suggested good solutions for structuring the vetoes. The formula describing the way in which the vetoes are allocated is often described in the legal documents as the *Investor Majority*.

Structure of the Board of Directors

Investors generally want to appoint someone to the board of directors. The board member can have some influence over the strategy pursued by the company, add value by introducing potential customers

Exhibit 10.1 Alternative Veto Structures

Company 1	Company 2	Company 3
Shareholdings post round B:	*Shareholdings post round B:*	*Shareholdings post round B:*
• Series A investor: 5%	• Series A investor: 20%	• Series A investor: 20%
• Series B investor 1: 30%	• Series B investor 1: 20%	• Series B investor 1: 10%
• Series B investor 2: 10%	• Series B investor 2: 15%	• Series B investor 2: 10%
		• Series B investor 3: 10%
Good solution: Series B investor 1 holds the vetoes, either named explicitly or Investor Majority defined as "the holders of 74%* or more of the Series B preferred stock."	*Good solution:* Any two of the three investors are required to approve a restricted transaction or Investor Majority defined as "the holders of 60%† or more of the Series A and B preferred stock combined."	*Good solution:* Any two of the four investors. Avoid using an Investor Majority defined as a percentage since the A investor would have too much power (which would probably be unacceptable to preferred the B investors).

*Series B investor 1 owns 75% of the B stock. The A stockholders are excluded from the vetoes completely since they own only a small share of the company.
†At least 35% of the 55% of stock held by the A and B investors combined.

and management recruits, and help to protect the investment made by the investor.

At all times, however, the primary responsibility of a director is his or her fiduciary duty to the company. This duty, at all times, has primacy over the responsibilities that such a person might have to the venture capital company that appointed him or her. The director attends the board meeting as an individual in his or her own right and is to pursue the best interests of the company rather than the interests of a specific investor. More on these potential conflicts below.

The following are the most important aspects of the board to be addressed in the term sheet.

Composition of the Board

A good board has a balance between representatives of the executives, the investors, and external, nonaligned third parties.

After the Series A investment round, the board might comprise one to two executives (the CEO and either the chief technical officer or the CFO), the lead investor in the Series A round (maybe the second investor if there are two roughly equal investors in the round), and an independent chairperson. Typically, both the executives and the investors must agree to the appointment of the chairperson.

At this stage, it is preferable to keep the board tight and small. The milestones to be met by the company are quite tangible (e.g., finish the product, get pilots in place, find early reference customers). As the company moves to a Series B round, the board needs the space to grow as the Series B investor(s) might require a board seat(s). If more than one board seat has been allocated to Series A investors, one of them may need to resign.

ENTREPRENEUR TIP

At the time of the Series A round, if two investor directors have been appointed, it would be good to identify and agree on which one of them will resign from the board if the Series B investor insists that there be no more than one.

Observer Positions on the Board

Where there is too much demand for board seats, it might be possible to appoint someone as an observer. An observer will attend the board meetings but will not have the right to vote. In theory, he or she has the right to observe rather than participate, but this is enforced only under extreme circumstances. The investment agreement might also state that the right to appoint an observer falls away after a defined period of time, say 12 months or the date of the next investment.

Automatic Loss of a Board Seat

It is good to avoid proliferation of board seats. One way to regulate the size of the board and match the board structure to the underlying shareholding and power base is with a formula that defines when an investor loses a board seat. The investment agreement might state that an investor loses the right to a board seat if he or she owns less than 5 to 8% of the share capital of the company. Thus, if a new Series B investor invests or the Series A shareholder sells part of his or her shareholding, this clause might be triggered and the Series A investor loses the seat.

One advantage of such a clause is that it avoids the inevitably awkward discussions associated with asking someone to resign from the board if he or she would prefer not to.

Remuneration and Audit Committees

Remuneration and audit committees are the bane of every venture capitalist's life, but it is necessary for the investors to be involved. The remuneration committee, under powers delegated by the board, sets the compensation package of each senior executive—base salary, bonus structure, and stock option allocation.

The typical composition of the committee is the chairperson (assuming this person is not also the CEO) and the lead investor(s). Decisions often need to be unanimous. The CEO makes proposals and may attend the meetings but shouldn't have a vote given the conflict of interest.

Because cash resources must be carefully preserved in every early-stage venture, the right compensation culture needs to be promoted. Excessive salaries at the top tend to cascade down the organization. Many venture capitalists expect the best CEOs to recruit high-quality people at below-market salaries and to enthuse them with the vision of the company and the potential financial upside inherent in the growth in value of their stock options.

The audit committee interfaces with the external auditors of the company to provide a point of reference independent of management.

Decision Rights Assigned to the Board

Directors of venture capital backed companies are often surprised by how rare it is for formal votes to be held at the board. This is not just because most boards operate collaboratively but because many rights typically reserved for a board will have been allocated to the preferred stockholders noted in the section above on restricted transactions.

The board might still need to make the decision, but this decision might need to be ratified by the investors.

In a public company, there are typically no preferred stockholders. Decision rights are balanced between the executive team, the board, and the shareholders. Since shareholders are consulted only in quite rare circumstances (e.g., very large acquisitions) boards tend to have a high degree of decision-making rights.

Conflict between Role as a Director and Representative of Investor

When appointed to a board, each director has a fiduciary responsibility to pursue the best interests of all of the stockholders, not to represent any particular stockholder, even if that stockholder has been instrumental in having that director appointed to the board. While the exact responsibilities may vary from country to country, this underlying principle remains the same. Failure to fulfill one's fiduciary responsibilities as a director may result in personal liability.

The person appointed to a board by a venture capital company is commonly known as an *investor director*. Investor directors will hopefully have very good relationships with the CEOs of the companies. However, many people on boards with investor directors complain that some investor directors seem primarily concerned with the narrow economic interests of the investor who appointed them to the board. As an employee of a venture capital company who has his or her own separate responsibilities to the limited partners in the venture capital fund, this concern is perhaps inevitable.

This conflict is most apparent when the company goes through difficulties, and an internal round of funding—by the existing investors—needs to be undertaken. There will be at least three camps in this discussion: those investors willing to invest more (fresh investors), those investors unwilling or unable to invest more, and management. A severe down round is often the proposed solution, with the fresh investors owning a very large share of the company (and management receiving new options to compensate them for the severe dilution). This can lead to a power play between the three camps that is played out, acrimoniously, on the board.

The investor director appointed by the fresh investors will want to push through the financing proposal and can legitimately argue (and threaten) that the company will fail without the new investment. The unwilling or unable investors will want the funding but also want to avoid penal terms; they might, in fact, threaten to put the company into liquidation if they have a veto over fund-raising. Management's overwhelming concern is to get the new funding, but also to soften the blow of the severe dilution of its shareholding, by being allocated new options.

Each of the parties will feel a tension between their fiduciary duty as a director and the strict interests of their own constituency. In the case above, the unwilling or unable investor has every right, in his or her shareholder capacity separate from the board, to veto the transaction when his or her approval is sought under the restricted transactions clause (see the section above titled, "Who Has the Vetoes?"). However, at the board table, fiduciary duty must predominate.

Sections titled "Restricted Transactions/Protective Covenants" and "Structure of the Board of Directors" above are concerned mainly with the way in which decisions are made.

Sections titled "Redemption," "Forced Sale," "Registration Rights," and "Tagalong Rights, Dragalong Rights" that follow are concerned mainly with the ability of the investors to force a liquidity event.

Venture capitalists sometimes liken themselves to passengers on a train, with the entrepreneur and executive management being the engineers. Passengers need the ability to be able to get off the train at some stage, and they need to make sure that the engineer does not get off the train before them.

The term sheet will include clauses that allow them to force an exit for their investment in a number of ways—even if the entrepreneur does not want them to—and to achieve a fair value for their position when they actually exit.

Investors can realize some return on their investment in a number of ways. The company may be sold or merged; it may undertake an initial public offering or be subject to a management buyout. It may even be put into liquidation and the proceeds distributed. Also, the investors might simply redeem their preference shares, perhaps collecting a coupon as well.

In general, investors get the best return through a sale or an IPO. They want to avoid selling their shareholding to management, who, of course, will want to buy it at a modest price. Liquidation of the company is generally the worst option; the business will lose any goodwill it has built up as a going concern. Redemption of the preferred stock caps the return the investor can get; it only makes sense if the company has performed poorly and investors would suffer even more if they converted their preferred stock to common stock.

Investors always want to ensure that the business does not turn into a "lifestyle" business for the founders and executive management, which allows the train engineers to earn very good current compensation, but which does not create much of a capital gain for the passengers. For example, often a software company set up to develop and sell a product evolves into a service business, selling consultants' time rather than a product. Such a business rarely creates a significant capital gain for investors because service businesses are harder to scale than product businesses due to the increasing demand for professional staff as revenues grow. In another instance, the founders and executives might prefer to be in control of their own business rather than be a division of a larger company or face the rigors of the public markets. This might lead them to oppose a sale or IPO of the company.

At the time of negotiating the term sheet, the investor and the entrepreneur need to agree on the expected period over which the company might achieve its potential. This is important because the length of this period will trigger a set of forced liquidity rights given to the investor. For a start-up or an early-stage company, this should be five years or more. A company rarely reaches its potential in a much shorter period than that. Where the company has been up and running for a few years, it may be appropriate to have a shorter prospective period, say four years or in certain circumstances even less than that. If the investor has an excessively short time horizon for achieving a return on his or her investment, this will lead to a suboptimal result for everyone if the forced liquidity clauses are activated. Entrepreneurs should look for as long a period as can be negotiated. The company can, of course, be sold earlier or undertake an IPO, if the key parties agree.

Both the entrepreneur and the investors do not want the exit of the company to be forced. They both want the company to stay in business long enough to achieve its full potential. The forced exit clauses exist to ensure that the entrepreneur does not tie the investors into the company forever and inhibit them from realizing a return on their investment.

Redemption

One of the advantages of buying preferred stock is that it can be redeemed—unlike common stock. While investing in loan stock (in conjunction with the purchase of common stock) would also provide the investor with a means of getting his or her capital back, it sits as a liability on the balance sheet.

The articles of association of the company normally include a paragraph like the following:

> *The Company may, on or after the fifth anniversary of the date of investment (subject to Corporate Law Acts and to the prior written consent of an Investor Majority), redeem such Series A Preferred Stock then in issue.*

The real advantage of the redemption clause to the investor is that it can be used as a threat. Since the business will not often have the cash resources to fund the redemption, the entrepreneur will be forced to sell the company or to borrow significant funds in order to fulfill his or her obligations. Any desire on the part of the entrepreneur to continue to run the business as a lifestyle business may be thwarted. Alternatively, if it is not possible to sell the business (e.g., an overhanging lawsuit), the entrepreneur will need to find the capital.

There might be a coupon rate on the preferred shares, and if any payments are outstanding, they will need to be paid on redemption.

ENTREPRENEUR TIP

Aim to have the redemption period start as late as possible, say four or five years from the date of investment. Also, stagger the redemption so that, say, one-third becomes redeemable in year 5, one-third in year 6, and the balance (including dividends) in year 7.

There are legal constraints on redeeming stock, which differ from country to country. In general, the company will need to have sufficient shareholder reserves (accumulated profits).

Investors activate redemption clauses extremely rarely. It is more likely that they will seek to activate the forced sale clause.

Forced Sale

The forced sale clause has a similar objective to the redemption clause. The investor needs the ability to sell his or her shares at some stage. But not many acquirers want to buy the minority position of an investor in a private company. In particular, a minority position will attract a poor price if the buyer believes that the entrepreneur in charge of the company has little interest in selling the company. Thus, minority positions tend to sell at a discount per share compared to majority positions or 100% of the company.

Investors will include in the term sheet the right to put the whole company up for sale after, say, five years, including the shares of people who might not want to sell. If the investors owned only 25% of the company, they could force the remaining 75% to sell. In practice, the forced sale clause will normally provide the noninvestor shareholders with the right to buy the investor's shares first, if they are willing to pay the price demanded by the investor.

A Typical Forced Sale Clause

Following is a typical forced sale clause:

> *In the event that a Realization does not occur prior to the fifth anniversary of the investment, and so far as the Investor Majority does not otherwise decide, all of the parties hereto shall use all reasonable endeavors to procure a purchaser for the entire issued stock of the Company as soon as possible thereafter. Within one month of that date, the Founders and the Investors shall appoint an investment bank. If the Founders and the Investors cannot agree on such a bank within such one-month period, then an independent advisor appointed by [body x]*

shall appoint such a bank. Such investment bank shall seek to procure a purchaser for the entire issued stock of the Company. The Company and the parties hereto agree that they shall cooperate with and assist fully such investment bank who shall have full access to all information of the Group to enable the stock of the Company to be sold and meet with such bank and/or prospective purchaser if required.

Each of the Parties hereto agrees that once a proposed purchaser (the "Acquirer") is found and a price agreed upon with the Investors for the entire issued stock of the Company, the Investors may by notice in writing require any of the other Parties hereto to sell all of the stock held by such parties to the Acquirer at a price per unit of stock not less than the price agreed between the Acquirer and the Investors save that in the case where Series A stock remains outstanding and has not been redeemed and/or converted in accordance with the provisions of the Articles of Association, the exit/liquidation provisions shall apply. If any of the parties hereto (other than the Investors) make default in transferring his stock pursuant to the provisions of this clause within a period of 14 days, or such longer period as the Investors may, if they think fit, reasonably allow for the purpose, any director of the Company or some other person appointed by the Board for the purpose shall be deemed to have been appointed attorney of that defaulting party with full power to execute, complete, and deliver in the name and on behalf of that defaulting party a transfer of its stock to the Acquirer, and the Board shall thereupon, subject to such transfers being properly stamped, cause the name of the Acquirer to be entered in the register of members of the Company as the holder of that stock, and the validity of the transaction shall not be questioned by any person. For the avoidance of doubt, the preemption provisions of the Articles of Association shall not apply to any transfer of stock pursuant to this clause.

The Parties shall seek to procure, so far as is possible and subject to the provisions of this Agreement and the Articles of Association, that the parties to this Agreement shall participate on the same terms in any Realization in which all of them are participating so that, for the avoidance of doubt, each of the Investors shall receive an amount in respect of the stock being sold by them equal to the relevant proportion of any other consideration payment receivable by the Founders as consideration for the stock being sold by them pursuant to the Realization. The Founders agree to disclose to each of the Investors all such consideration and any benefits received or receivable by them pursuant to a Realization.

ENTREPRENEUR TIP

Ensure that the Investor Majority required to trigger a forced sale clause comprises all or the vast majority of the preferred stockholders. A few years into the investment, some preferred stockholders might have liquidity problems and might be willing to sell their investment at a low price, thus forcing everyone else to sell at the same level.

The forced sale of the company still triggers the exit preference clause. For example, if the investors have an exit preference of $15M and the best price achievable through the forced sale is $10M, all the proceeds will go to the holders of the preferred stock.

Registration Rights

Registration rights are a part of legal documents that few people other than the lawyers truly understand or focus on. They determine how the preferred stock will be treated in the event of an initial public offering (IPO). As a result, they end up being relevant only for a small percentage of all companies that receive investment; the majority of them are sold to larger companies, if they succeed.

The rights will include "demand rights," whereby the investors can insist that the company undertake an IPO. They will also include "piggyback rights" that allow the investors to include their shares in the first batches of stock to be sold to investors in the public markets.

If your company is considering an IPO, you will need to delve into this topic in far greater detail. But, at start-up or a very early stage, registration rights do not deserve a lot of attention when you are signing the term sheet—unless your lawyer suggests that the investors are looking for extremely preferential treatment.

Tagalong Rights, Dragalong Rights

Tagalong Rights

Continuing with the train analogy, if the founders want to sell some or all of their stock, the passengers (i.e., the investors) will often want the right to sell the same proportion of their stock. For example, if the founder owns 40% and wants to sell 30% to another company, then the term sheet might say that the founder must also procure an offer from the same acquirer at the same price for three-quarters of the position owned by the investors. Essentially, the investors can "tag along" with the sale of stock by the founder.

Often, this clause must be read in conjunction with two other clauses:

1. A blanket prohibition on the founders selling[1] their stock, without the express approval of the Investor Majority.
2. The vesting provisions for stock and options (see Chapter 11). The stock must be vested for the founder to be able to sell it.

Following is a typical tagalong rights clause:

Each of the parties to this agreement (other than the Company and the Investors) hereby covenants with and undertakes to each of the Investors that in the event of his receiving any offer for the purchase of all or any of his stock and wishing to accept such offer then notwithstanding any other provision of this Agreement or anything contained

---

1 The founders are not allowed to grant any rights of ownership to their stock.

in the Articles of Association that party (hereinafter referred to in this clause as the "Selling Stockholder") shall procure that it shall be an express term of any such agreement for the sale and purchase of his said stock, that each of the Investors shall have the option (for a period of thirty days after receiving written notice of such offer) of selling to the purchaser thereof at the same time the same proportion of the stock held by each of the Investors and/or their Permitted Transferees as the proportion being sold by the Selling Stockholder. The terms of the sale shall be the same for each of the Investors (and their respective Permitted Transferees), as the terms of sale upon which the Selling Stockholder is selling.

Dragalong Rights

When an offer to buy a company is made, some minor stockholders might object. This is not surprising. If, because of the exit preferences, the small stockholders will receive little or no value, they will prefer to sell the company later when they have a chance of realizing more value.

The dragalong clause provides that, where a certain percentage of the shareholder base (say 75 to 80%) or where certain specific shareholders agree, the remaining shareholders can be forced to sell their shareholdings. This clause should be read in conjunction with the forced sale clause, which allows the investors to force a sale of the company after, say, five years. Dragalong rights can be invoked typically at any stage in the company's life, but they normally require the vast bulk of the shareholder base to agree. The forced exit clause at a late stage in the company's development might require only a majority of the investors who themselves might own only a minority of the company.

Similar to the definition of Investor Majority regarding the restricted transactions in Chapter 9, it is critical to understand who can be dragged and who can block a dragalong clause.

For example, investor A owns 40%, investor B owns 36%, founder 1 owns 15%, and founder 2 owns 9%. If the dragalong threshold is set at 75%, the investors can drag the two founders. Note that neither of the investors can be dragged without their consent, even if all the other shareholders vote together. If the threshold is set at greater than 76%, the investors will need one of the founders to agree to the sale in order to drag the other founder. This requirement to put together a coalition becomes important when some of the smaller shareholders are troublesome. It is particularly important when the proceeds of the sale are to be allocated according to exit/liquidation preferences and the investors are getting all or most of the proceeds of the sale. In such a case, not surprisingly, the founders will probably oppose the sale of the company.

The following is a typical dragalong clause:

Each of the parties hereto hereby covenants with and undertakes to the Investors that in the event of a bona fide third party offer (the "Offer") being made by any person (the "Purchaser") to acquire stock comprising more than [80] percent of the issued stock of the Company such party will immediately notify the Investors thereof. If such Offer is in terms acceptable to the Investors but is not acceptable to any other Party (a "Nonaccepting Party") the Investors shall have the option to require the Nonaccepting Party to transfer the same proportion of stock in the Company then held by such Nonaccepting Party to the Purchaser (the person to whom stock is to be transferred being hereinafter referred to as the "Acquirer"), as the proportion of the stock in the Company held by the Investors as is being sold to such person and, subject to the exit/liquidation preference provisions, at the same price per unit of stock as is being offered to other holders of stock of the same class as those held by such Nonaccepting Party by giving notice to that effect to such Nonaccepting Party. If such Nonaccepting Party makes default in transferring his or their stock pursuant to this clause, the Chairman or failing him one of the Directors or any other person appointed by the Board for that purpose shall forthwith be deemed to be the duly appointed attorney of such Nonaccepting Party with full power to execute, complete, and deliver in the name and on behalf of such Nonaccepting Party all such documentation as is required to transfer the relevant stock to the Acquirer and give a good discharge for the price paid for such stock and enter the name of the Acquirer, or such person as he directs, in the register of members as the holder or holders by transfer of the stock so purchased. The Board shall forthwith pay the consideration for the stock into a separate bank account in the Company's name and shall hold such money on trust (but without interest) for such Nonaccepting Party until he or they shall deliver up his or their certificates for the stock so transferred.

Information Rights

Investors will outline, explicitly, the basic information they expect to receive. This will include regular (monthly or quarterly) financial statements. Founders and executives should have no problem providing such information to investors. The reason this is stated explicitly is to provide for situations such as a breakdown in relations between the founders/executives and the investors.

Right of Access to the Premises and Records and Right to Appoint a Consultant

Where the investor does not believe he or she is receiving accurate or timely information, the legal agreement will include the right for the investor or his or her representative to have access to the premises of the company and to examine records. It will generally also include the right to appoint a consultant to examine the company's activities and records and for the company to bear the costs for this.

Preemption Rights

Investors and other shareholders will want the right to subscribe for (acquire) stock in the company in the event of future rounds of fundraising or issues of stock. Preemption rights are normally constructed to allow each shareholder to purchase the same percentage of each upcoming investment round as he or she currently holds in the company. This is a basic protection for stockholders that enables them to cover the possibility of the company selling stock at a reduced price to favored parties.

Transfer Provisions

The transfer provisions establish the process to be followed when a stockholder wishes to sell stock in the company. The investors might have a veto on the founders or executives selling any stock. To the extent that they are allowed to sell stock, there might be tagalong rights in place whereby the seller (e.g., a founder) must procure an offer for a similar proportion of the investor's shares at the same price. The investors will have determined a definition of *permitted transferees*—people or organizations to whom the investor may sell the stock, without being subject to the transfer provisions. In a similar vein, the other stockholders (founders and executives) will have permitted transferees; normally, these are constrained to close family members.

ENTREPRENEUR TIP

Keep the definition of "permitted transferees" narrow. Investors should be able to transfer their stock to other entities or persons within the same ownership or management group, but they should not be able to transfer or sell their stock to other entities. The remaining stockholders will be keen to ensure that the stock is not sold to competitors or other conflicted entities without their having the possibility of acquiring their position through the transfer provisions.

Other than permitted transfers, when a stockholder wishes to sell stock to a third party, the transfer provisions ensure that it is offered around to the other existing stockholders at a set price. Each stockholder will be told the size of his or her preemption right but will typically also have the right to apply for more in the event that other existing stockholders do not pick up their preemption rights. If the existing stockholders do not wish to buy the stock, the selling stockholder is free to sell his or her position to an outside party at a price no less than that offered to existing shareholders.

Exclusivity Clause

The exclusivity clause defines the period of time during which the company agrees to talk to no other investor; the investor uses this time to complete commercial due diligence, negotiate the detailed legal documents, and complete the investment. Exclusivity periods can vary from four to eight weeks, occasionally a little longer.

Term sheets represent indicative terms on which an investor and a company agree to try to complete an investment. A term sheet is not legally binding except in relation to one item—the exclusivity clause. If the company breaches the exclusivity clause by engaging in discussions with other parties, it leaves itself open to a claim from the investor.

The grant of exclusivity to one investor is a point of extreme risk to a company. Up to that time, a company might have been entertaining rival offers, and the balance of power between the two sides might have rested with the company. Once exclusivity is granted, the balance of power moves to the investor. The investor is not compelled to complete the investment and, of course, is not obliged to continue with the same terms. Some investors are notorious for "deal creep"—locking up the deal with an exclusivity clause and adjusting the terms in their own favor as completion approaches. The company might have no option but to go along with the less favorable terms. It might be running short on cash. It might be fearful of having to approach other investors after the exclusivity period; it risks being perceived as damaged goods, failing to close the investment with their chosen investors. Any investor subsequently approached will ask, "Why did the prior investor not close? Did they discover some problem only apparent in detailed due diligence?" "What do they know that we don't know?"

Entrepreneurs will be very cognizant of closing risk prior to signing a term sheet with exclusivity. There are a few tactics for mitigating closing risk:

- Get the investor to do as much due diligence as is possible prior to term sheet terms being discussed. Venture firms with good reputations will aim to do the vast bulk, if not all, of their commercial due diligence prior to discussing terms or putting a term sheet on the table. The closing risk and risk of deal creep is minimized. Many entrepreneurs make the mistake of forcing investors to put term sheets on the table at a premature stage to see what they are thinking in terms of valuation. This is a mistake. Term sheets from investors who have done limited work provide only false comfort to entrepreneurs.

- Keep the exclusivity period as short as possible.
- Talk to other entrepreneurs. Good venture capital companies will be protective of their reputations and will want to be seen to be delivering on their term sheets.
- Get the investor to split the exclusivity period in two. If there are some remaining commercial due diligence items (for example, the company might want to limit customer calls to the one chosen investor and try to delay these until after the signing of the term sheet), the first period of exclusivity, say four weeks, might cover the period to complete this. At this point, the investor might be compelled to give a go/no-go decision and a final confirmation of the terms, after which the only items for discussion are legal points. While lawyers might argue that this sort of arrangement represents semantics and has no real legal basis, it does put some moral pressure on the investor not to move the goalposts late into the exclusivity period.

CHAPTER 11

ALIGNING THE INTERESTS OF FOUNDERS/MANAGEMENT AND INVESTORS

One of the analogies used in Chapter 10 was that of the train engineer and the passengers—the founders and key executives being the engineer, and the investors being the passengers. The train engineer and the passengers need to be going in the same direction.

The legal agreements will encompass a wide variety of provisions to align the interests of the founders/key executives and the investors. These provisions aim to achieve the following:

1. *Reward the founders and key executives for value creation.* Founders will get founders' stock and key executives will be rewarded handsomely from the option pool.
2. *Ensure that the founders and key executives do not try to sell the company before the investors are ready.* There will probably be a blanket prohibition on insiders selling stock without investor consent and, to the extent that they are allowed, the tagalong provisions discussed earlier would make such a sale hard to undertake.
3. *Tie the key people in long enough to give the company a good chance to succeed.* Vesting of stock and options is the common practice for motivating the key people to stay around.
4. *Ensure that the full energy of the founders and key executives is committed to the venture rather than any other activities.* Often, when founders have suffered a few rounds of dilution and own a lot less of the company than they started with, they start to think

about ways of capturing more of the potential prize for themselves. They might think about starting a new company or joining a competitor. Noncompete clauses are required to stop this. All intellectual property relevant to the venture needs to be assigned to it. Also, investors tend to dislike entrepreneurs who have interests in multiple companies. When times get tough in the venture—as they often do—entrepreneurs riding multiple horses might decide to divert their attention from the struggling company.

Founders' Stock

The position of a founder—one of the small number of individuals who establishes the company—offers the potential for significant wealth generation. The first investors normally aim for a significant minority stake, leaving the remainder of the equity for the founders and to be allocated to an option pool for key hires. It is not unusual for the founders to hold 50 to 70% or more of the equity in aggregate after the seed or Series A round. This founders' stock is bought for a nominal amount, unless investment had been required to get the company up and running prior to the investors coming on board.

Option Pool

The option pool, after the seed or Series A investment, is normally set at 10 to 15% of the fully diluted share capital of the company. It may be a lot higher if the founder group has big management gaps that will need to be filled quickly. But the pool is not normally set at a level that contains sufficient options to reward all employees hired on the five- to seven-year journey to an exit. Rather, it will be set at a level that will allow the board (the remuneration committee) to allocate options to all the expected hires over the coming 12 to 24 months or at minimum until after the next round of investment.

The investor and the founders should agree on a broad template for allocating the options in the pool. While this is not normally done prior to the closing of the investment round and will not form part of the legal agreement governing the investment, it is a good test to ensure that the pool will be sufficient.

One way to do this is to identify the expected allocation of options to senior positions yet to be filled. For example, if the pool represents 15% of the company, 2% might be reserved for a CFO, and a further 3% might be reserved for a vice president of sales. The remaining 10% should be sufficient to cover all other general hires for the subsequent 18 to 24 months.

A matrix of allocations by position and by time of hire can help the remuneration committee of the board and the CEO set guidelines for the number of options each type of hire will get. It might be along the lines of Exhibit 11.1.

You will see that the allocation depends on the seniority of the person hired and the date on which the person is hired. Early hires get more options because they take the higher risk of coming onboard earlier.

Future investors, Series B and beyond, will often ask for the size of the option pool to be increased if it has been depleted or if it looks insufficient for the coming 12 to 18 months. If they ask for the pool to be increased by the existing investors, prior to their investing, all the dilution falls on the existing investors. This dilution helps the Series B investors because they can benefit from the existence of a large pool without suffering the associated dilution. This benefit is twofold. First, a larger pool provides money that will attract great employees. Second, if there are any unallocated options in the pool at the time of sale of the company, the effective ownership share of all of the stockholders, including the Series B investors, will receive a minor increase.

Most investors and boards of very early-stage venture-backed companies are not interested in making money out of employees through

Exhibit 11.1 Sample Grid for Allocation of Options

Position	Hired in Next Six Months	Hired in Following Six Months	Hired in Year 2
Senior engineer	0.5% (1 hire)	No hires	0.2% (2 hires)
Junior engineers	0.1% (10 hires)	0.05% (5 hires)	0.03% (10 hires)
Senior salespeople	—	—	—
Junior salespeople	—	—	—

options. Therefore, they will typically aim to have the exercise price on the options be as low as will be allowed by the tax authorities. A critical aspect of an option scheme is the vesting arrangements.

Vesting Arrangements

Vesting is one of the most important provisions in any venture capital agreement, yet is treated in a cursory manner on some term sheets, only to rear its head as a highly contentious issue when negotiating the detailed legal documents.

While there are many different ways of constructing vesting arrangements, the basic goal is to bind founders and option holders to the company by ensuring that their ownership position is earned over time. For example, after the Series A round, a founder might own 20% of the company. But, if this shareholding is subject to vesting over four years, he or she only gets beneficial ownership of 5% if he or she stays for one year, 10% for two years, 15% for three years, and the full 20% for four years.

Legally, this is effected by a set of vesting clauses. Vesting compels the founders and option holders[1] to sell back a percentage of their stock, typically at a nominal value. This percentage declines over time, motivating the founder/option holder to stay with the company.

Many founders are happy to have vesting applied to option holders, but balk when it is applied to founders' stock. Their reticence is hardly surprising; they run the risk of being forced out of "their" company and having a large share of their ownership position taken away. Investors have a very different view. If the founder delivers on the promise of building a valuable company, then vesting will not cause a problem. However, if the founder leaves (or is forced to leave by the board because of underperformance) during the vesting period, this unvested stock will be required as an incentive for the founder's replacement.

---

1 In the case of option holders, when their options are vested, they have the right to exercise them.

Vesting works particularly well when there is a small group of founders. Take, for example, the situation in which three colleagues start a company and own 20% of the company each after the first round of investment. A few months later, two of them would be very upset if their third colleague left the company for a high-paying job, leaving them to slog through the building of the company over the next five to seven years. The 20% shareholding of the departing founder is a deadweight on the company. Vesting solves this problem.

Different law firms and different venture capital companies utilize slightly different legal approaches to vesting. However, rather than worry about the legal niceties, the entrepreneur should focus on the commercial questions regarding vesting.

How Much of the Stock Will Be Subject to Vesting?

The starting point of most institutional investors is that all stock owned by founders and all options allocated to key executives must be subject to vesting. The capitalization table in Chapter 8 (Exhibit 8.1) is now shown as Exhibit 11.2.

The founder stock owned by Smith, Jones, and Davis (7%, 10%, and 10%, respectively) and any options allocated from the pool (13%) would be subject to vesting. The options would vest from the time of allocation of the option to the option holder. Sometimes this is the date

Exhibit 11.2 Capitalization Table for Company X

	Initial Stock Position	Initial Ownership	Series B Stock Issued	Issued Share Capital	Percent Ownership	Fully Diluted Share Capital	Percent Ownership
Founders/Executives							
J. Smith	10,000	10.0%	0	10,000	8%	10,000	7%
M. Jones	15,000	15.0%	0	15,000	12%	15,000	10%
A. Davis	15,000	15.0%	0	15,000	12%	15,000	10%
Investor A	40,000	40.0%	10,000	50,000	38%	50,000	33%
Investor B	0	0.0%	40,000	40,000	31%	40,000	27%
Option pool	20,000	20.0%		0	0%	20,000	13%
Total stock	100,000	100.0%	50,000	130,000	100%	150,000	100%

of employment, and sometimes it is the date of formal establishment of the option scheme.

Seed and first round investors, in a recently established company, want all the founder equity and options to be subject to vesting. Since the company is new and all the value is yet to be created, the founders should have to "earn" all their shareholding. If any of them decide to leave shortly after the investment is made, why should they get a free ride on the invested dollars and the hard work of other founders and executives? Vesting requires fairly elaborate legal drafting, and so is often not put in place until the first institutional investment is made. If the company does an early angel round, angel investors do not necessarily demand it. They might assume that the institutional investors will put it in place later.

In the case of a Series B or Series C round, the founders and executives have a better case for having only a portion of the stock subject to vesting from the date of the B or C investment. The starting point of some B and C investors is that the vesting clock must start again, but this can be demoralizing for executives who have already worked through two of their five years of vesting after the Series A investment. The rationale of the B or C investors in seeking to reset the clock tends to be, What happens if a key person decides to leave shortly after our investment? However, the founders and key executives should be able to make a strong argument for their holdings being at least partially vested if they have been in the business for some years.

Over What Time Period Will the Vesting Occur? What Is the Vesting Schedule?

A typical vesting period is four to five years. Seed and first round investors might ask for five years since five to seven years is not an unusual time frame for the company to achieve its ambitions. Later investors might agree to a shorter period. The starting point for many investors is to have the vesting work in yearly increments over the agreed time frame. If skillfully negotiated, the founders can typically

Exhibit 11.3 Sample Five-year Vesting Schedule

Length of Time Executive Remains as an Employee	Proportion of Stock to Be Sold Back at Nominal Value (Unvested Stock)
1 year	80%
15 months	75%
18 months	70%
21 months	65%
24 months	60%
60 months	0%

get this changed to a "one-year cliff with quarterly vesting thereafter." A five-year vesting schedule might be as shown in Exhibit 11.3.

At What Price Is the Stock Sold Back?

The price to be paid for the stock is normally very low—maybe the higher of nominal value or the price per share subscribed to by the founder (if the founder paid for his or her stock).

Under What Circumstances Will the Vesting Be Accelerated?

Most vesting schedules allow for automatic acceleration in the case of the death or certified disability[2] of the founder/executive. The person (or their estate) would not be required to sell back any unvested shares at a nominal value.

There is typically much more negotiation around acceleration of the vesting schedule in the event of sale or IPO of the company. When

---

2 Requiring the founder or executive to depart from the company.

the company is sold, the acquiring company will want to buy 100% of the stock of the company. However, they will also wish to lock in key employees for some period of time. They may wish to roll over the vesting arrangements in place in the company (e.g., if the vesting schedule has two years to run, the stock in the purchasing company allocated to the founders and executives of the acquired company might vest over two years).

At the time of sale of the company, founders and executives tend to be in a position of power vis-à-vis outside investors; they know they will probably be required to sign new employment contracts with the purchaser, committing them for one to three years. They might demand some concessions from the outside investors who probably face no, or a limited, lock-up period[3] (if they received stock rather than cash as the purchase price). If the board of the company being acquired has the right, but not the obligation, to accelerate the vesting schedule at the time of acquisition, this should give it the flexibility to solve this issue.

Similar considerations come into play at the time of an IPO. The underwriters will want the key executives to commit to staying with the company after the IPO; one piece of leverage for the board of the company in extracting this commitment is the discretion over the acceleration of the unvested portion of the executive's stockholding.

Is There a "Good-Leaver/Bad-Leaver" Override in the Vesting Provisions?

One feature seen in Europe more than in the United States is the use of good-leaver/bad-leaver provisions. These provide discretion to the board of the company to designate the person as a good leaver, in which case the person leaving gets to hold vested stock, or as a bad leaver, in which case the person leaving is compelled to sell back all stock at nominal value.

---

3 The selling shareholders might be bound not to sell their shares to the purchaser for 3, 6, or 12 months after the sale.

There are a few other variations on the good-leaver/bad-leaver condition. Founders and executives tend to resist good-leaver/bad-leaver provisions because such provisions jeopardize their entire stockholding since their holding can be subject to the discretion of a board that might have lost confidence in them.

Noncompete Agreements

Naturally, when investors invest in a business, they are heavily dependent on management performing and being committed to the business. The investors will want to ensure that the founders and executives cannot abandon the business and go into competition with it. There will be a noncompete agreement, either in the employment contract with the executives or in the shareholders' agreement—maybe in both.

The noncompete clause will define the "relevant business," which will cover current activities and likely future activities of the company. It will also define the "relevant geography"—the territory in which the executive is prohibited from competing. It is important to define these carefully. If defined too broadly (e.g., the relevant geography is defined as the world), there is a danger that if a company tries to pursue the executive for breach of the noncompete clause, the court will deem the provision null and void because it effectively prohibits the executive from earning a living. If defined too narrowly, the business might find a disgruntled executive (e.g., if he or she suffered aggressive dilution of his or her stockholding) in competition with it.

Similarly, the period of the noncompete clause should not be too onerous. Two years from the date of departure often ends up as the compromise period. One point of note for investors: it is useful to define the noncompete period as starting from the date of resignation of the executive or him or her being a stockholder in the company, whichever is later. This closes off the possibility of an executive or founder starting a new competitive business while still having the right to receive confidential information about the company because of his or her shareholding.

Intellectual Property Assignment

Naturally, all intellectual property (IP) developed by an executive, founder, or employee while associated with the company should belong to the company. If it doesn't, the company might be forced to enter into a costly license agreement to get access to the IP. Similarly, any IP developed by the founders prior to joining the company that is relevant to the business will need to be assigned to the business, if it has not already been.

Warranties and Representations

At the time of making the investment, the investor will be concerned that there are problems that he or she does not know about, but of which the founders and executives are aware. These might include liabilities not on the balance sheet, threatened lawsuits, faulty or challenged intellectual property, lack of proper title to real estate assets, and major problems with customers. Over the years, law firms have built up a big standard inventory of items that they want the founders and key executives to warrant. The list is too long to include here.

The company will then prepare a disclosure letter listing the relevant facts relating to the warranty list. For example, it might cover known patents of competitors that might conflict with the company's intellectual property, receivables that might not be collected, possible claims against the company, and so on. The disclosure letter is the one final opportunity for the company and the individual warrantors to tell the investors about every item they need to be aware of.

The investors will typically ask all founders to be warrantors—even if they are not executives (assuming they hold a material shareholding). They will also likely ask the CEO to be a warrantor because he or she is in the best position to know if there are any items the investors need to be aware of.

If it turns out that the warrantors (company and individual) have not told the truth, the investors may pursue a legal case against them. This is extremely rare in practice. The only times when warranties are pursued are when there has been fraud or a gross violation of the principle that investors need to be made aware of highly material actual or contingent liabilities or other issues.

The company and the individual warrantors should keep the following in mind:

- Always fully disclose everything of which you are aware.
- Limit the size of the claim that the investors can make. Typically, the company will be liable for the entire amount of the investment. Individual warrantors might be able to cap their liability at a multiple of their salary.
- Keep the period as short as possible, perhaps one year or the final sign-off of the next set of financial statements by the auditors, whichever is later. Tax warranties will run for longer—often five to six years.
- Try to raise the minimum amount of a warranty claim. In practice, a warranty claim should be for at least 5% or more of the amount of an investment.

PART V

EXERCISES

CHAPTER 12

TERM SHEET EXERCISES

P art V turns the theory of the prior chapters on term sheet clauses into the practice of term sheets seen regularly in venture capital deals. If entrepreneurs are going to negotiate effectively with investors, they need to understand how the investors are thinking. A term sheet gives clues to an investor's view of a business—the potential ultimate value in the business, the importance of different founders, the time frame over which the investor expects to see an exit, the types of downside risks, and so on. By uncovering these clues in the term sheet, the entrepreneur will see what the investor is trying to achieve. This will make it easier to reach a win-win deal. The entrepreneur will also be able to concentrate on the terms that are likely to be negotiable rather than running head-on into the must-haves for the investor.

The term sheet will reflect the level of competition that the investor perceives from other investors in relation to the deal. A term sheet from an investor who believes that other known and unknown investors are also circling the company will inevitably be more benign in comparison to one in which the investor thinks that he or she has a monopoly on the deal. In addition to more favorable terms, the deal will close faster.

The best thing that any CEO or CFO can do when dealing with investors is to manage the perception of the potential investors regarding the competitive tension around the deal. Of course, this is perception rather than reality. The smart investor will ask seemingly friendly questions such as: "Who else is looking at the deal? Are other investors keeping you busy? Have you had to prepare this analysis before? Have other investors talked to these customers?" This friendly investor is trying to test out the level of competition and feel his or her way to the low end of the valuation range that the entrepreneur will accept.

The following Creditica term sheet mini cases are hypothetical and simplified, but they represent common situations faced by entrepreneurs and investors.

MINI CASE ONE: TERM SHEETS 1, 2, AND 3

Creditica is at its start-up stage and needs $2M to achieve its first major commercial and technical milestones. You are the CEO, and over the past three months you have been cultivating a few potential investors for the company.

Three term sheets (1, 2, and 3) have been given to the company.

- What is each investor aiming to achieve with the term sheet?
- Which terms in each term sheet should you (the CEO) aim to negotiate with the investors? What should you be aiming for?

	Term Sheet 1	Term Sheet 2	Term Sheet 3
Investor	Small VC ($20M fund)	Large VC ($200M fund)	Bank of Northeast States • Fifth-largest credit card issuer in the United States • Key prospect for Creditica
Ownership	$2M for 20%	$2M for 25% Option to invest additional $2M at $20M valuation within next two years	$2M for 15%

(Continued)

	Term Sheet 1	Term Sheet 2	Term Sheet 3
Instrument	Participating preferred stock (12% coupon rate) Full ratchet antidilution without pay-to-play	Convertible preferred stock (10% coupon rate) No antidilution	Convertible preferred stock (0%) No antidilution
Vesting provisions	Founders: • 50% vested up front • Remaining 50% over four years CEO and others: over four years	All managers: over four years	All managers: over three years
Decision rights	Normal vetoes	Normal vetoes	Normal vetoes Right of first refusal on sale of company Influence over product road map
Other factors	Good at nurturing early-stage ventures	Lots of experience and contacts in financial services software sector	First-class reputation

In a perfect world you (the CEO) would have been able to line up parallel term sheets and pick the clear winner. In practice, this is incredibly difficult to achieve. Some investors move fast through their due diligence. Others might be tied up on another deal. An ideal investor with a great reputation and good contacts might have come late to the deal. In practice, each term sheet will have its own advantages and disadvantages.

What is each investor aiming to achieve with the term sheet?
The **small VC** has given a good valuation ($8M premoney). He has also been quite generous in relation to the vesting provisions—allowing 50% up front. His overall goal is to cozy up with the founders and to position himself as the benign, helpful VC in comparison to the large VC. One of his primary concerns (which, of course, he hasn't communicated to the

founders and CEO) is his inability to follow his investment in future rounds. He will have committed 10% of his fund to this company in this round; he won't want to invest any more. If the company misses its milestones, he won't be there to bridge the gap.

The vetoes will give him a lot of comfort, and the antidilution provision will provide him a weapon for negotiating a preferential deal in the event that the company doesn't perform well.

The **big VC** has given the poorest valuation (premoney valuation of $6M). In addition, she has carved out a very nice option to invest more money. While the $20M valuation looks high compared to the current valuation of $6M, it is a one-sided bet. Only if the company does exceedingly well will she exercise it. She is not too concerned about antidilution and protecting herself. The best way to protect one's investment is to have lots of reserves—she knows this. With a $200M fund, she might be expecting to put $10M or more into the company over time. Her main concern is to get a high ownership position in the early rounds (when the price of the stock is hopefully at its lowest point) that she knows she can protect against dilution in future rounds.

The **bank's** main goal in investing is to learn from the company and to build a stake that will give it an implicit option to buy the company. In the event that Creditica's product truly delivers the value it promises, it could prove to be a huge competitive weapon for the bank in the strategy to move from number 5 position in the United States to number 1.

The bank has paid the highest valuation and is not worried about it. While it might pay a high relative price for its initial 15%, it knows that, if the product proves to be good, it might have to pay only a modest price for the remaining 85%. Its power to write more checks will distort future investment rounds and allow it to manipulate events. Its main concerns are to get the vetoes, the right of first refusal, and the influence over the product development road map. The right of first refusal is particularly pernicious—no other buyers will invest the large amount of time and effort into conducting due diligence if they know they can be trumped by an inside buyer. The inside buyer, of course, will have the best information set regarding the prospects of the company, and the third-party buyer will know this. Venture capital insiders call this sequence of events a *creeping acquisition*.

Which terms in each term sheet should the CEO aim to negotiate with the investors? What should you be aiming for?

Small VC. The CEO should be concerned that the small VC will have little or no more money to invest in the company after the first round. If the company does well, then the problem is reduced, but not eliminated. Future investors will want the existing investors to invest in the Series B round to show good faith in the prospects for the business and to demonstrate that the price per unit of stock the Series B investor is paying is not unreasonably high. If the company does poorly and the price per unit of stock in the second round is lower than it was in the first round, then the small investor will seek to exercise his antidilution rights. Both investor B and the founders/executive management will want to avoid this. Events can come to a stalemate with the A investor wanting to exercise his or her antidilution rights (and also having lots of vetoes over new issues of stock, etc.) and the B investor wanting the A investor to take aggressive dilution or even to be wiped out. All VCs have been in these situations, and they are not pleasant. A good solution here would be for the small VC to split the investment with another small VC—each owning 10% and each subject to the pay-to-play provisions.

Rather than trying to squeeze the valuation a little higher, the CEO would be better served by aiming to get the antidilution provision out of the term sheet. If the small VC won't accept this, the CEO should insist on a pay-to-play provision in which the small VC only gets his antidilution rights if he invests his pro rata share of the round.

The participating feature of the preferred shares offered by the small VC is less attractive than that offered by the other two investors. The entrepreneur should aim to have the participation capped at, say, three times the price per share proposed or perhaps have the stock redesignated as convertible preferred stock. Either way, the entrepreneur should concentrate on solving the antidilution problem first.

Large VC. The terms here (other than the valuation) are relatively benign. The large VC will be able to look after herself in any future fund-raising rounds. The CEO should first work on getting the option taken out. The option is a free ride for the large VC. The CEO should then work on the valuation, perhaps targeting to raise the valuation to the level of the small VC, from, say, $6M to $8M.

This is the cleanest deal and, if skillfully negotiated, you as the CEO should be able to get a better valuation by using the two other term sheets as leverage.

Bank of Northeast States. This is the hardest one of all. Executives in early-stage companies are often dazzled when they get the attention of a large strategic investor. The strategic investor is always generous with promises of sales, access to additional customers, and the ultimate carrot of perhaps acquiring the company at an early point.

As CEO, you need to be very careful. You want the Bank of Northeast States as a reference customer and don't want to antagonize the people there. In your negotiation, you should focus exclusively on the softer issues. The right of first refusal must be taken out. No deal, irrespective of the valuation, should be accepted with it included. Your negotiating goal should be to make the bank a passive investor. No seat on the board. Limited information rights. No right of first refusal. No influence over the product development road map, other than maybe a right of consultation.

It might be worth accepting the valuation but reducing the amount of money accepted from the investor, say to $1M, thus reducing its shareholding to below 10% and aim to bring in a purely financial investor alongside. While strategic investors are best avoided, it would be far preferable to have two strategic investors at 10% each rather than one at 20%. They might keep each other honest.

The shareholding given to the bank should be small enough to allow it to be subject to dragalong rights. For example, the bank can be forced to sell its shareholding if the vast majority of the other shareholders find a good offer that the bank is unwilling to match. A good term to negotiate into the deal would be that the other shareholders in Creditica have a right to buy back the bank's shareholding for $1M if it doesn't conclude a deal to purchase Creditica's software for $0.5M within 12 months.

You, the CEO, should consider whether to combine the small VC and the bank into one investor consortium and aim to create competition for the deal between this consortium and the big VC.

Mini Case Two: Term Sheet 4

It is the fourth quarter of 2009. Creditica has achieved the milestones established in the case (product finished, two early customers). The initial $2M ($0.50 per share) had been raised in 2008 from Gamma Ventures, a Chicago-based VC firm with a $40M fund, in return for a 25% share of the company (in preferred stock). However, the new funding, planned for late 2009, has not been closed because commercial progress had not been made fast enough to bring in a new investor prior to the end of 2009. Gamma has offered to put up an additional $1M to cover the capital needs of the company over the next six months. It is expected to take four months to close a new $3M round of investment from a new investor.

Why did Gamma structure the financing as proposed in term sheet 4? How should the founders respond to the proposal?

Term Sheet 4

Investor:	Gamma Ventures
Date of investment:	December 31, 2009
Amount of investment:	$1M
Form of investment:	Convertible loan
Conversion terms:	Convertible into same class of shares (at a 25% price discount) purchased by a third-party investor on an investment of at least $3M
Repayment and interest terms:	Repayable on demand by Gamma after June 30, 2010, if not converted and subject to an interest rate of 10% per annum
Security:	Gamma will take security over the assets of the business (tangible, current, and intellectual property assets)

Why did Gamma structure the financing as proposed in term sheet 4?

Gamma is probably broadly satisfied with the way its investment has progressed to date. The company has met its milestones, albeit a bit behind schedule, which is not unusual for an early-stage company. Gamma's main goal is to see the company safely raise the new round from a third party on favorable terms.

Gamma's investment is a bridge to a future round.

Structuring the investment as a loan convertible into the next round is smart. Rather than buy more Series A stock, Gamma wants to try to get the $1M included into the Series B round. The Series B round will be higher in the layers of exit preferences and will have more say in the decision rights. The 25% discount on the next round price is a little kicker to reward Gamma; the $1M invested in the bridge round will have been at risk in the company for longer than the money coming from a new investor.

Gamma is worried about a few issues. Failure to raise a new round on time might lead to the company running out of money and being forced into liquidation. A delay in raising the round beyond the next six months would require another internal financing by Gamma. With a modest fund size of $40M, Gamma is already concerned about the amount of money ($3M) it has invested in the deal. If the new investor perceives that the company is running out of money and that the existing investors are tapped out, he or she may try a washout round or a down round—even if the underlying business is not performing poorly.

This is the reason that Gamma has included two relatively harsh fallback terms. First, the loan becomes repayable on demand in six months. If no new funding is in place at that time, the repayment condition can become a strong bargaining tool versus the founders. Taking security over the assets will also work in Gamma's favor. If the business goes into liquidation, the loan from Gamma would rank above most other payables. In theory Gamma could get hold of the key asset (the source code to the software product) and either restart the company or sell it. If Gamma had invested the $1M in preferred stock convertible into the next round rather than as loan stock, it would not have been able to take security over the assets. It also wouldn't have been able to make the money repayable. Preferred stock can be redeemed only if the business has accumulated profits, which Creditica clearly hasn't at this point.

How should the founders respond to the proposal?

The founders do not have a lot of options because the company is nearly out of money. The convertible loan proposal is not unreasonable, and it avoids a hard discussion about the valuation (price per unit of stock) of the company in Q4 2009; it lets a third-party investor set the price. If, instead of being convertible into the next round, Gamma had set a low stock price in Q4 2009, this would have given a signal to the new investor to put in a low valuation in the Series B round. This is not in Gamma's or the founders' interests.

The founders might seek to have the repayment clause extended beyond June to give themselves a little more room, although the cash would be starting to run out around that point.

In reality, the real negotiation around the $1M bridge loan will take place when the new investor puts down a term sheet. Will the B investor let the $1M convert into the B round? How will he view the 25% discount? Will he ask Gamma for fresh cash beyond the $1M loan into the new round to show good faith and continued belief in the business? While the letter of Gamma's term sheet states how the conversion should work, the relative negotiating power and inclination of the new investor will determine exactly how the B round is constructed.

MINI CASE THREE: TERM SHEET 5

It is November 2009. In 2008, Gamma Ventures invested $2M for 20% of Creditica in Series A preferred stock (at $50 per share—40,000 shares) with full ratchet antidilution protection.* Management owns the remaining 80%.

---

* If there is a subsequent issue of shares at a lower price, the shares purchased by Gamma are to be repriced as if they had been originally issued at the lower price. See Chapter 9 for variants on this formula.

Creditica has not achieved the commercial milestones set out in the case but has made some progress nonetheless. However, the company will run out of money in December 2009. A new investor, Hard Rock Partners, has presented term sheet 5.

Term Sheet 5	
Investor:	Hard Rock Partners
Date of Investment:	December 31, 2009
Amount of investment:	$3M
Form of investment:	Series B convertible preferred stock
Ownership:	50% of the company
Board seats and decision rights:	Hard Rock to nominate one director to the board. Most decision rights to be reserved for the Series B investor.

What shareholding will the founders, Gamma, and Hard Rock own after Hard Rock's investment?

The best place to start is by working out the new shareholdings assuming that there is no antidilution protection in place for Gamma. See Exhibit 12.1.

Exhibit 12.1 Without Antidilution Protection: Capitalization Table after Hard Rock Investment

	Series A			Series B		
	Amount Invested (million)	Number of Shares	Percent of Ownership	Amount Invested (million)	Number of Shares	Percent of Ownership
Management	0	160,000	80.0%		160,000	40.0%
Gamma Ventures	2	40,000	20.0%		40,000	10.0%
Hard Rock Partners		0		3	200,000	50.0%
Total		200,000	100.0%		400,000	100.0%
Price per share	$50.00			$15.00		

Since Hard Rock is to own 50% of the company, it must be issued stock equivalent to the total amount of stock already outstanding. Gamma has 40,000 shares, and management has 160,000. Hard Rock will receive 200,000 shares.

This situation changes dramatically when the antidilution protection on Gamma's Series A stock is taken into account. In the Series A round, Gamma negotiated full ratchet antidilution protection for its investment. This means that the money Gamma invested in the A round is viewed as issued at the B round price, if the B round investor invests at a lower price. Gamma's stock remains as Series A stock rather than being converted into Series B stock. It is issued more Series A stock as a bonus. See Exhibit 12.2.

The new capitalization table is complicated to work out. The simplest way is to allocate 50% of the company to Hard Rock in accordance with its term sheet. Gamma's shareholding has to be two-thirds of Hard Rock's because it invested $2M and its stock will be deemed to be issued at the same price as Hard Rock's $3M. Gamma gets 33.33%. All that remains is 16.67%, which belongs to management. As management has 160,000 shares, it is possible to solve for the number of shares to allocate to Hard Rock (480,000) and the bonus shares (280,000) to allocate to Gamma in satisfaction of its antidilution rights.

This gives a price per share to both Hard Rock and Gamma of $6.25.

Exhibit 12.2 With Antidilution Protection: Capitalization Table after Hard Rock Investment

	Series A			Series B		
	Amount Invested (million)	Number of Shares	Percent of ownership	Amount Invested (million)	Number of Shares	Percent of Ownership
Management	0	160,000	80.0%		160,000	16.67%
Gamma Ventures	2	40,000	20.0%		320,000	33.33%
Hard Rock Partners		0		3	480,000	50.00%
Total		200,000	100.0%		960,000	100.00%
Price per share	$50.00			$6.25		

As you can see, the impact of the antidilution is very severe on management. Management's share is diluted severely from 80% to 16.67%. If no antidilution protection were in place, management's position would have gone from 80% to 40%—still a big reduction.

What are the consequences of Hard Rock's investment?
Management will move from the position of true owner of the business to a small stockholder. While the managers are probably disappointed with the valuation offered by Hard Rock, they are probably angry with Gamma. A natural alliance between management and Hard Rock would not be unusual to prevent or mitigate the impact of the antidilution clause. Hard Rock wants the managers to own a significant share—to keep them motivated to build the business. Hard Rock might insist that Gamma not exercise its antidilution rights or that it limit itself to, say, 25% of the business. Since Hard Rock is the party with the power to walk away from the deal, its views will prevail if it negotiates effectively. It could, for example, insist that an option pool be created equivalent to 30% of the fully diluted share capital of the company—this 30% would be used to reset the ownership position of the management team.

This example shows the potentially corrosive effect of antidilution when the stock price of a company declines between private funding rounds. It can be hard for a management team to argue against an antidilution clause in initial legal arrangements. It is easy for the investor to make the point that if management believes the valuation of the business, it shouldn't be concerned about antidilution protection that comes into effect only if the business proves to be overvalued.

Mini Case Four: Term Sheet 6

It is the fourth quarter of 2009. Gamma Ventures, the $40M fund from Chicago, invested an initial $2M in Creditica in 2007. The original plan had been to raise a second round of investment from new investors in late 2008. But, as investment sentiment for technology companies was very weak at the time, it fell to Gamma Ventures to invest the second round of $3M in Q1 2009. Gamma Ventures now owns 60%, and management owns 40%.

The company grew extremely rapidly in 2009 as the market took off. Creditica scaled up its cost base to take advantage of the opportunity. However, a number of very large sale opportunities have been delayed for a few months. There is an unforeseen immediate cash need for $1M. Gamma proposed the following term sheet. Why?

Term Sheet 6

Gamma Ventures

Instruments:	Guarantee of bank loan up to $1M.
	Option to purchase 6% of company for $300K.
Option:	Option is exercisable for two years after which time it lapses.
Board membership:	Two founders
	Two Gamma Ventures representatives
	One independent chairperson (appointment to require the approval of Gamma)

Why did Gamma propose this term sheet?

Gamma is simultaneously very worried and very excited about this investment. On the positive side, Creditica has scaled up its revenues (and costs) and has the potential to be a very big hit for Gamma. If it is sold for $67M or more, it will pay back Gamma's entire fund (60% = $40M). In practice, it would only need to be sold for less than the $67M because of Gamma's exit preferences. If the company continues on its current business trajectory, it has the potential to be sold for $100M or more.

On the negative side, Gamma has too much money committed to this deal. The $6M represents 15% of its fund, and more might be required. Under normal circumstances no one deal should take up more than 10% of the fund. A good spread within a portfolio would suggest 15 plus companies. Therefore, it has become too big and important for Gamma to fail. This is dangerous because it can cloud the rational judgment of the principals of the fund.

Gamma has no alternative but to put up the additional $1M in capital. This has been done as a guarantee of a bank loan rather than as a straight equity investment or as a loan or preferred stock convertible into the next round. This may make sense for a few reasons:

1. Gamma may have taken the view that it owns enough of the company—at 60%. Since the company desperately needs the cash, Gamma could have insisted that its share be raised to 70%. But any new investor will almost certainly insist that management get re-upped in options, thus negating any ownership benefit that Gamma might have received.

2. Gamma doesn't want to put up any cash unless it has to. If a new Series B round occurs in a quarter or two, the loan might be repaid without Gamma having to put up any cash. Also, if the outstanding sales opportunities close quickly, the cash position of the company might improve without the need to draw on Gamma's loan guarantee or to close another round of investment. If the capital went in as a convertible loan or as convertible preferred stock, its money would definitely be in the company.

3. Gamma has taken an option to invest $300K more. This could have a lot of value if, by the time the option to invest $300K runs out, Creditica is clearly a winner and Gamma would be happy to have a larger percentage of its fund invested.

Gamma has restructured the board to give itself a lot of power. The independent chairman is subject to the approval of Gamma.

MINI CASE FIVE: TERM SHEET 7

It is the fourth quarter of 2009. Gamma Ventures invested an initial $2M in Creditica in 2008. At that time Gamma Ventures received 40% of the equity of the company in Series A convertible preferred stock (4M shares at 50 cents each) with an exit preference. It received full ratchet antidilution protection for its shares.

Progress in the company was slow because of software development problems and difficulties in lining up reference customers. The company will be out of money in two months. Sigma Ventures has agreed to invest $1M in the company based on term sheet 7.

Term Sheet 7

Sigma Ventures

Amount of investment:	$1M
Instrument:	Series B convertible preferred stock with an exit preference. The exit preference on the Series A stock is to be eliminated.
Price per share:	1 cent
Board membership:	Sigma to have two board members
Option pool:	An option pool representing 25% of the total equity (post Sigma investment) will be put in place
Vesting:	Any founders' shares or options will vest over a period of five years starting from Q1 2010
Antidilution:	Sigma will have full ratchet antidilution protection on its shares

What will the ownership structure of the company be after this round?

Sigma wants to restart the company. It has set the price per share at a nominal level so that the money it invests will buy 100% of the company. It has provided for management to be re-upped to a 25% ownership position through options. These options will vest over five years from the date of the investment. No credit will be given to the managers for the two prior years in which they worked for the company. The board will be dominated by Sigma. Sigma also wants to eliminate the liquidation/exit preference on the Series A stock.

Gamma is in a tough position. It has antidilution rights, and it has a legal right to receive a very large bonus issue of stock that, in effect, would protect its shareholding. But this is only a theoretical right. If Sigma is to put up all the capital, it can rewrite most terms of the prior agreement by simply refusing to invest the new capital, thus letting the company fail.

The only protection for Gamma in reality is to invest its pro rata pre-emption rights, which come to 40% of the $1M being subscribed.

One alternative open to Gamma (if it decides not to take up its pre-emption rights) is brinkmanship. It can refuse to sign the new legal agreement governing the subscription of stock by Sigma. The legal agreement with Gamma almost certainly will require the approval of Gamma for any new issue of stock. If Sigma is extremely keen to do the deal with Creditica, it might make some concessions. It might raise the price per share and let Gamma hold onto a modest percentage of ownership.

Alternatively, Sigma might reduce Gamma's ownership percentage to virtually zero through aggressive dilution but allow it to hold onto its liquidation/exit preference. In effect, if the company is sold, Sigma will receive the first $1M, Gamma will receive the next $2M, and Sigma and management will share the remaining proceeds at a 75/25 ratio. Gamma will have a chance of getting its capital back, but no more than that.

SECURITY PORTAL INC.

T he case in this appendix illustrates the wide variety of options facing the entrepreneur when deciding how to take a new venture forward.

SECURITY PORTAL INC. (SPI)

J ohn Smith worked in materials research in the defense industry for 20 years. From the research he undertook over that period, he believes he can develop technology to screen vehicles automatically for weapons, explosives, and hazardous materials (nuclear, chemical, biological, etc.). By exposing the vehicle to radio waves previously unexploited in security screening, he believes it should be possible to develop a profile of all the materials in the vehicle. Such a scanner might be deployed at shipping ports or access routes into cities.

John and his team have the expertise to develop the radio front-end module for such a system, although they have limited experience in large customer-ready scanning systems for deployment in the field.

In light of terrorist and criminal threats, John expects the market for such a scanner to grow rapidly. There are no products on the market today that can screen vehicles for so many threat objects. John believes that his approach for designing such a product will be unique and that the intellectual property will be defensible.

Access to customers in the market will be very challenging. There are three to four large, established companies selling to the transportation security authorities today, and these authorities seem to prefer products from established companies rather than untested newcomers. They are notoriously conservative, having been burned before by recommended products that didn't work or that broke down too easily. The buyers of the product will be city governments, airports, and the like. But they will buy based only on recommendations from the transportation security authorities—in fact, given the high cost, they may need to be mandated to buy such equipment.

The prize is clearly very big. The market is large, and a business selling $50M to $100M of equipment each year might be sold for $200M to $400M to a large security equipment company or might have the potential to undertake an IPO. But getting to this stage involves extraordinary risks for investors asked to invest today.

The investors have lots of questions: Will John and the team be able to develop the technology? Even if the raw technology can be developed, can it be converted into a product and strengthened for use in the real world? At a low enough cost that it can meet a target price point for sale? Will the transportation security authorities in the major countries test it and sign off on it? Within a reasonable time frame? Will they ultimately mandate its use? Will competitors come up with something better in the meantime? Will there actually be a market for this type of equipment?

The aggregate amount of funding required to take the project all the way through a market rollout is likely to be $30M to $50M.

John is wondering how to take the project forward.

Raising the $30M to $50M in one investment round is almost certainly impossible—absent the perennial investment fools who occasionally raise their heads! If the project is to get the finance required over its life, the plan needs to be broken down into a series of logical stepping-stones.

If John were to adopt the cookie-cutter strategy for an early-stage technology business, it might look something like Exhibit A.1.

Exhibit A.1 Security Portal Inc. (SPI): Likely Plan

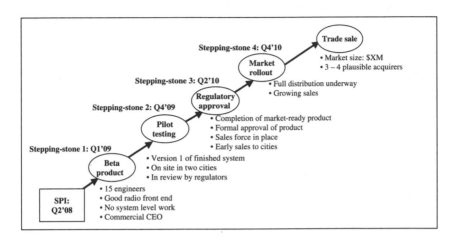

Under this plan, the company would develop a beta product using a Series A investment round, focusing on the key technical differentiators (the radio front end). The team would recruit a CEO, probably from the security equipment business, who has prior relationships with the regulatory authorities or the cities. The Series B round might allow the system to be completed and put into pilot testing with one or two cities, under the close oversight of the regulatory authorities. If the product proves itself in the field, with the Series C round the company would push the regulators to approve the product and, hopefully, to mandate its use in specific situations. A sales force would be established to push the products to the city and local governments. The final two rounds of investment would be used to build top line revenue.

But the possibilities are a lot more complex than the linear plan suggested above. There are a number of big things that can go wrong:

- Can the team develop a system, not just a radio front end?
- Will the regulatory authorities approve the product? How can a small company get "airtime" with them?
- Can SPI access the market, given the distribution power of the large security equipment companies?

On the positive side, a number of new business opportunities may present themselves, if the basic product can be made to work at a cheap enough price:

- *Human portal products.* Products such as the metal detectors currently in place in airports today might take off as a separate market.
- *Handheld detectors.* A portable handheld detector would be useful for customs, police, and city officials
- *Cargo screening.* Similar to vehicle screening, the transportation security authorities might determine that it is also necessary to screen all cargo moving by ship, train, or truck. This would be an entirely new market segment, fairly similar to the vehicle screening product.

There are many potential first stepping-stones that John could take to move the project forward initially:

- *Quick-to-market independent prototype.* John believes that, in six to nine months, he can have a very rough prototype of the radio front end. If all goes well, this radio front end could then be linked to an off-the-shelf imaging system. This prototype would be a long way from being ready to sell, but it should be able to demonstrate the validity of the technology. However, showing this to others in the industry would expose the concept to potential competitors, including the large security equipment companies.
- *Best-in-class product.* Within 18 months, if the development plans went according to schedule, the company might be able to come to market, preemptively, with a very sophisticated product that is fully proven.
- *Development relationship with a large security equipment company.* One way to engage seriously with the regulatory authorities and to have a good chance of attacking the market is to make an early choice to work with one security equipment company. However, this may limit the team's exit options at a later

Exhibit A.2 SPI Map

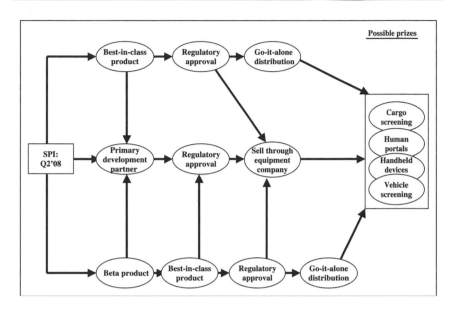

stage if it wanted to sell the company to someone other than the security equipment company with whom it had been working.

The map of alternatives open to SPI might look like those shown in Exhibit A.2.

There are a lot of paths open to the company. One recurring issue will be whether it goes for an independent existence all the way to a large market position or whether it engages much earlier with a large equipment company. There are a number of different points at which this could happen. SPI could link up with a security equipment company up front as a development partner. A second alternative would be to develop a beta product and then join up with a security company. A third would be to develop a best-in-class product and then join up. And, finally, the company could gain regulatory approval and then join up.

There is no right answer. It will depend on the circumstances of the company. But the entrepreneur should be able to form a view by looking at two factors. First, the investment capital required to jump between each stepping-stone (on an independent path) and, second, the likely boost in the value of the company at each point if it goes alone to develop the beta, finish the best-in-class product, get regulatory approval, and undertake market rollout.

STANDARD TERM SHEET CLAUSES

Company X Inc.
Term Sheet
Series A Preferred Stock Financing

Transaction Structure

Investment:	$X
Form of investment:	Preferred stock
Investors:	Lead investor: $X
	Investor two: $X
Price per unit of stock:	$X
Timing of investment:	$X will be committed on closing. $X will be committed on completion of an agreed-upon set of milestones.
Capitalization:	See attached capitalization table
Closing:	Later of September 15, 20XX or legal completion date

1. **Rights and Preferences of Series A Preferred Stock:**
    a. *Dividends:* The preferred stock will carry no right to dividends other than as described below. No dividends on common stock will be payable without the consent of

the preferred stockholders. If dividends are declared, the preferred stockholders shall be entitled to receive their portion of dividends as if they had converted their preferred stock into common stock.

b. *Liquidation and Exit Preference:* In the event of any liquidation, dissolution or exit of the Company, the holders of Preferred Stock will, at a minimum, be entitled to receive an amount equal to their original issue price per unit of stock, plus an amount equal to all declared but unpaid dividends thereon (the *"Preference Amount"*). If there are insufficient assets to permit the payment in full of the Preference Amount to the holders of Preferred Stock, then the assets of the Company will be distributed to the holders of the Preferred Stock in proportion to the Preference Amount each holder is otherwise entitled to receive.

After the full Preference Amount has been paid on all outstanding shares of the Preferred Stock, any remaining funds and assets of the Company legally available for distribution to shareholders will be distributed among the holders of the Preferred Stock and Common Stock on an as-converted basis.

A merger or consolidation of the Company in which its shareholders do not retain a majority of the voting power in the surviving Corporation, or a sale of all or substantially all of the Company's assets, will be deemed to be a liquidation, dissolution, or winding up.

c. *Voting Rights:* Each unit of Preferred Stock carries a number of votes equal to the number of units of Common Stock then issuable upon its conversion into Common Stock. The Preferred Stock will generally vote together with the Common Stock and not as a separate class except with respect to those matters identified under the Protective Provisions set out in this document. In addition, holders of the Preferred Stock shall vote separately on matters that by law are subject to a class vote.

d. *Board of Directors:* The Board of Directors shall consist of five (5) persons. The Preferred Stock investors shall elect two

(2) Directors: one (1) Director shall be appointed by the Lead Investor and one (1) Director shall be appointed by Investor Two. The Management shall have the right to appoint two (2) representatives to the Board. Within three (3) months of closing this transaction a nonexecutive chairman will be appointed with the agreement of the executives and the preferred stockholders.

e. *Redemption:*   Any time after five (5) years from the date of purchase, Preferred Stock holders shall have the right (unless converted) to require the Company to redeem the Preferred Stock at 100% of cost plus 10% simple interest per annum, plus declared but unpaid dividends to the date of redemption. Redemption shall be called for and paid in three equal installments: upon the date of redemption and the first and second anniversary of the date of redemption.

f. *Right of First Refusal:*   If the Company proposes to offer any new securities [other than (i) Employee Stock Option, (ii) the Conversion Stock, (iii) stock issued in connection with a stock split, stock dividend, or recapitalization, or (iv) stock issued in a Public Offering or an Acquisition of the Company at a price and minimum raising as referred to in paragraph (i) below], Preferred Stock holders shall have the right to purchase such portion of the new securities as is necessary to allow Preferred Stock holders to maintain their pro rata ownership in the Company. This right of first refusal shall terminate upon the closing of an initial public offering. Should any stockholder decide to sell their stock, they must first offer to existing stockholders on a pro rata basis, treating both classes of stock as the same class.

g. *Conversion:*   The holders of the Preferred Stock shall have the right to convert the Preferred Stock at any time into shares of Common Stock. The initial conversion rate for each series of Preferred Stock shall be one for one.

h. *Automatic Conversion:*   The Preferred Stock shall be automatically converted into Common Stock, at the then applicable conversion rate, upon the closing of an underwritten public offering of shares of Common Stock of the Company at the public offering of not less than five (5) times current issue price per share and for a total public offering amount of not less than $25 million new money.

i. *Antidilution Provisions:* Stock splits, stock dividends, and so forth shall have proportional antidilution protection. The conversion price of the Preferred Stock shall be subject to adjustment to prevent dilution on full ratchet basis in the event that the Company issues Common Stock or Common Stock Equivalents at a purchase price less than the applicable conversion price: except that, without triggering antidilution adjustment, Common Stock may be sold or reserved for issuance to employees, directors, consultants or advisors of the Company pursuant to stock purchase, stock option or other agreements approved by the Board in amounts not to exceed that set forth in the capitalization table.

j. *Protective Provisions:* Consent of holders of a majority of the outstanding Preferred Stock will be required for:

  i. Any action that alters or changes the rights, preferences, or privileges of the Preferred Stock.

  ii. Any increase in the authorized Preferred Stock.

  iii. Any action that authorizes, creates, or amends any class of stock having rights senior to or parri passu with the Preferred Stock.

  iv. Any amendment of the Company's Articles of Incorporation that adversely affects the rights of Preferred Stock.

  v. Any action that effects a reclassification of the outstanding capital stock of the Company.

  vi. Repurchase of Common Stock other than pursuant to stock purchase agreements providing for such rights in connection with a service termination.

  vii. Any merger, liquidation, dissolution, or acquisition of the Company or sale of substantially all of its assets.

  viii. Any issuance of new stock.

k. *Right of Cosale:*   Preferred Stock holders will have standard cosale rights in connection with any Common Stock holder sale to a third party (tagalong rights).

l. *Information Rights:*   The Company shall deliver to the investor; (i) annual financial statements within 90 days after the end of each fiscal year; (ii) unaudited monthly financial statements within 21days of the end of each month; (iii) an annual budget and operating plan within 30 days prior to each fiscal year, and (iv) each qualifying investor shall also have the right to inspect Company books and facilities and talk to the Company's personnel upon reasonable notice. These information rights shall terminate upon the Company's initial public offering.

2. **Closing:**   Closing shall be on September 15, 20XX or legal completion date.

3. **Other Covenants:**   All employees and consultants of the Company will sign a customary Confidentiality, Invention Assignment and Noncompete Agreement. Key employees will sign employment contracts with suitable covenant protection. Stockholders will be bound by standard covenants to protect investors. The details of these covenants are subject to final legal agreement.

4. **Expenses:**   Legal fees of the investors relating to the financing of up to $30,000 shall be paid by the Company.

5. **Stock Purchase Agreement:**   The investment shall be made pursuant to a Preferred Stock Purchase Agreement which shall contain, among other things, appropriate representations and warranties of the Company and relevant management, covenants of the Company and shareholders reflecting the provisions set forth herein, and appropriate conditions of closing which shall include, among other things, proper shareholder and Board approvals, completion of standard due diligence (both market and technical), creation of remuneration, stock option, and audit committees which will comprise nonexecutive directors only (remuneration of founders to be agreed before completion), key-man insurance on founders which will be payable to the company,

documentation in a form acceptable to investors' counsel, and a legal opinion from counsel to the Company.

6. **Stock Vesting:** Post our financing, the Company will have an Employee Option Pool, which will constitute the equivalent of 12% of the total Common Stock outstanding postfinancing. Stock from the Employee Option Pool may be issued from time to time to employees, officers, directors, and consultants pursuant to arrangements approved by the Board of Directors and a Company repurchase right over any unvested stock upon a resignation, termination, or conclusion of service. No other options will be created or issued beyond the equivalent of 12% until Exit, unless bonus stock is issued to Preferred Stock holders to maintain their percentage holding post creation or issuance. The stock options will be subject to a four (4) year vesting schedule.

7. **Founder Shares:** Common stock owned by the founders of the company will be subject to a four (4) year quarterly vesting schedule but will be regarded as fully vested in the event of the sale of the company or in the event of death or permanent disability of the Founder. In the event that any of the founders leave the Company, the Company will have the option of purchasing up to 50% of the vested stock owned by the departing Founder at a price to be set by an independent party.

8. **Registration Rights:** The investors shall be entitled to (i) unlimited "piggyback" registration rights on all registrations by the Company for its own account, other than for employee plans or Rule 145 transactions, (ii) unlimited S-3 registration rights, with a $750,000 minimum, if available, and (iii) demand registration rights, subject to customary underwriter cutback provisions. Investors shall have two demand registrations commencing on the earlier of six months after an IPO, or four years after the close of this financing. The Company shall bear all expenses of the registrations, except underwriting, discounts, and commissions. A Registration Rights Agreement will be signed on First Closing. Shareholders will agree to a lockup on shares for a reasonable period following an IPO, if required by the sponsor.

9. **Exit Provision:**   It is agreed that Preferred Stock holders shall be entitled to offer their stock for sale to other stockholders at any time after the fifth anniversary of the completion of this investment. If the stock is not acquired by the other stockholders or persons nominated by them, all the stockholders agree that the entire stock of the Company will be offered for sale. An investment banker will be appointed by all stockholders to find a purchaser and to determine a fair market value for the offered stock. The other stockholders will have the right of first refusal to purchase the offered stock at this fair market value. If the other stockholders do not elect to purchase the offered stock, the entire share capital of the Company will be offered for sale, provided that the price paid by the purchaser is not less than the fair market price.

10. **Nonbinding:**   This Memorandum of Terms creates no liability or obligation on the part of either party, except for the obligations of exclusivity set forth below. Neither party will be otherwise bound unless and until definitive agreements are executed.

11. **Exclusivity:**   In consideration of the Lead Investor committing time and expenses to put in place this investment, upon acceptance of this term sheet by the Company, the Company agrees that until the earliest to occur of (i) September 15, 20XX or legal completion date, the Company will negotiate only with the Lead Investor regarding an investment and will not directly or indirectly discuss, negotiate with, or provide information to any other party in connection with any potential merger, reorganization, sale of assets, or similar transaction or the issuance of debt or equity. In the event of withdrawal by the company or the investors, all parties will pay their own legal expenses incurred by the new investors.

12. **Expiry:**   This offer expires on June 23, 20XX.

Offered by: Accepted by:

_____   _____

John Smith   Mary Jones
Partner   CEO
Venture Capital Company   Company X Inc.

INDEX

ABOUT THE AUTHOR

Dermot Berkery is a general partner with Delta Partners, a leading European venture capital company that invests in Ireland and the United Kingdom. He has led investments in early-stage companies in sectors such as software, electronics, mobile services, medical equipment, components, and security equipment.

Prior to Delta Partners, he was a senior manager at McKinsey & Co., one of the world's premier management consulting organizations. He served clients throughout the United States, Europe, and Australasia, focusing mainly on financial services and energy. Prior to his working with McKinsey & Co., he was with Arthur Andersen.

He developed and teaches a course on entrepreneurial finance on the MBA program at University College Dublin.

He is a graduate of Harvard Business School and University College Dublin and is trained as a chartered accountant. Dermot resides with his family in Dublin, Ireland.